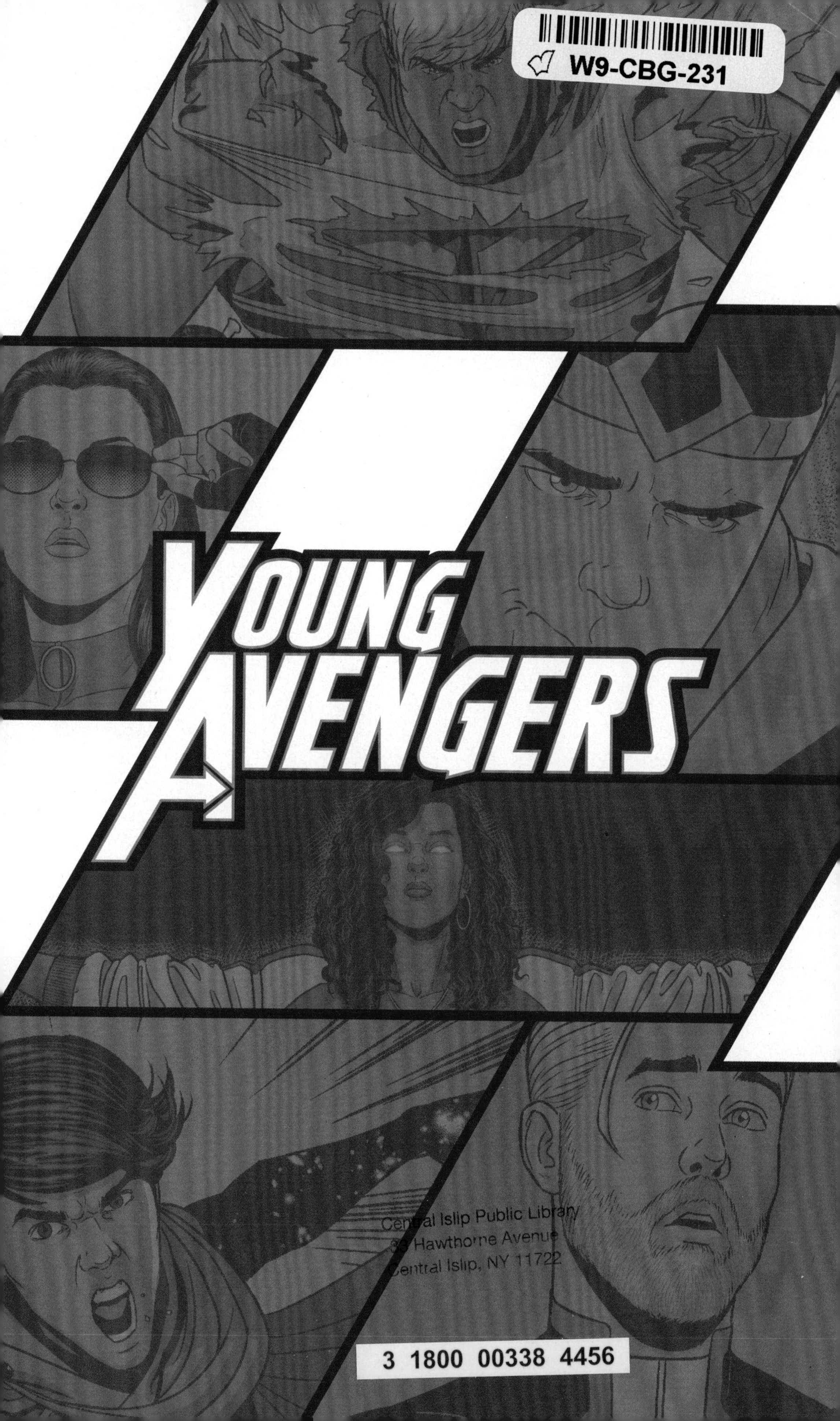
YOUNG AVENGERS

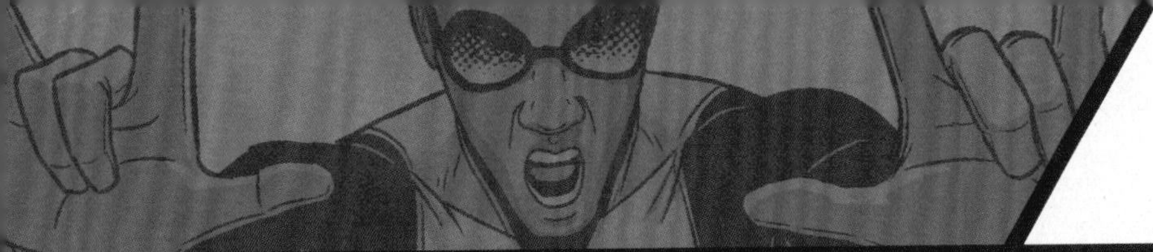

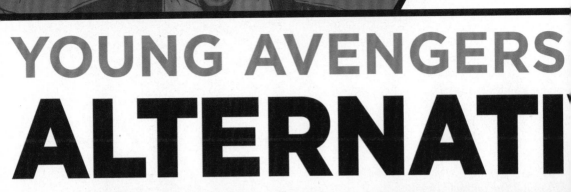

YOUNG AVENGERS
ALTERNATI

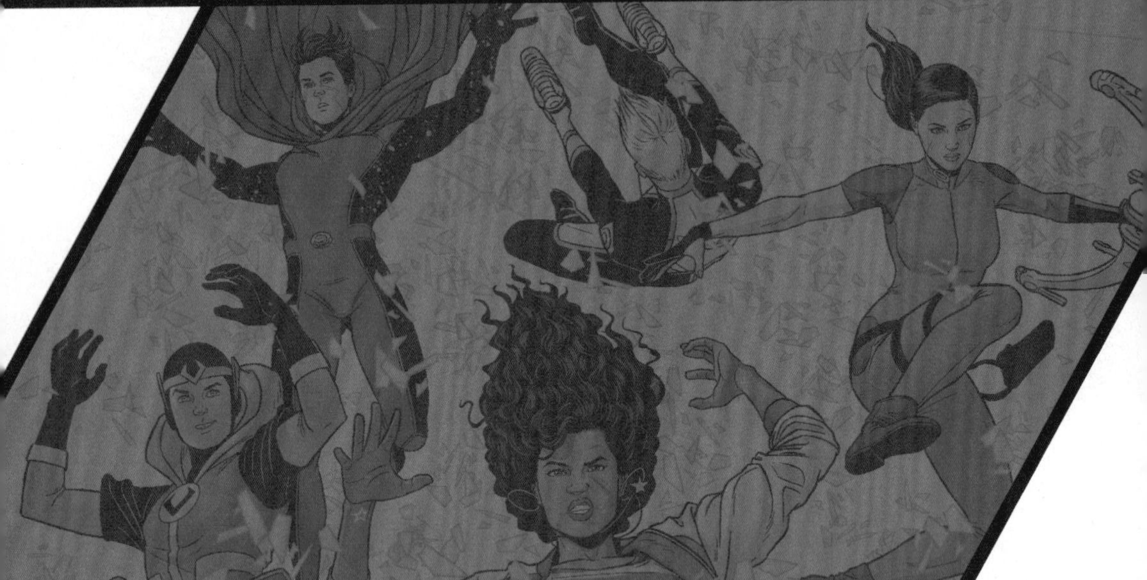

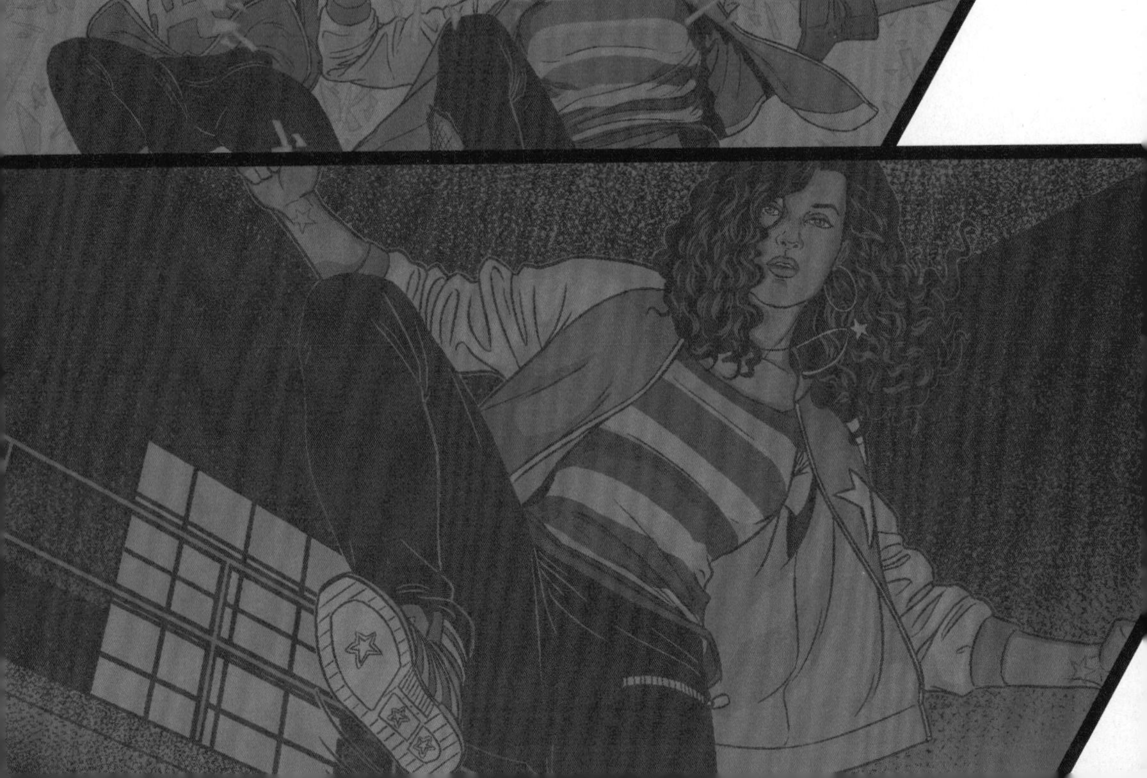

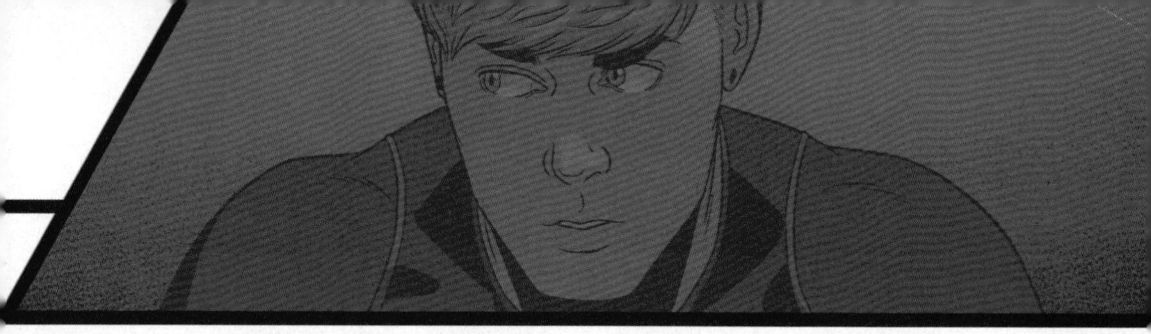

E CULTURE

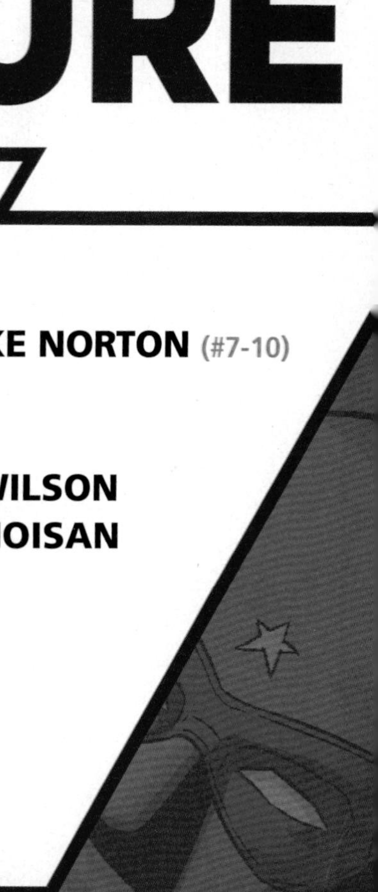

writer: **KIERON GILLEN**
artists: **KATE BROWN** (#6)
JAMIE McKELVIE with **MIKE NORTON** (#7-10)
color artist: **MATTHEW WILSON**
letterer: **VC'S CLAYTON COWLES**
cover art: **JAMIE MCKELVIE & MATTHEW WILSON**
assistant editors: **JACOB THOMAS & JON MOISAN**
editor: **LAUREN SANKOVITCH**

collection editor: JENNIFER GRÜNWALD
assistant editors: ALEX STARBUCK & NELSON RIBEIRO
editor, special projects: MARK D. BEAZLEY
senior editor, special projects: JEFF YOUNGQUIST
svp of print & digital publishing sales: DAVID GABRIEL
book design: JEFF POWELL

editor in chief: AXEL ALONSO
chief creative officer: JOE QUESADA
publisher: DAN BUCKLEY
executive producer: ALAN FINE

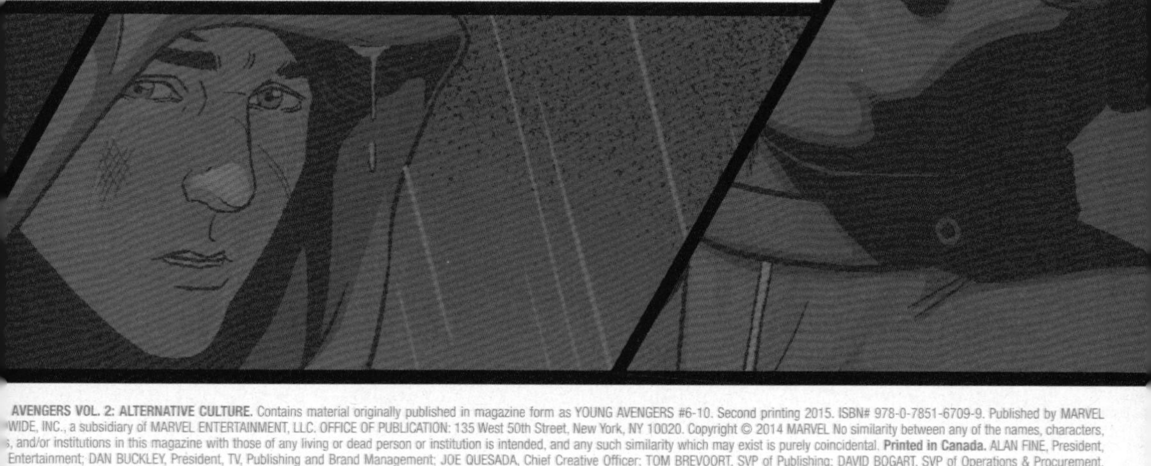

AVENGERS VOL. 2: ALTERNATIVE CULTURE. Contains material originally published in magazine form as YOUNG AVENGERS #6-10. Second printing 2015. ISBN# 978-0-7851-6709-9. Published by MARVEL WIDE, INC., a subsidiary of MARVEL ENTERTAINMENT, LLC. OFFICE OF PUBLICATION: 135 West 50th Street, New York, NY 10020. Copyright © 2014 MARVEL No similarity between any of the names, characters, s, and/or institutions in this magazine with those of any living or dead person or institution is intended, and any such similarity which may exist is purely coincidental. **Printed in Canada.** ALAN FINE, President, Entertainment; DAN BUCKLEY, President, TV, Publishing and Brand Management; JOE QUESADA, Chief Creative Officer; TOM BREVOORT, SVP of Publishing; DAVID BOGART, SVP of Operations & Procurement, ing; C.B. CEBULSKI, VP of International Development & Brand Management; DAVID GABRIEL, SVP Print, Sales & Marketing; JIM O'KEEFE, VP of Operations & Logistics; DAN CARR, Executive Director of Publishing logy; SUSAN CRESPI, Editorial Operations Manager; ALEX MORALES, Publishing Operations Manager; STAN LEE, Chairman Emeritus. For information regarding advertising in Marvel Comics or on Marvel.com, contact Jonathan Rheingold, VP of Custom Solutions & Ad Sales, at jrheingold@marvel.com. For Marvel subscription inquiries, please call 800-217-9158. **Manufactured between 11/4/2015 and 12/7/2015 by O PRINTERS, SCOTT, QC, CANADA.**

765432

6

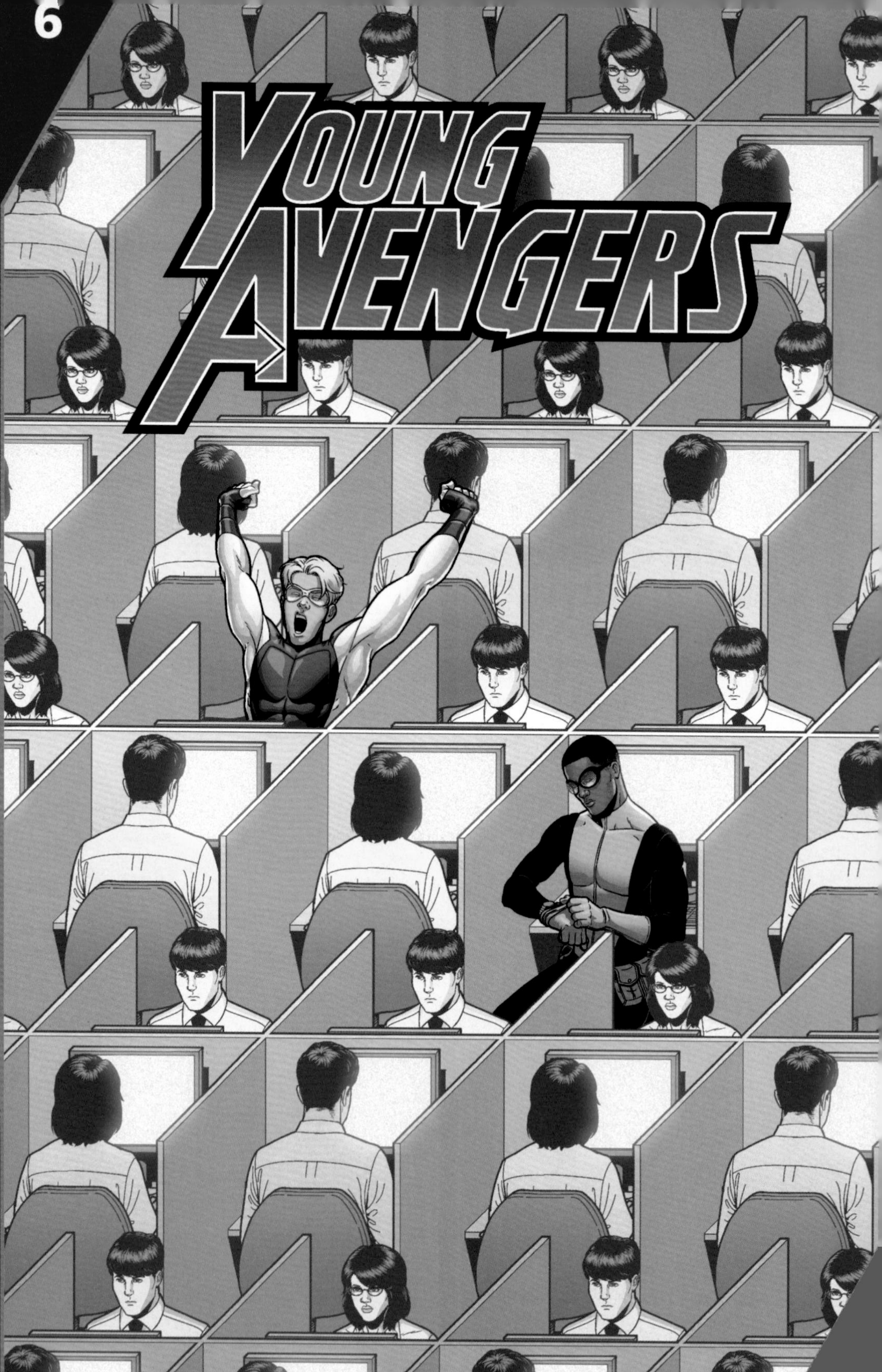
YOUNG AVENGERS

THE TOLL

AVAILABLE POSITION

WANTED:

[ON]E YOUNG SPEEDSTER SUPER HERO

JOB #:

[0]06.1

QUALIFICATIONS:

[A]bility to multitask, exceed the speed of sound, and resist detrimental side effects of [p]hysics and momentum.

EXPERIENCE:

Several years' experience in inappropriate wisecracking; history of juvenile delinquency a plus; experience and knowledge in young avenging a must. Twin brothers of reality warpers named Wiccan desirable.

SALARY:

Adventure, love and adoration of grateful citiz[ens]

NOTES:

quat
null
exer
mol o
eum i
conse

To try

"SPEED"
IDEAL CANDIDATE!
😉

RECOMMENDED CAND[IDATE]

SUPER STAFFING

AVAILABLE POSITIO[N]

WANTED:

ONE GENIUS DEPOWERED MUTANT

JOB #:

006.2

QUALIFICATIONS:

This position is looking for an organized and detail-oriented worker, with an extensive, genius-level knowledge of miscellaneous skills. Must be comfortable with long hours and working with teen heroes.

EXPERIENCE:

Looking for a former mutant with experience in X-Men-ing who may have sided with Cyclops during the mutant schism but has no current allegiance to either of the new mutant camps.

SALARY:

The thrill of do-gooding. The satisfaction of having a positive influence on the world at large.

NOTES:

"PRODIGY"
HIGHLY RECOMMEND!
☺

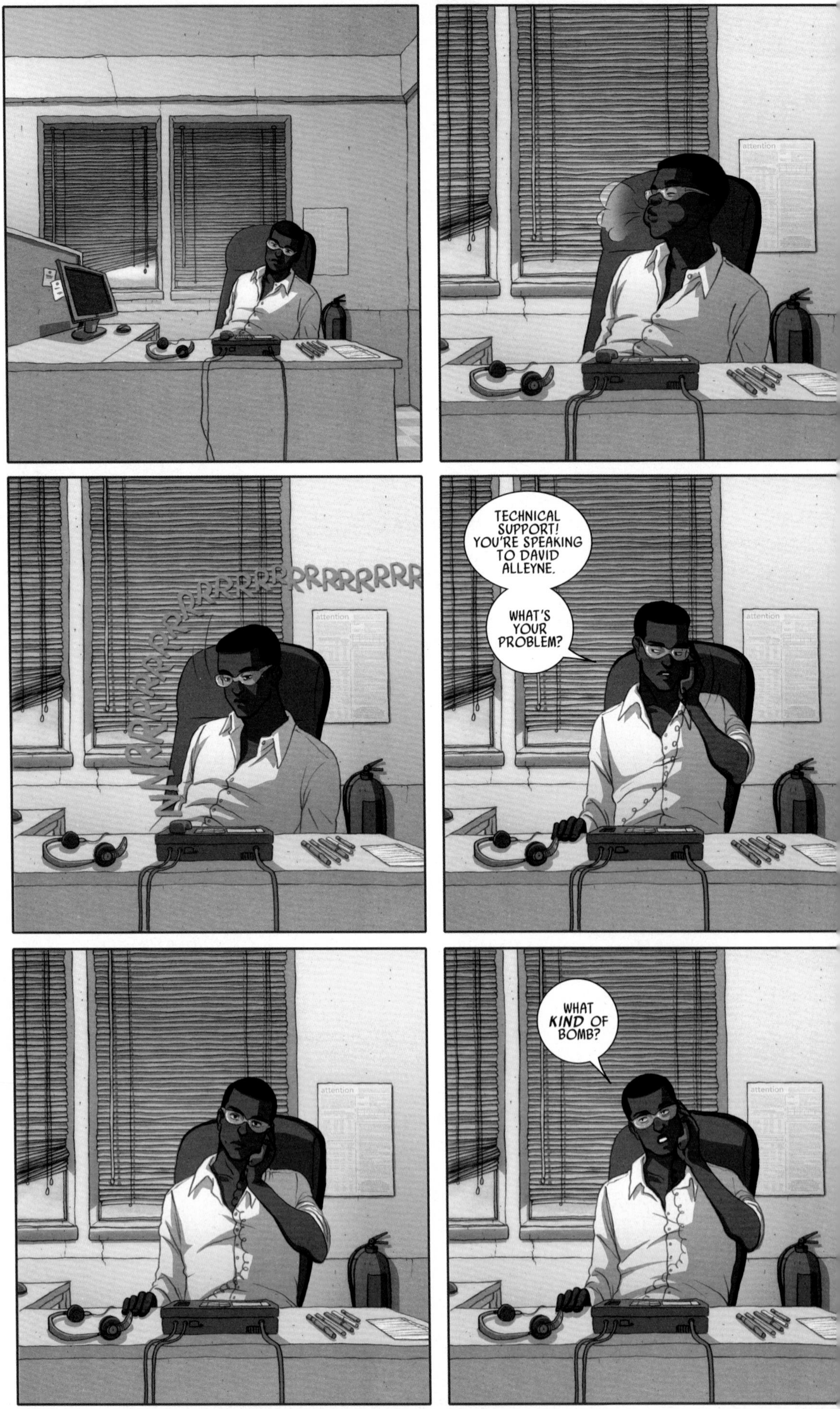
NNRRRRRRRRRRRRRRRRRRRRRRRRRR
TECHNICAL SUPPORT! YOU'RE SPEAKING TO DAVID ALLEYNE.
WHAT'S YOUR PROBLEM?
WHAT *KIND* OF BOMB?

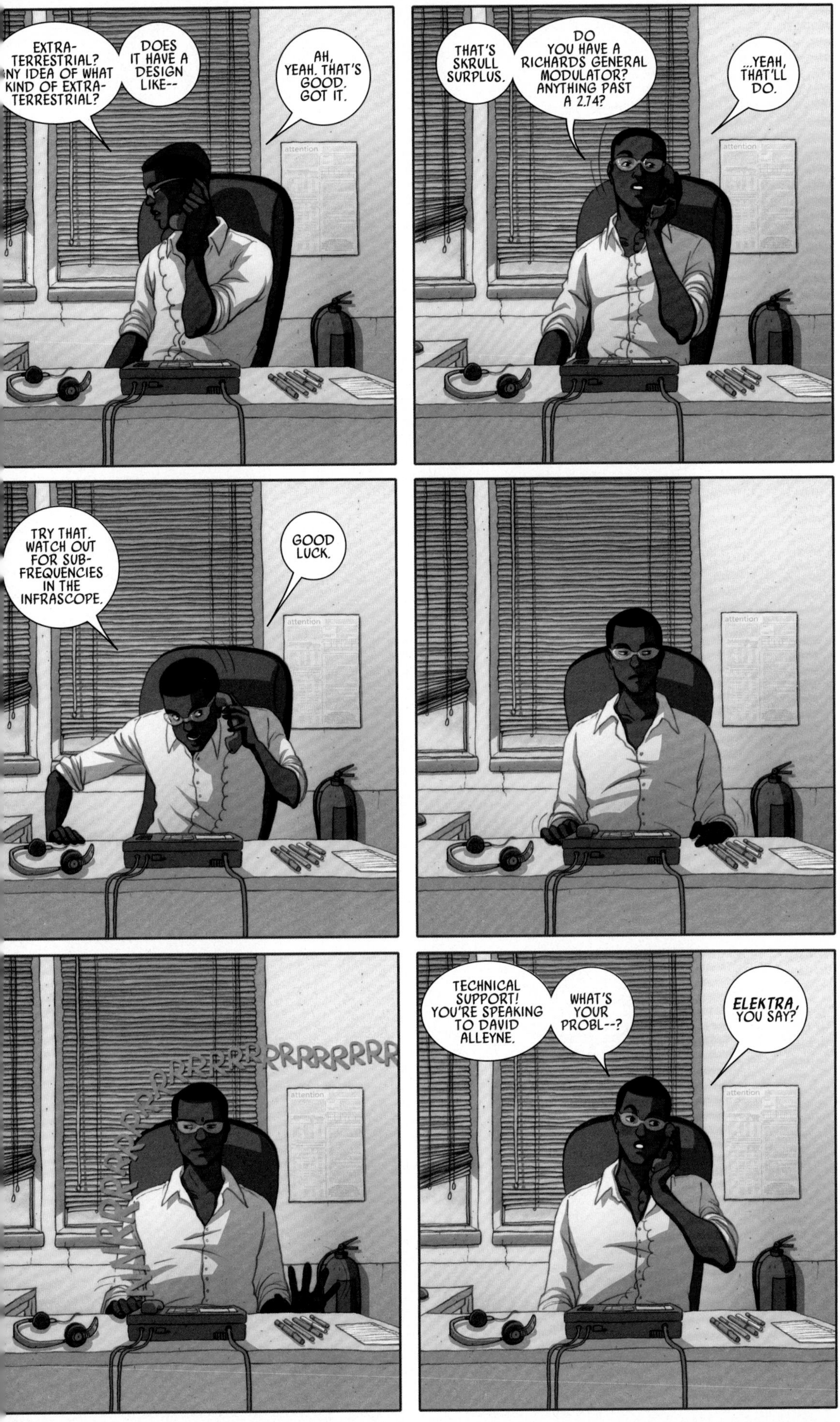
EXTRA-TERRESTRIAL? ANY IDEA OF WHAT KIND OF EXTRA-TERRESTRIAL?
DOES IT HAVE A DESIGN LIKE--
AH, YEAH. THAT'S GOOD. GOT IT.
THAT'S SKRULL SURPLUS.
DO YOU HAVE A RICHARDS GENERAL MODULATOR? ANYTHING PAST A 2.74?
...YEAH, THAT'LL DO.
TRY THAT. WATCH OUT FOR SUB-FREQUENCIES IN THE INFRASCOPE.
GOOD LUCK.
BRRRRRRRRRRRRRRRRRRRRRRRRR
TECHNICAL SUPPORT! YOU'RE SPEAKING TO DAVID ALLEYNE.
WHAT'S YOUR PROBL--?
ELEKTRA, YOU SAY?

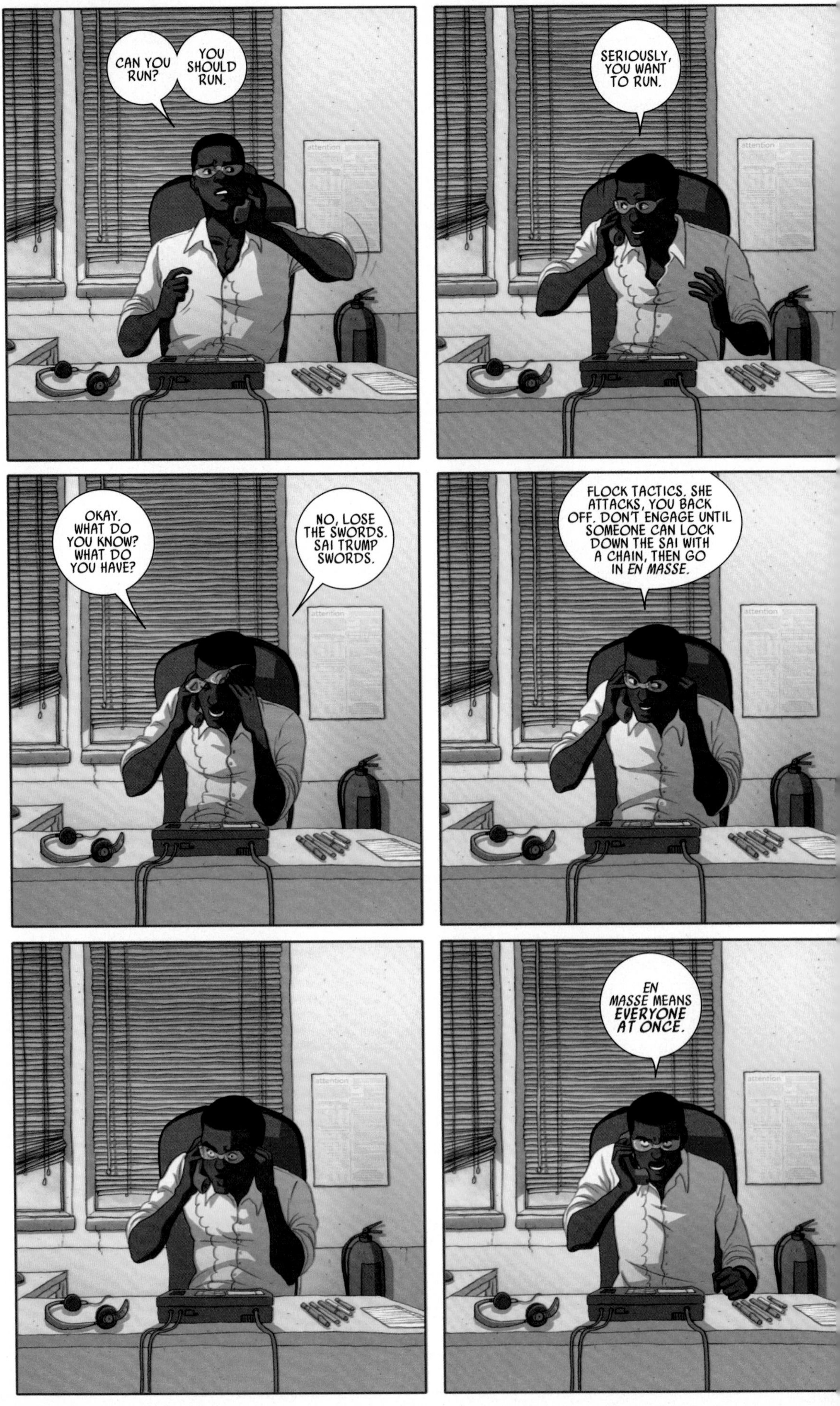
CAN YOU RUN?
YOU SHOULD RUN.
SERIOUSLY, YOU WANT TO RUN.
OKAY. WHAT DO YOU KNOW? WHAT DO YOU HAVE?
NO, LOSE THE SWORDS. SAI TRUMP SWORDS.
FLOCK TACTICS. SHE ATTACKS, YOU BACK OFF. DON'T ENGAGE UNTIL SOMEONE CAN LOCK DOWN THE SAI WITH A CHAIN, THEN GO IN EN MASSE.
EN MASSE MEANS EVERYONE AT ONCE.

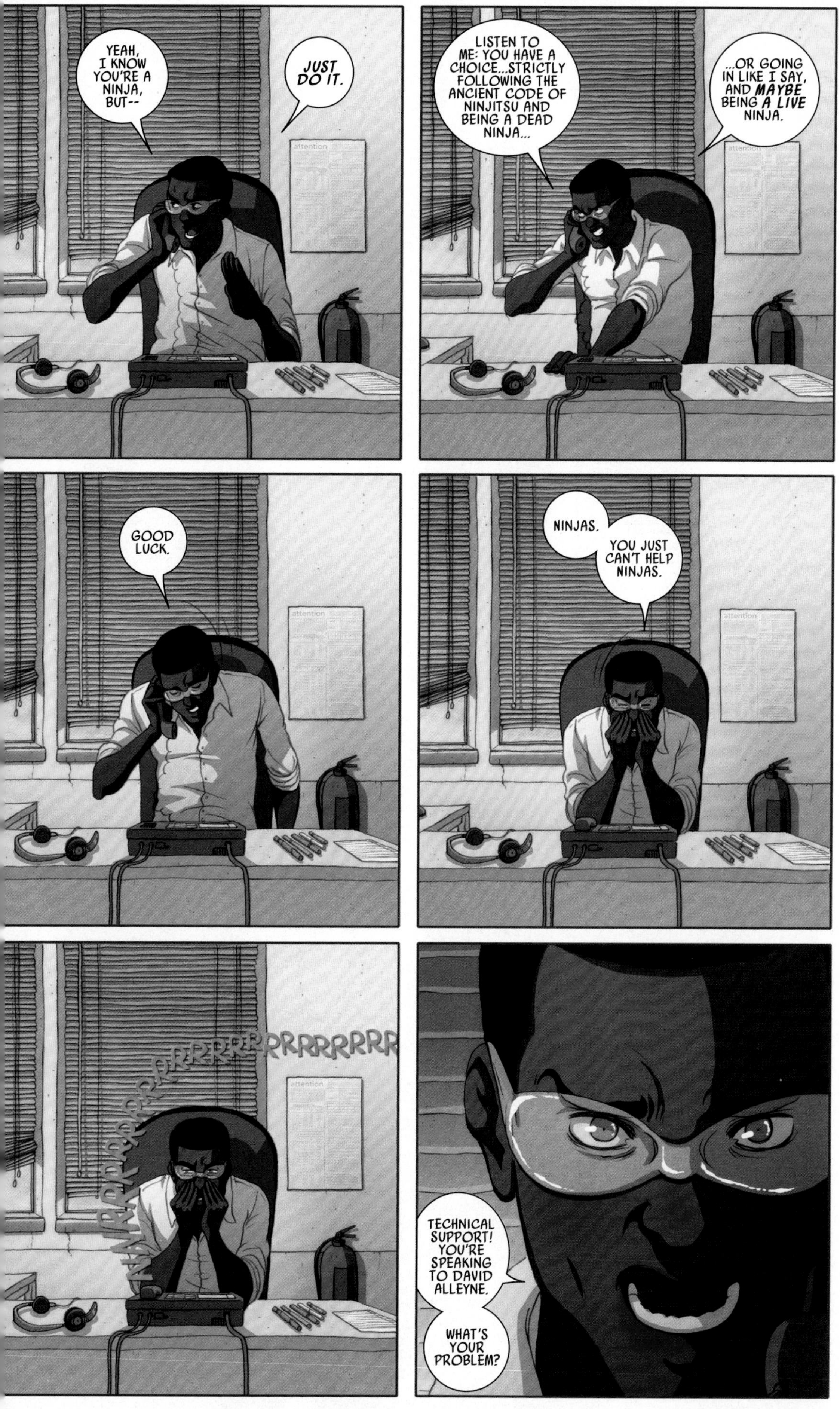
YEAH, I KNOW YOU'RE A NINJA, BUT--
JUST DO IT.
LISTEN TO ME: YOU HAVE A CHOICE...STRICTLY FOLLOWING THE ANCIENT CODE OF NINJITSU AND BEING A DEAD NINJA...
...OR GOING IN LIKE I SAY, AND MAYBE BEING A LIVE NINJA.
GOOD LUCK.
NINJAS.
YOU JUST CAN'T HELP NINJAS.
NNYARRRRRRRRRRRRRRRRRRRRRR
TECHNICAL SUPPORT! YOU'RE SPEAKING TO DAVID ALLEYNE.
WHAT'S YOUR PROBLEM?

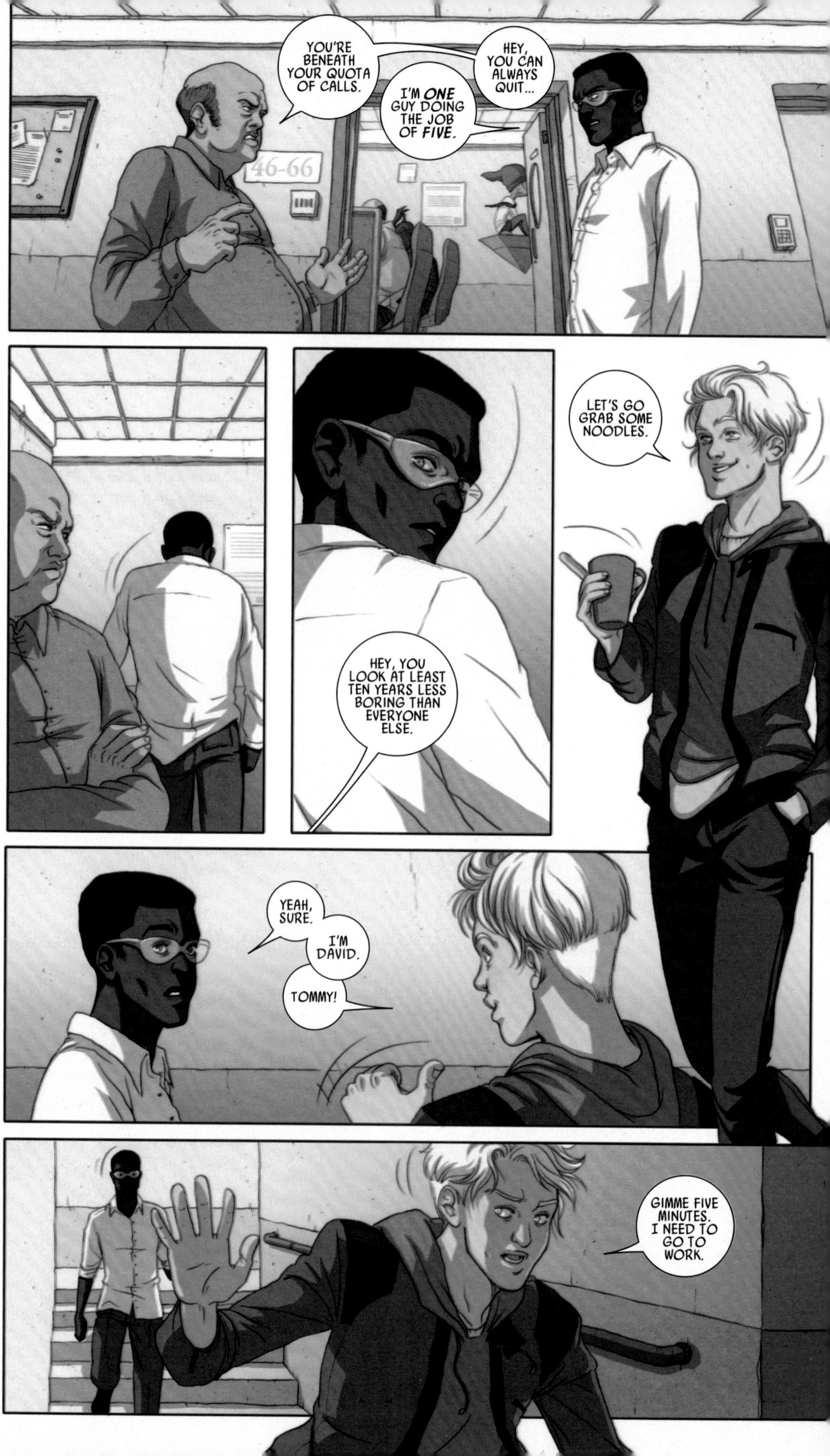
YOU'RE BENEATH YOUR QUOTA OF CALLS.
HEY, YOU CAN ALWAYS QUIT...
I'M ONE GUY DOING THE JOB OF FIVE.
46-66
HEY, YOU LOOK AT LEAST TEN YEARS LESS BORING THAN EVERYONE ELSE.
LET'S GO GRAB SOME NOODLES.
YEAH, SURE.
I'M DAVID.
TOMMY!
GIMME FIVE MINUTES. I NEED TO GO TO WORK.

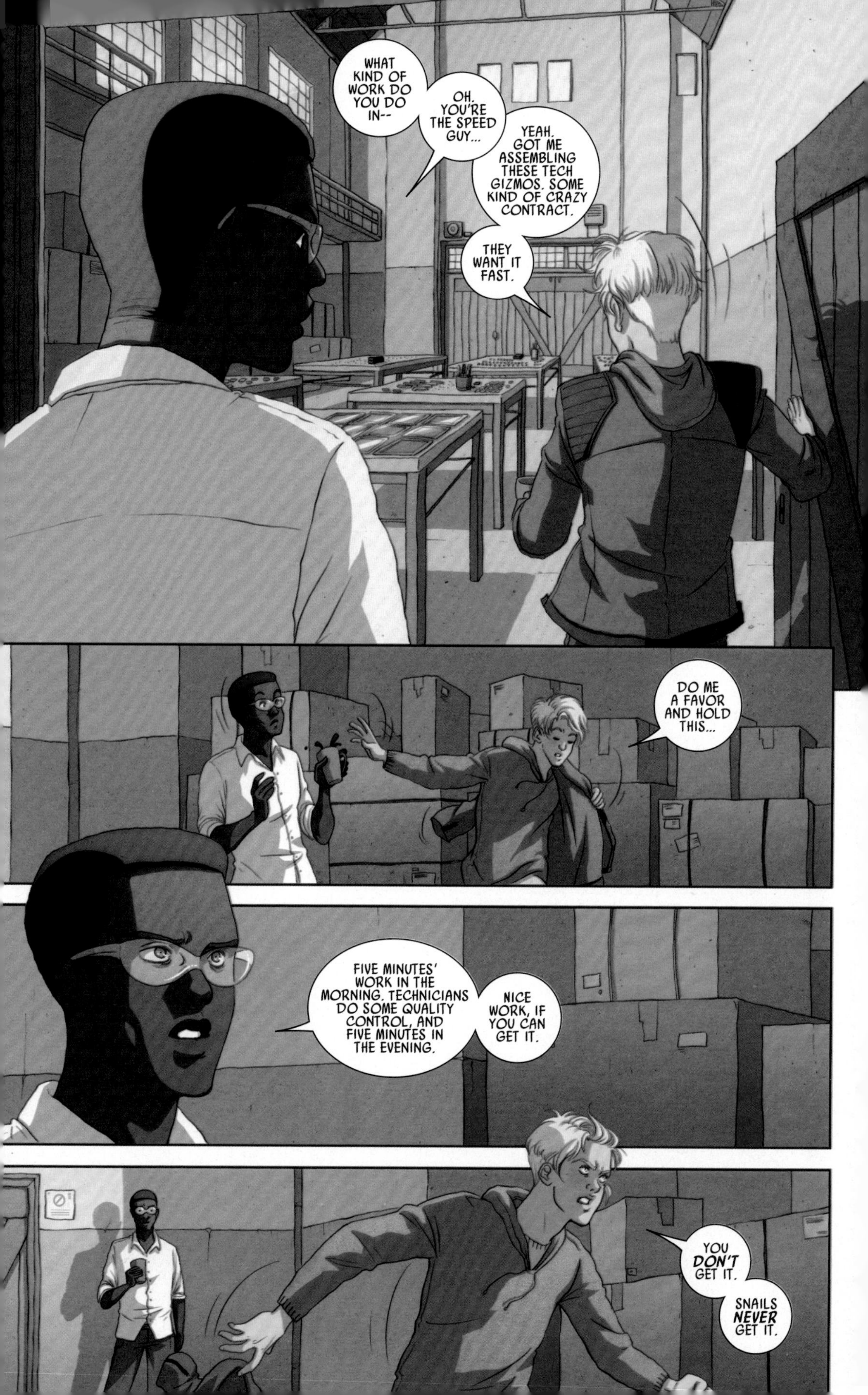
WHAT KIND OF WORK DO YOU DO IN--
OH, YOU'RE THE SPEED GUY...
YEAH, GOT ME ASSEMBLING THESE TECH GIZMOS. SOME KIND OF CRAZY CONTRACT.
THEY WANT IT FAST.
DO ME A FAVOR AND HOLD THIS...
FIVE MINUTES' WORK IN THE MORNING. TECHNICIANS DO SOME QUALITY CONTROL, AND FIVE MINUTES IN THE EVENING.
NICE WORK, IF YOU CAN GET IT.
YOU ***DON'T*** GET IT.
SNAILS ***NEVER*** GET IT.

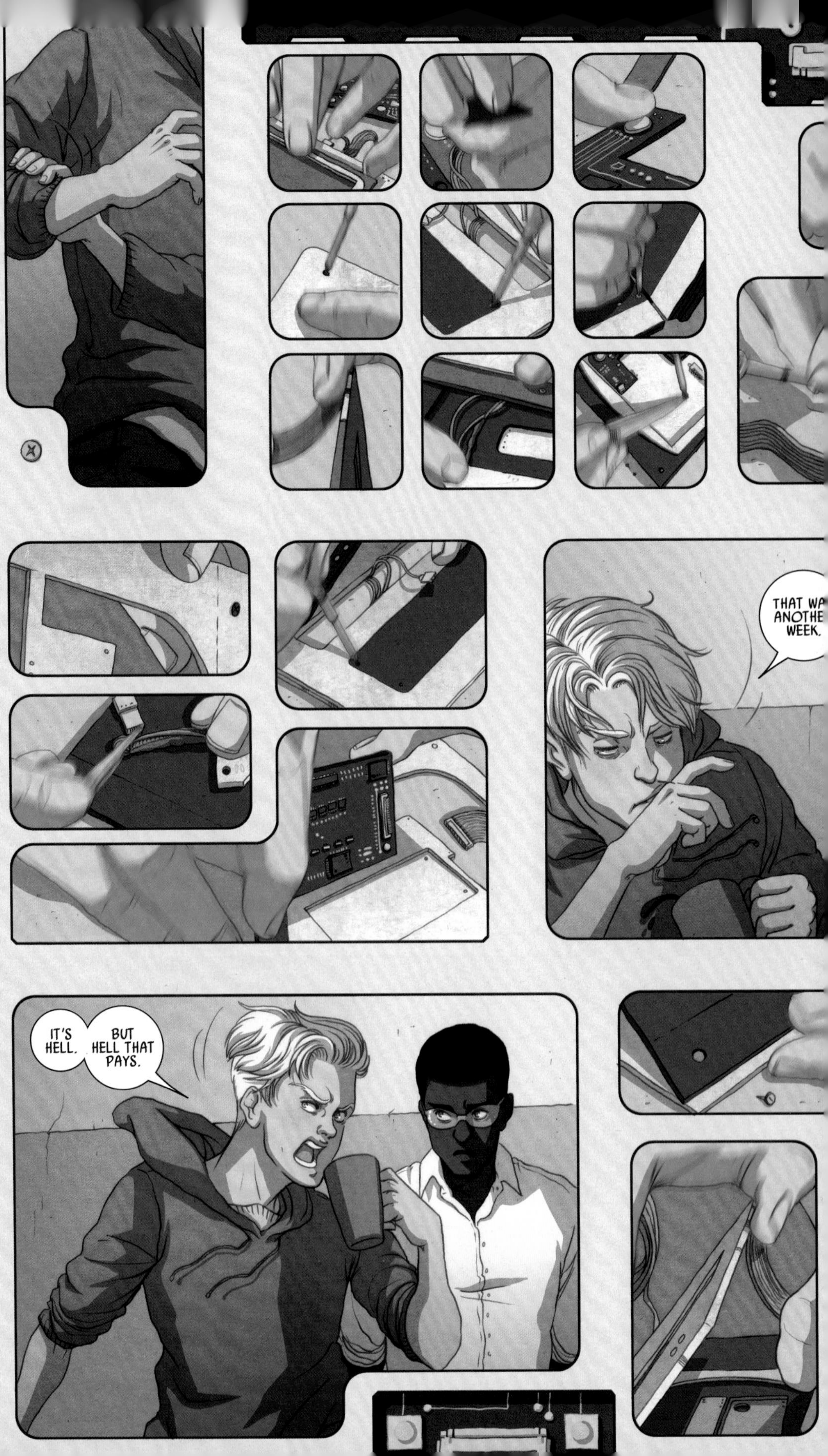
THAT WA
ANOTHE
WEEK.
IT'S HELL.
BUT HELL THAT PAYS.

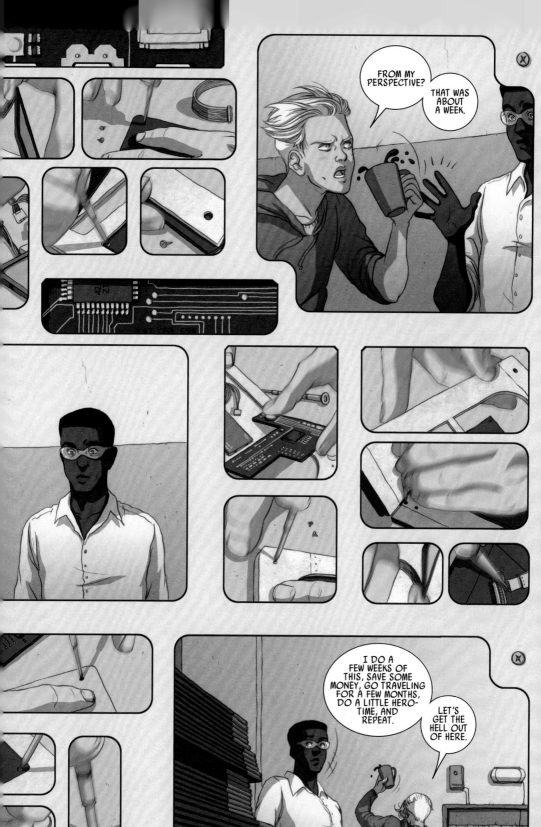

FROM MY PERSPECTIVE? THAT WAS ABOUT A WEEK.

I DO A FEW WEEKS OF THIS, SAVE SOME MONEY, GO TRAVELING FOR A FEW MONTHS, DO A LITTLE HERO-TIME, AND REPEAT.

LET'S GET THE HELL OUT OF HERE.

"I TRIED SETTLING DOWN FOR A WHILE, BUT THEY JUST DROVE ME CRAZY. NICE KIDS, BUT SO SHELTERED."

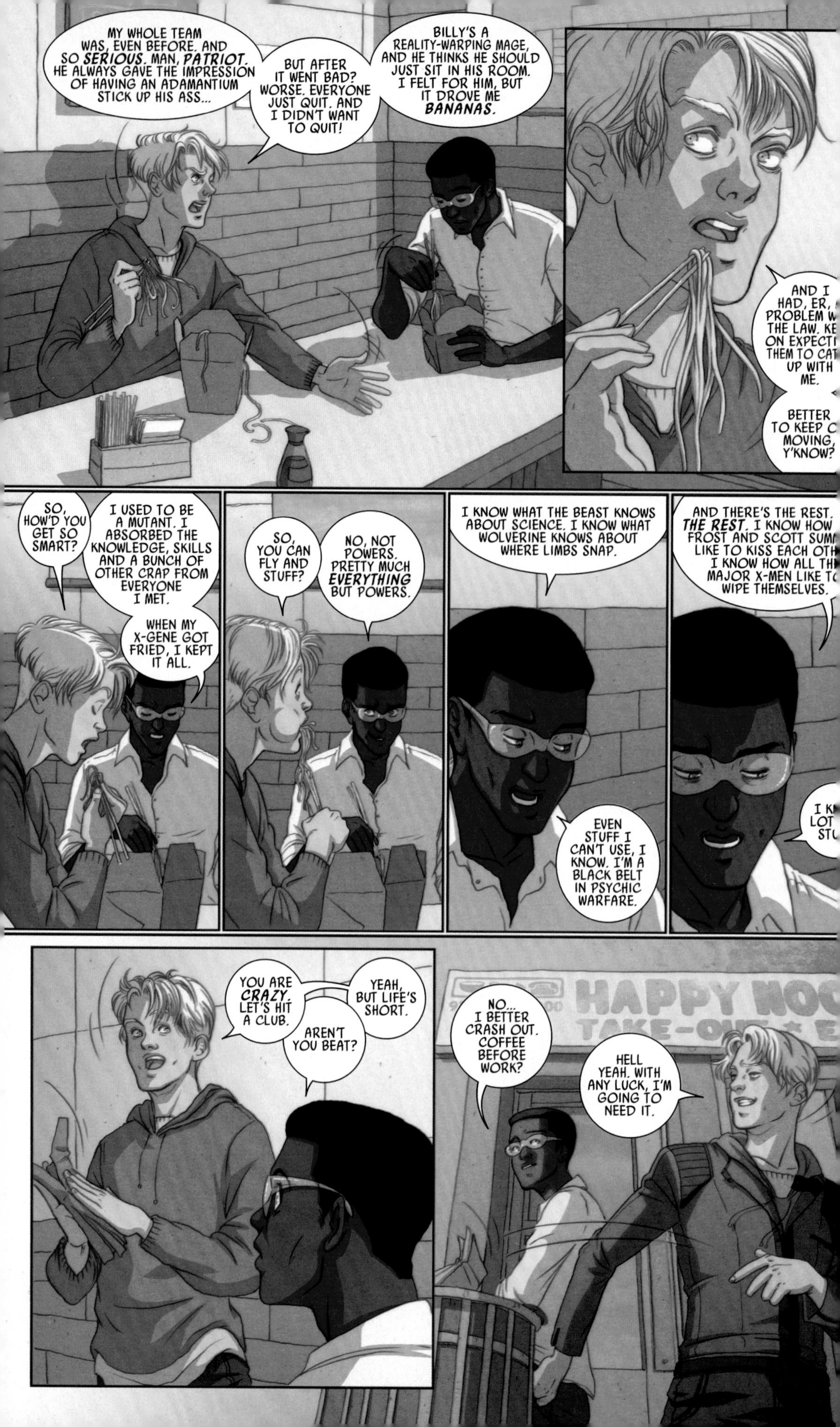
MY WHOLE TEAM WAS, EVEN BEFORE. AND SO SERIOUS. MAN, PATRIOT. HE ALWAYS GAVE THE IMPRESSION OF HAVING AN ADAMANTIUM STICK UP HIS ASS...
BUT AFTER IT WENT BAD? WORSE. EVERYONE JUST QUIT. AND I DIDN'T WANT TO QUIT!
BILLY'S A REALITY-WARPING MAGE, AND HE THINKS HE SHOULD JUST SIT IN HIS ROOM. I FELT FOR HIM, BUT IT DROVE ME BANANAS.
AND I HAD, ER,
BETTER TO KEEP
SO, HOW'D YOU GET SO SMART?
I USED TO BE A MUTANT. I ABSORBED THE KNOWLEDGE, SKILLS AND A BUNCH OF OTHER CRAP FROM EVERYONE I MET.
WHEN MY X-GENE GOT FRIED, I KEPT IT ALL.
SO, YOU CAN FLY AND STUFF?
NO, NOT POWERS. PRETTY MUCH EVERYTHING BUT POWERS.
I KNOW WHAT THE BEAST KNOWS ABOUT SCIENCE. I KNOW WHAT WOLVERINE KNOWS ABOUT WHERE LIMBS SNAP.
EVEN STUFF I CAN'T USE, I KNOW. I'M A BLACK BELT IN PSYCHIC WARFARE.
AND THERE'S THE REST.
YOU ARE CRAZY. LET'S HIT A CLUB.
YEAH, BUT LIFE'S SHORT.
AREN'T YOU BEAT?
NO... I BETTER CRASH OUT. COFFEE BEFORE WORK?
HELL YEAH. WITH ANY LUCK, I'M GOING TO NEED IT.
HAPPY
TAKE-OUT

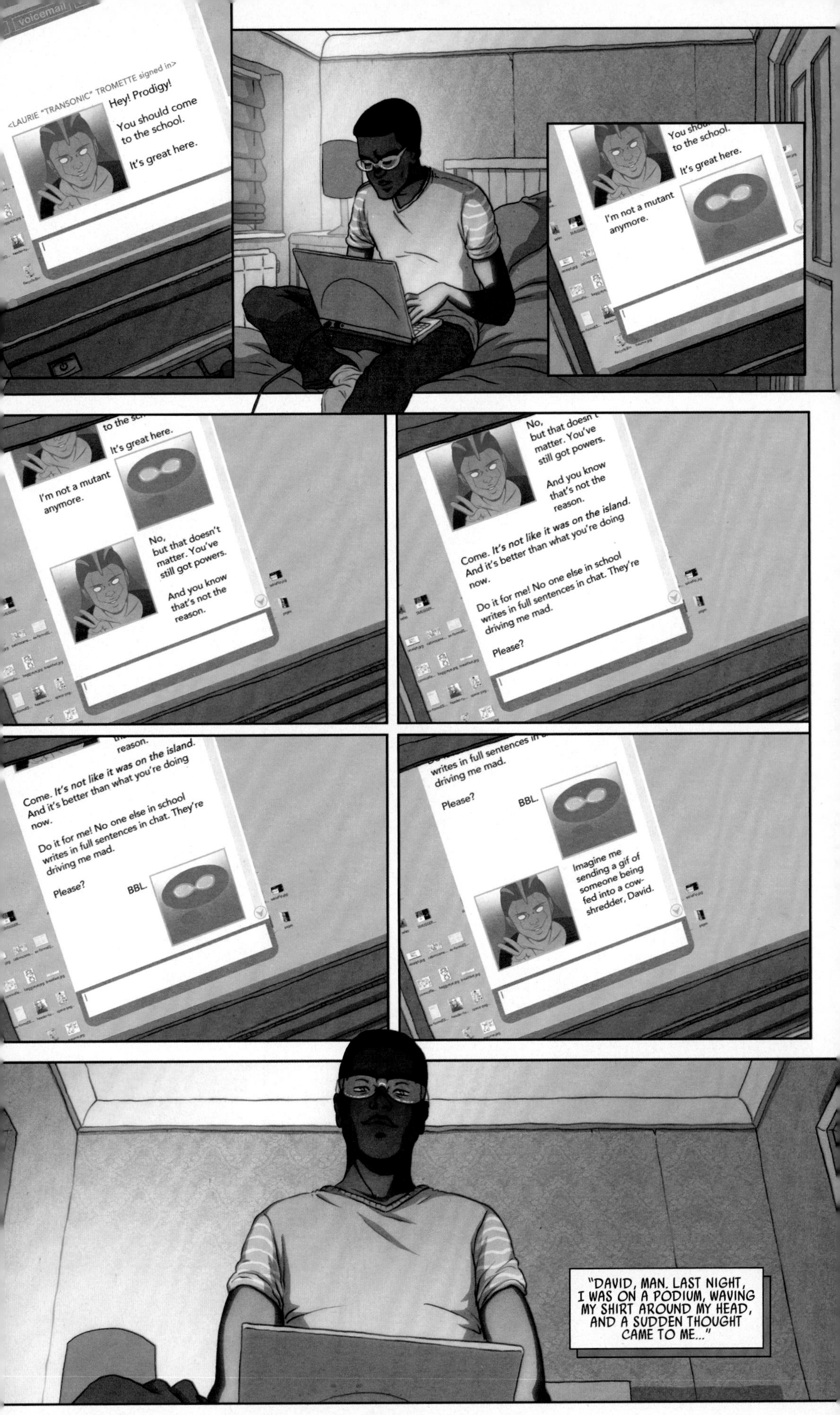
voicemail
<LAURIE "TRANSONIC" TROMETTE signed in>
Hey! Prodigy!
You should come to the school.
It's great here.
I'm not a mutant anymore.
No, but that doesn't matter. You've still got powers.
And you know that's not the reason.
Come. *It's not like it was on the island.* And it's better than what you're doing now.
Do it for me! No one else in school writes in full sentences in chat. They're driving me mad.
Please?
BBL.
Imagine me sending a gif of someone being fed into a cow-shredder, David.
"DAVID, MAN. LAST NIGHT, I WAS ON A PODIUM, WAVING MY SHIRT AROUND MY HEAD, AND A SUDDEN THOUGHT CAME TO ME..."

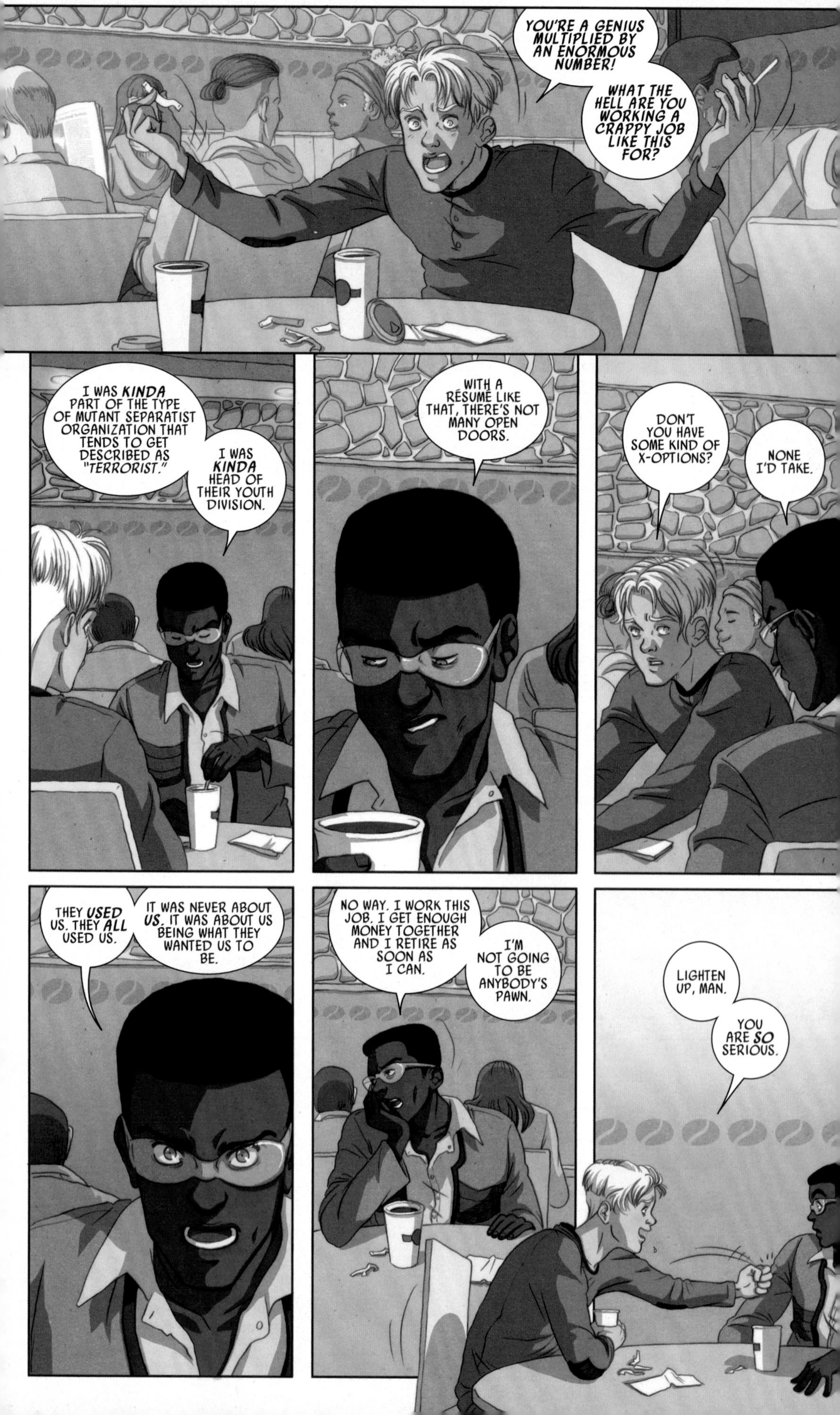
YOU'RE A GENIUS MULTIPLIED BY AN ENORMOUS NUMBER!
WHAT THE HELL ARE YOU WORKING A CRAPPY JOB LIKE THIS FOR?
I WAS KINDA PART OF THE TYPE OF MUTANT SEPARATIST ORGANIZATION THAT TENDS TO GET DESCRIBED AS "TERRORIST."
I WAS KINDA HEAD OF THEIR YOUTH DIVISION.
WITH A RÉSUMÉ LIKE THAT, THERE'S NOT MANY OPEN DOORS.
DON'T YOU HAVE SOME KIND OF X-OPTIONS?
NONE I'D TAKE.
THEY USED US. THEY ALL USED US.
IT WAS NEVER ABOUT US. IT WAS ABOUT US BEING WHAT THEY WANTED US TO BE.
NO WAY. I WORK THIS JOB. I GET ENOUGH MONEY TOGETHER AND I RETIRE AS SOON AS I CAN.
I'M NOT GOING TO BE ANYBODY'S PAWN.
LIGHTEN UP, MAN.
YOU ARE SO SERIOUS.

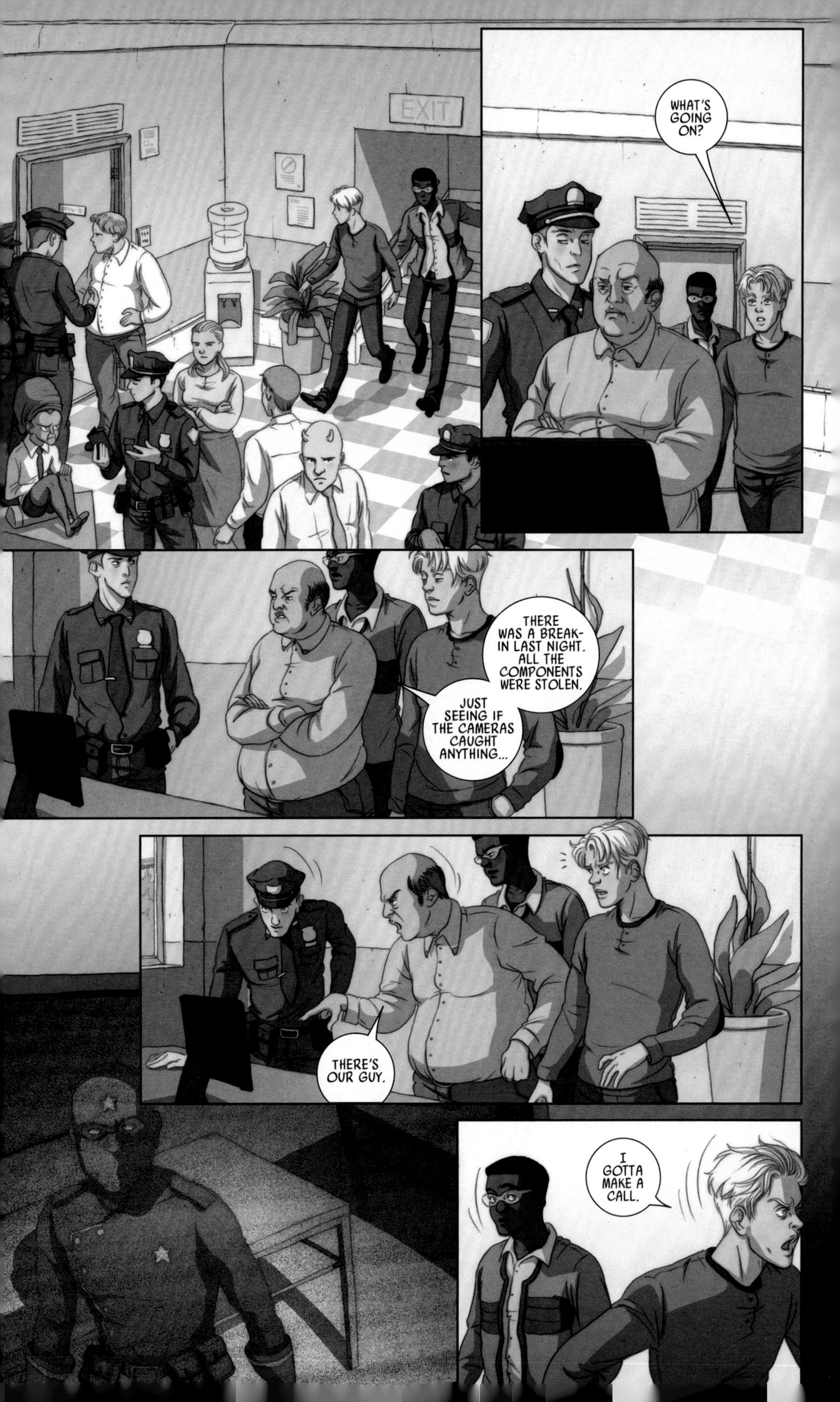
EXIT
WHAT'S GOING ON?
THERE WAS A BREAK-IN LAST NIGHT. ALL THE COMPONENTS WERE STOLEN.
JUST SEEING IF THE CAMERAS CAUGHT ANYTHING...
THERE'S OUR GUY.
I GOTTA MAKE A CALL.

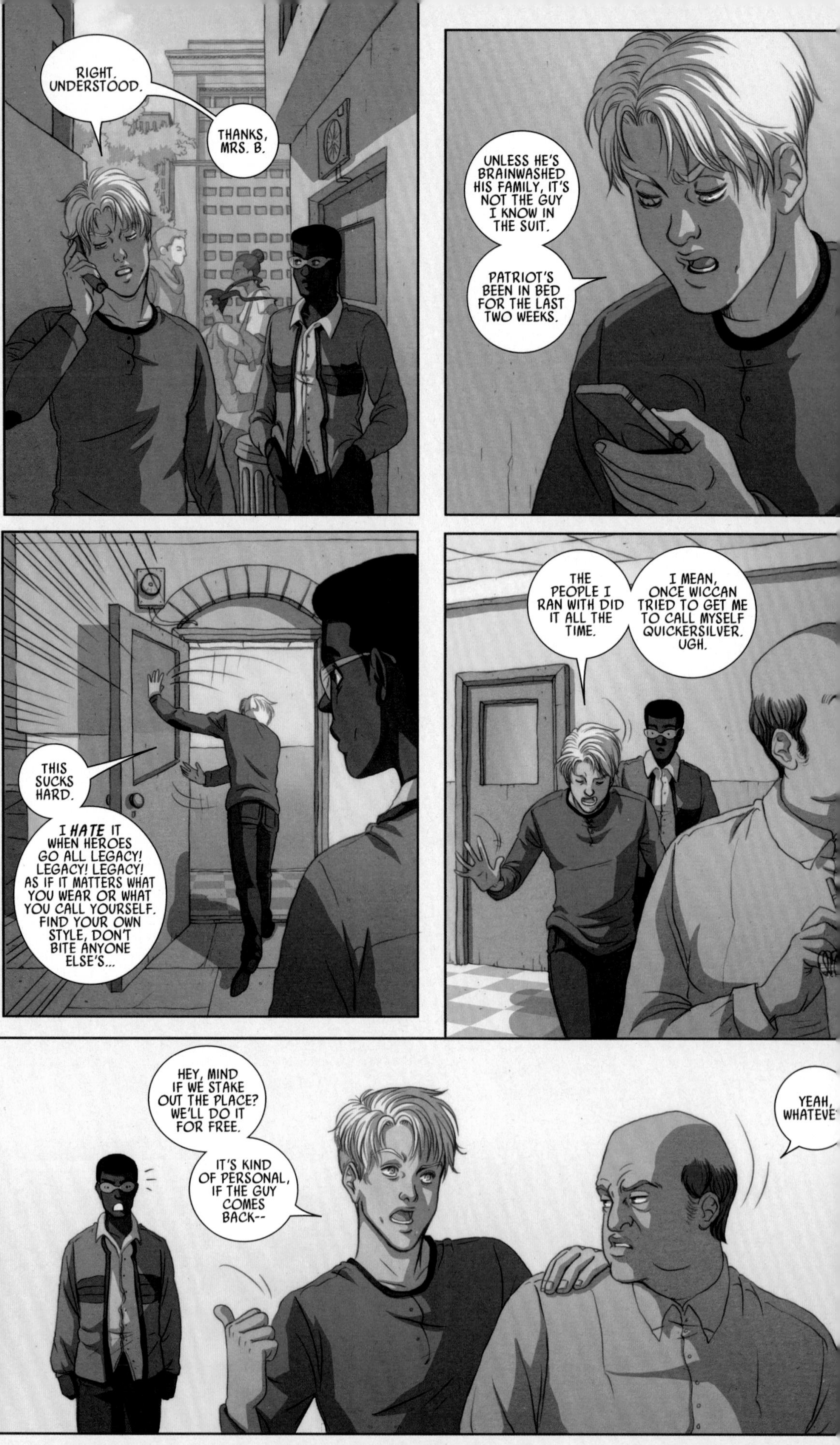
RIGHT. UNDERSTOOD.
THANKS, MRS. B.
UNLESS HE'S BRAINWASHED HIS FAMILY, IT'S NOT THE GUY I KNOW IN THE SUIT.
PATRIOT'S BEEN IN BED FOR THE LAST TWO WEEKS.
THIS SUCKS HARD.
I HATE IT WHEN HEROES GO ALL LEGACY! LEGACY! LEGACY! AS IF IT MATTERS WHAT YOU WEAR OR WHAT YOU CALL YOURSELF. FIND YOUR OWN STYLE, DON'T BITE ANYONE ELSE'S...
THE PEOPLE I RAN WITH DID IT ALL THE TIME.
I MEAN, ONCE WICCAN TRIED TO GET ME TO CALL MYSELF QUICKERSILVER. UGH.
HEY, MIND IF WE STAKE OUT THE PLACE? WE'LL DO IT FOR FREE.
IT'S KIND OF PERSONAL, IF THE GUY COMES BACK--
YEAH, WHATEVE

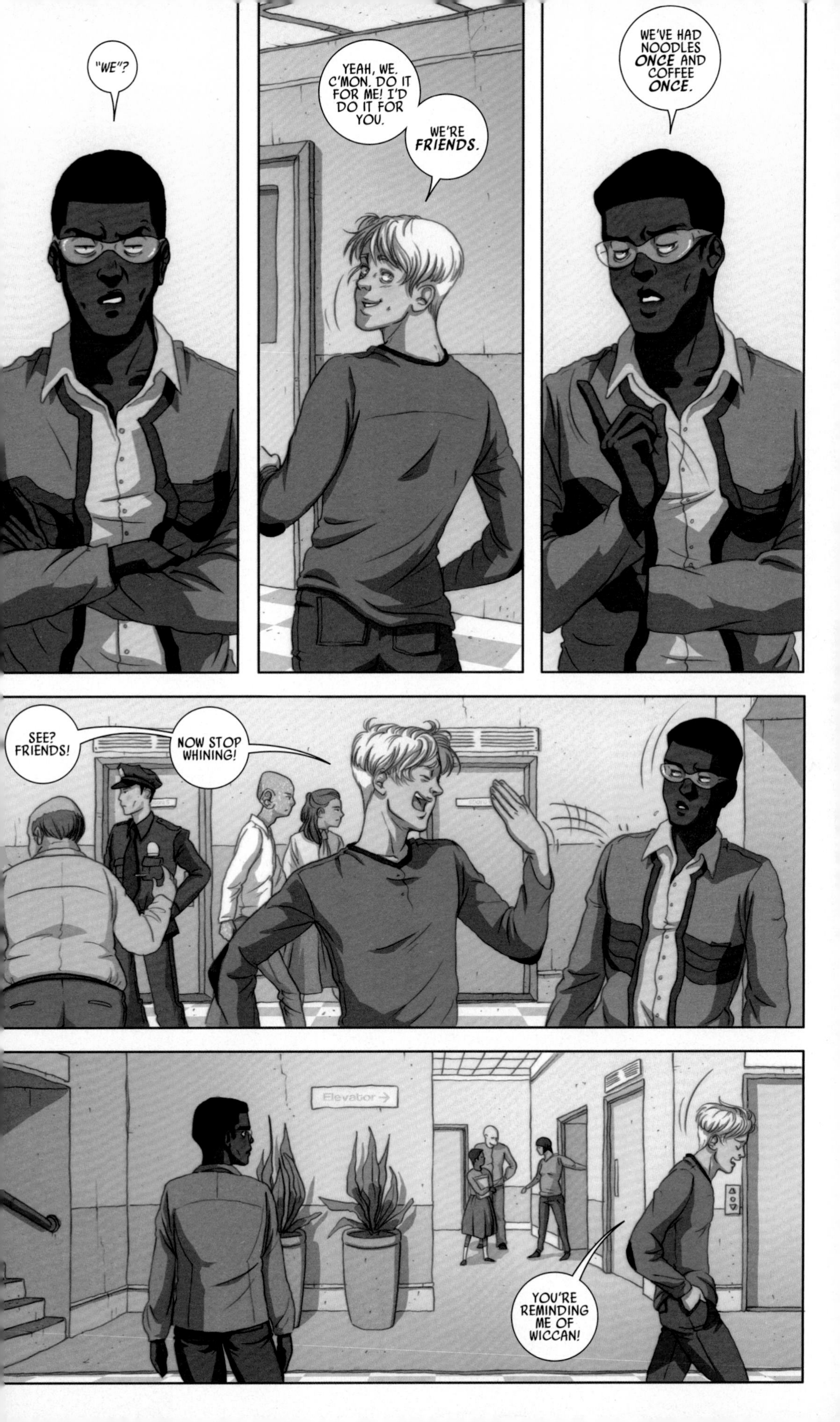
"WE"?
YEAH, WE. C'MON. DO IT FOR ME! I'D DO IT FOR YOU.
WE'RE FRIENDS.
WE'VE HAD NOODLES ONCE AND COFFEE ONCE.
SEE? FRIENDS!
NOW STOP WHINING!
Elevator
YOU'RE REMINDING ME OF WICCAN!

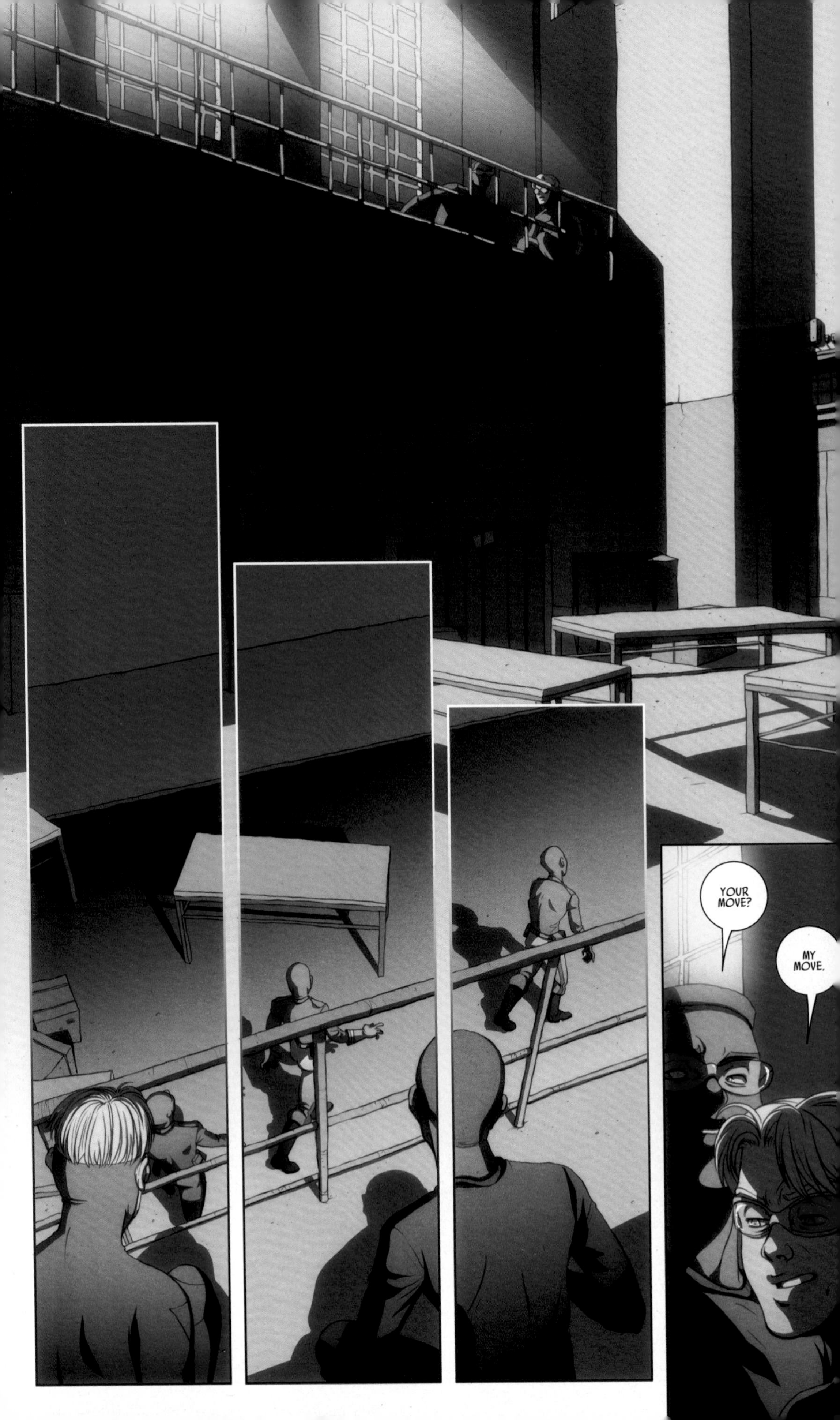
YOUR MOVE?
MY MOVE.

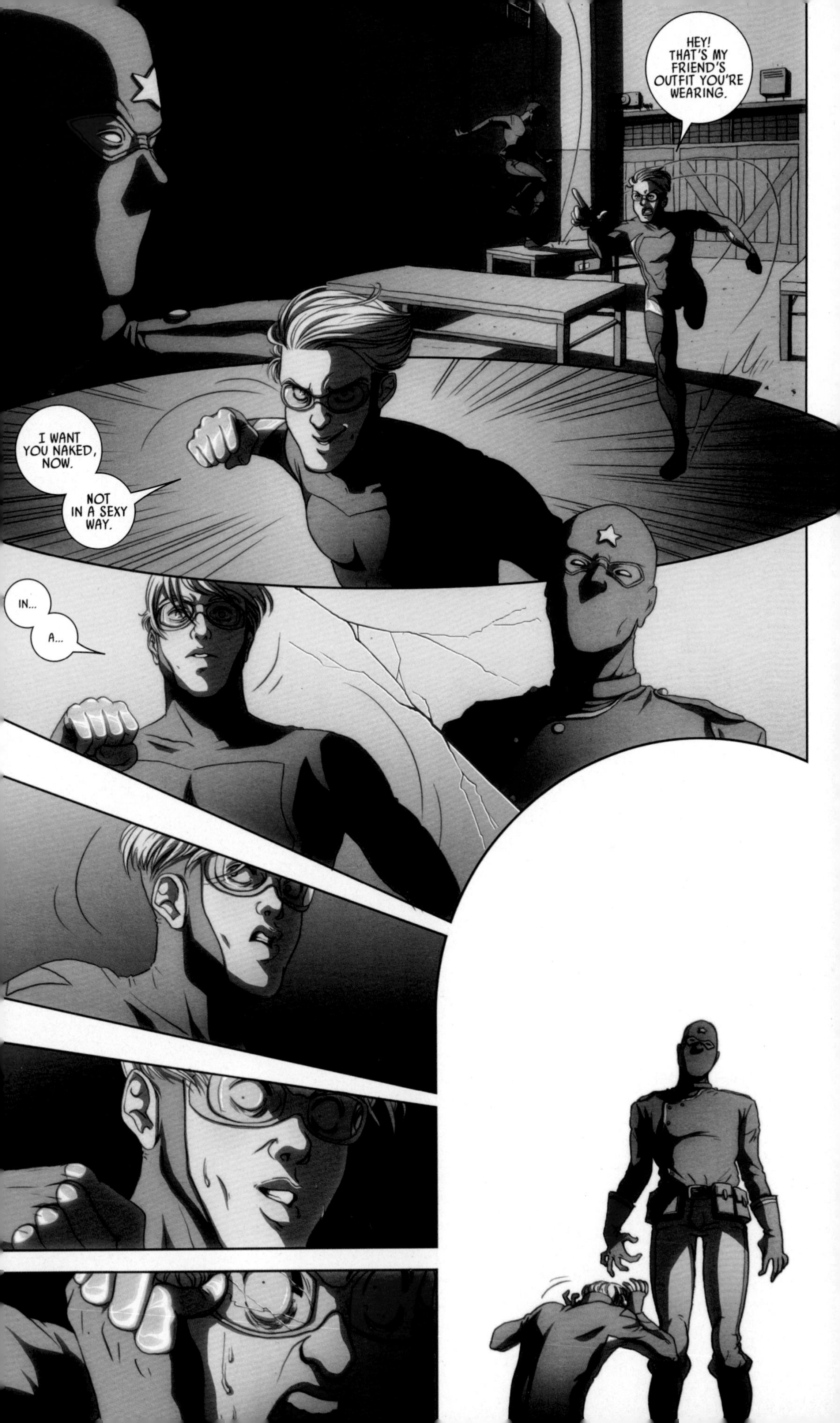
HEY! THAT'S MY FRIEND'S OUTFIT YOU'RE WEARING.
I WANT YOU NAKED, NOW.
NOT IN A SEXY WAY.
IN...
A...

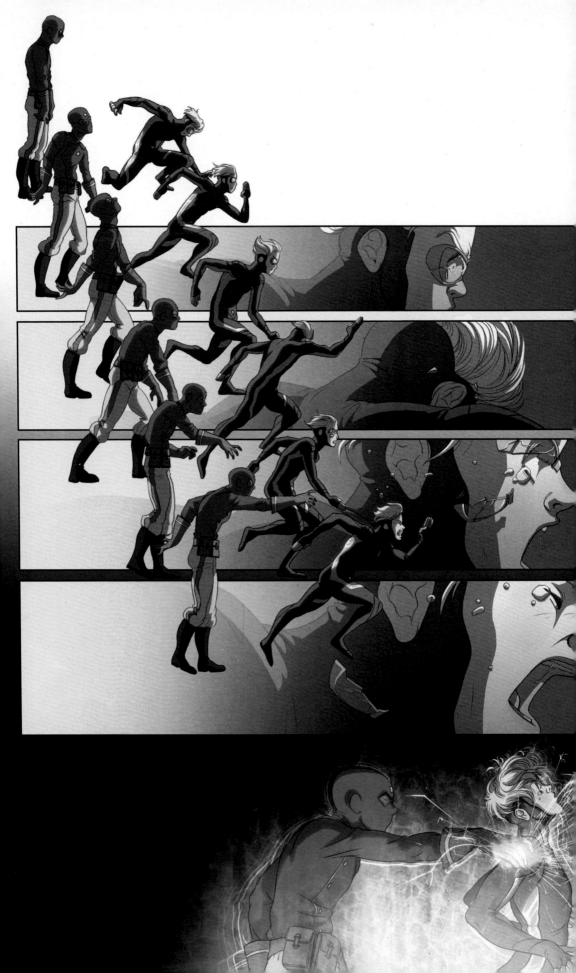

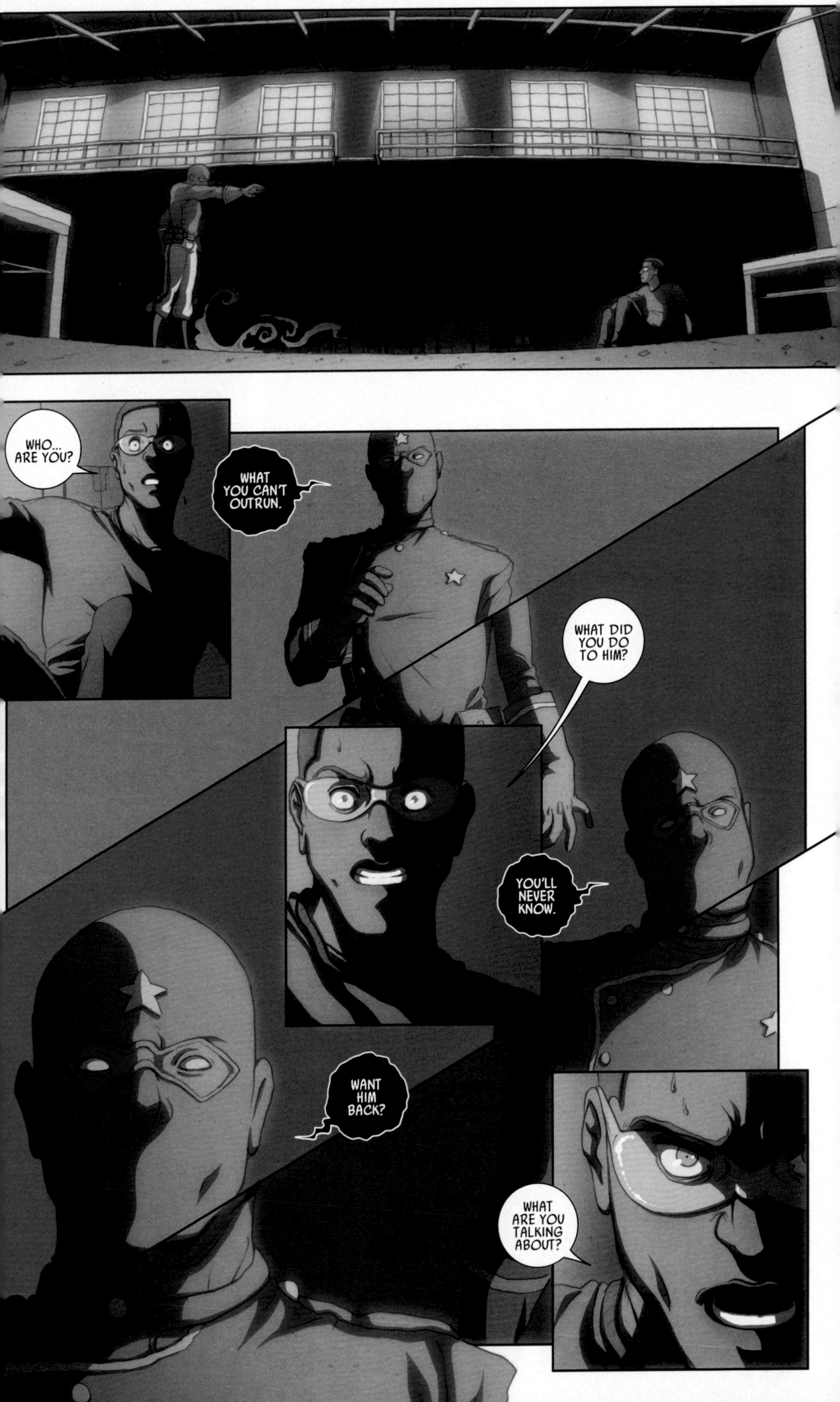
WHO... ARE YOU?
WHAT YOU CAN'T OUTRUN.
WHAT DID YOU DO TO HIM?
YOU'LL NEVER KNOW.
WANT HIM BACK?
WHAT ARE YOU TALKING ABOUT?

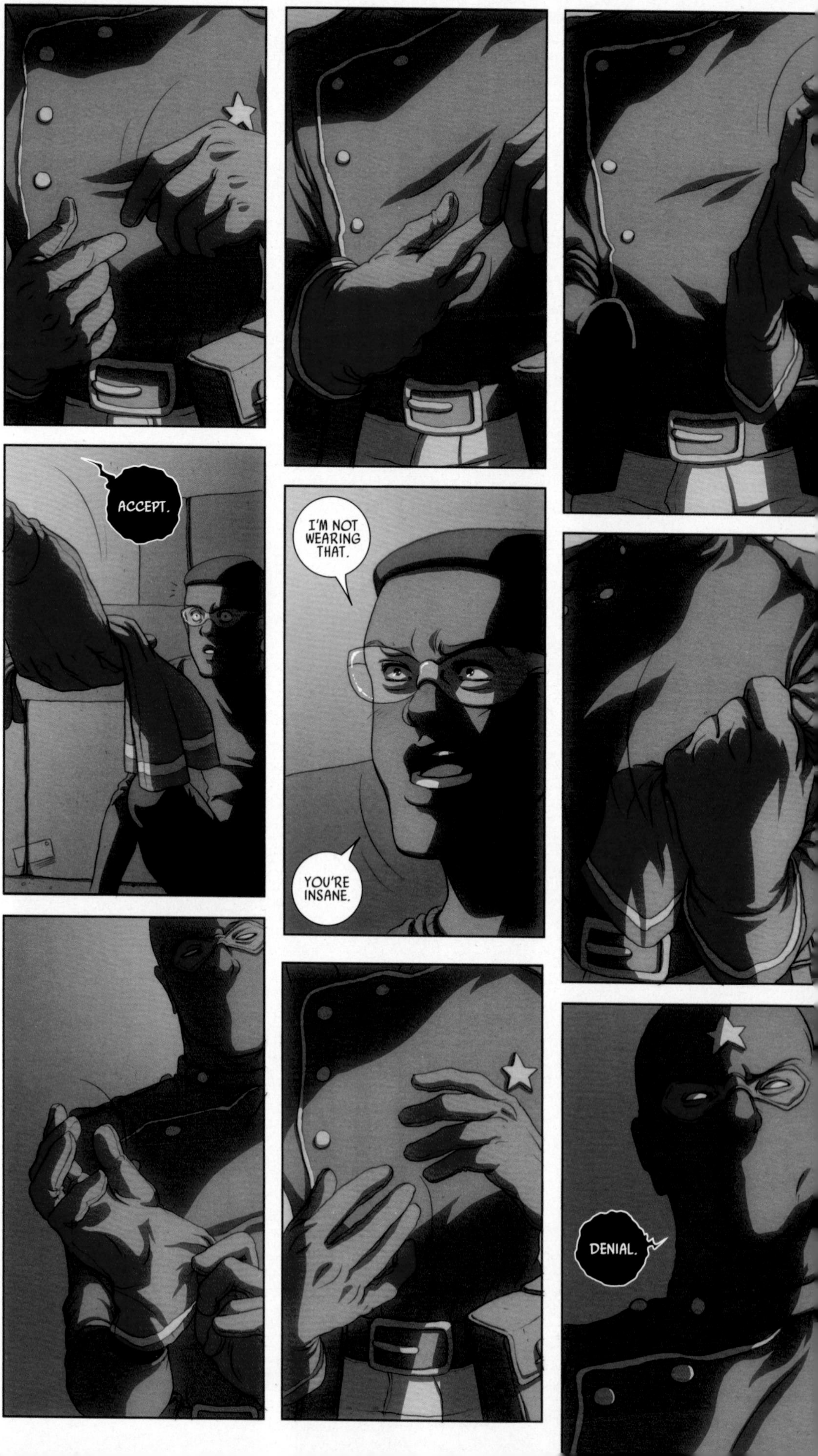
ACCEPT.
I'M NOT WEARING THAT.
YOU'RE INSANE.
DENIAL.

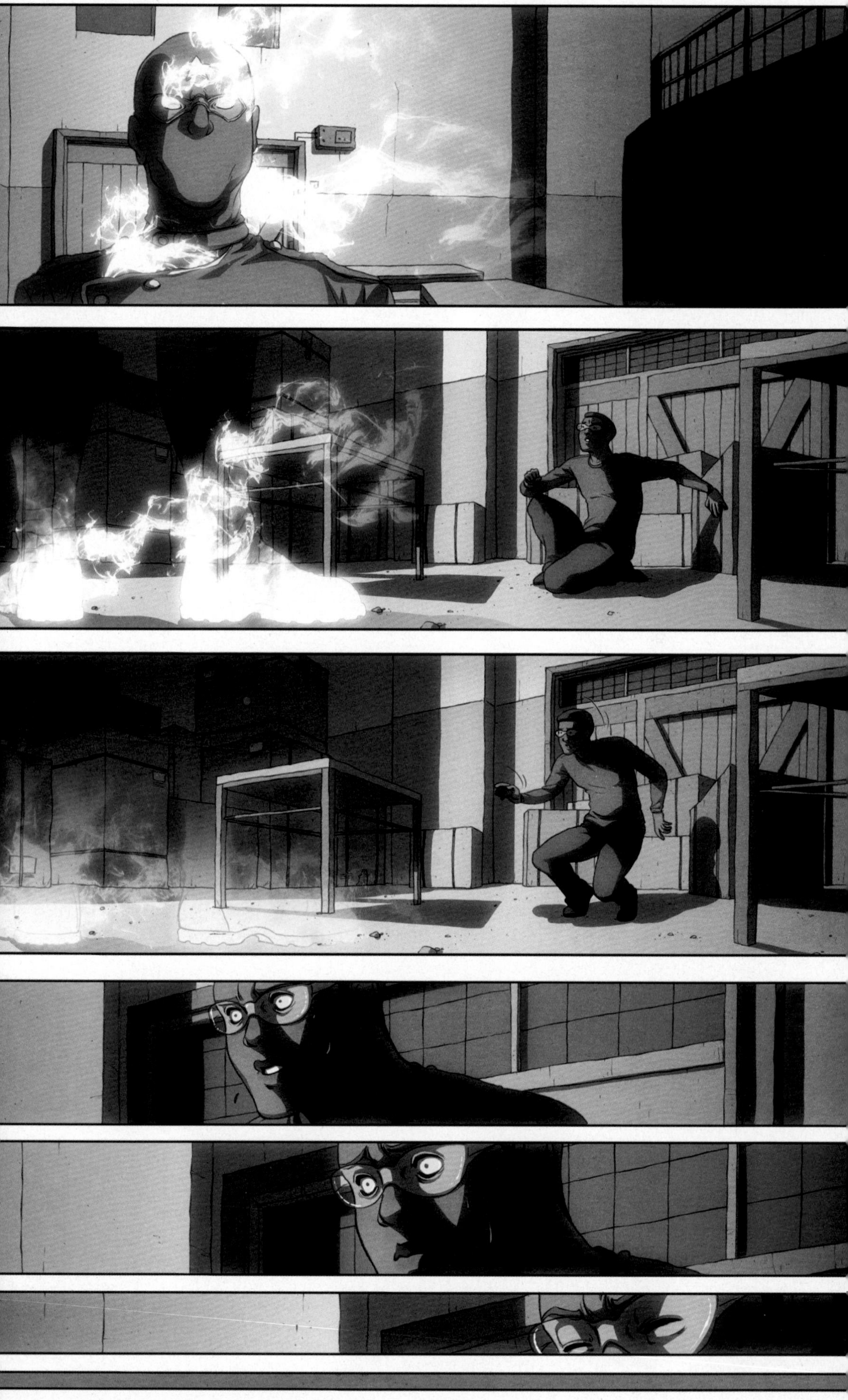

7

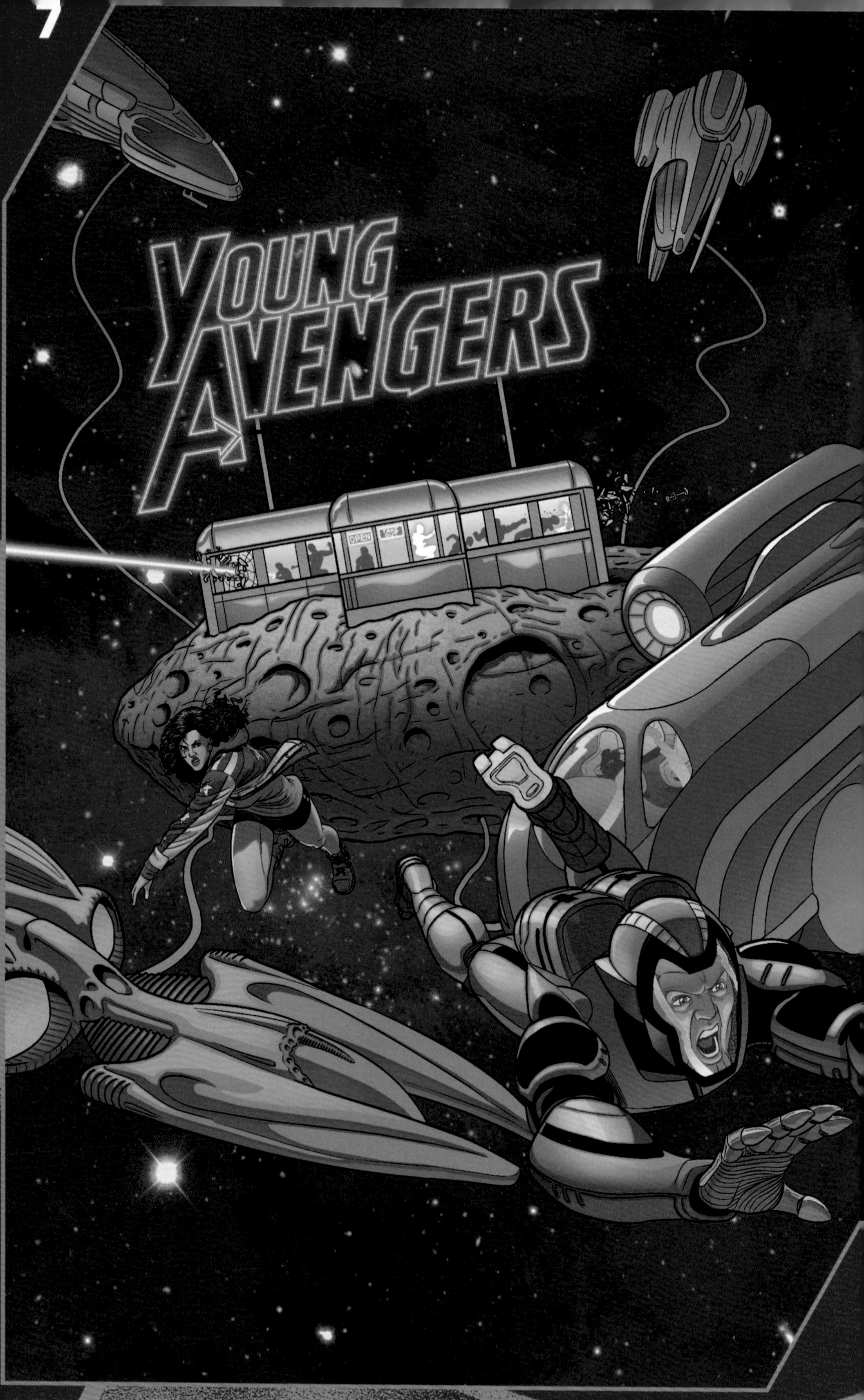
YOUNG AVENGERS
OPEN

BREAKFAST MEET

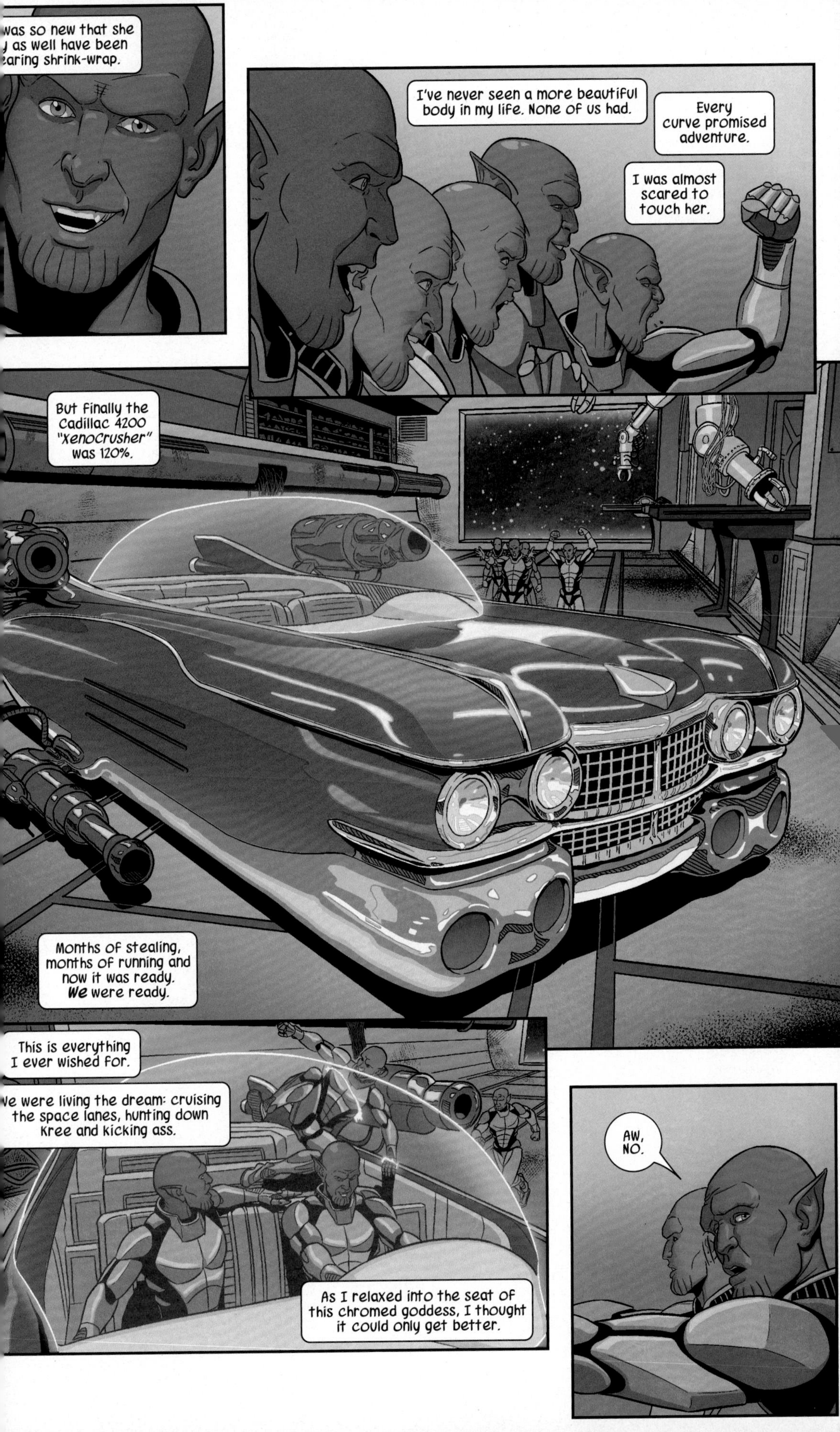
was so new that she
as well have been
aring shrink-wrap.
I've never seen a more beautiful body in my life. None of us had.
Every curve promised adventure.
I was almost scared to touch her.
But finally the Cadillac 4200 "Xenocrusher" was 120%.
Months of stealing, months of running and now it was ready. **We** were ready.
This is everything I ever wished for.
e were living the dream: cruising the space lanes, hunting down Kree and kicking ass.
As I relaxed into the seat of this chromed goddess, I thought it could only get better.
AW, NO.

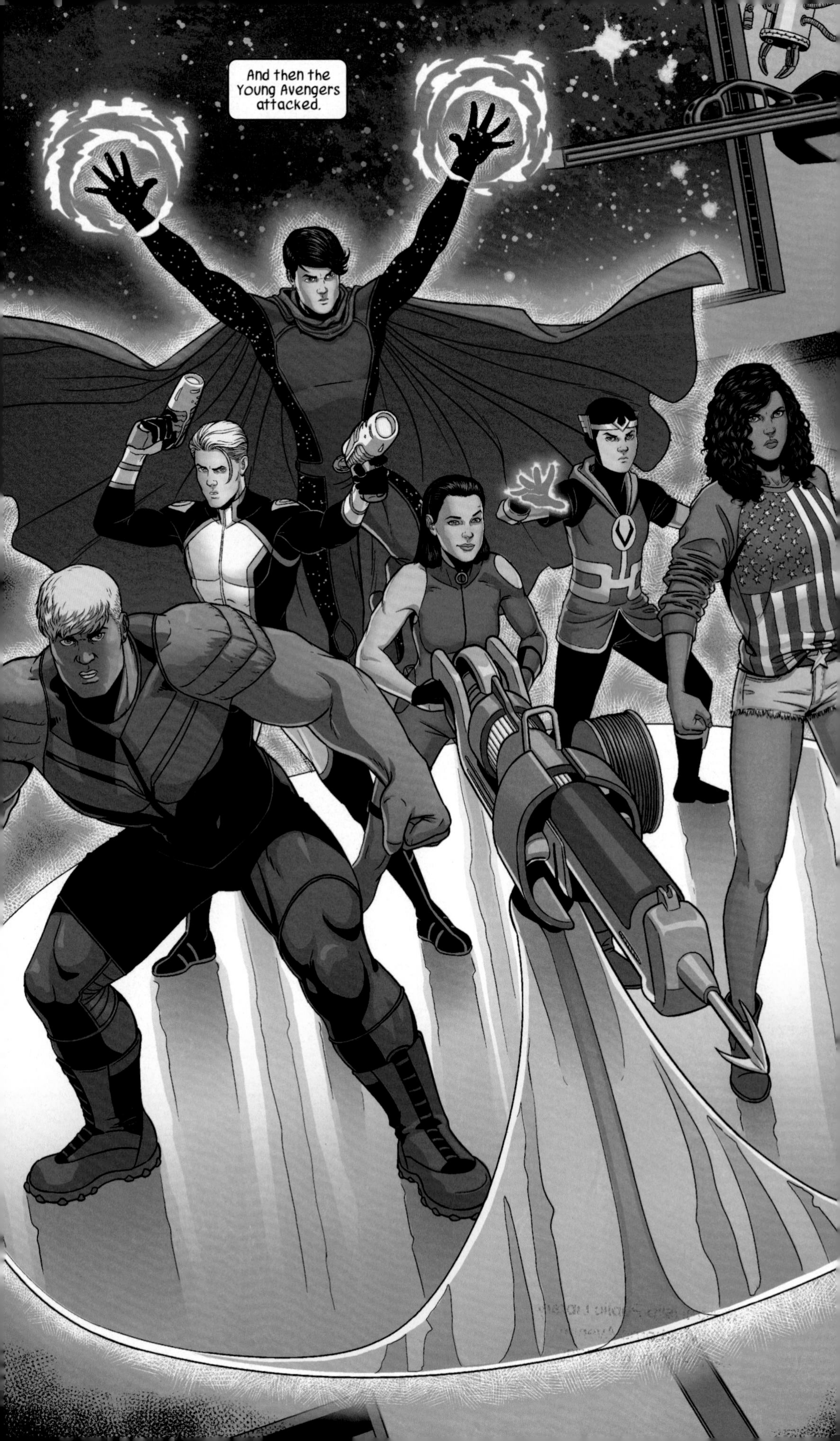
And then the Young Avengers attacked.

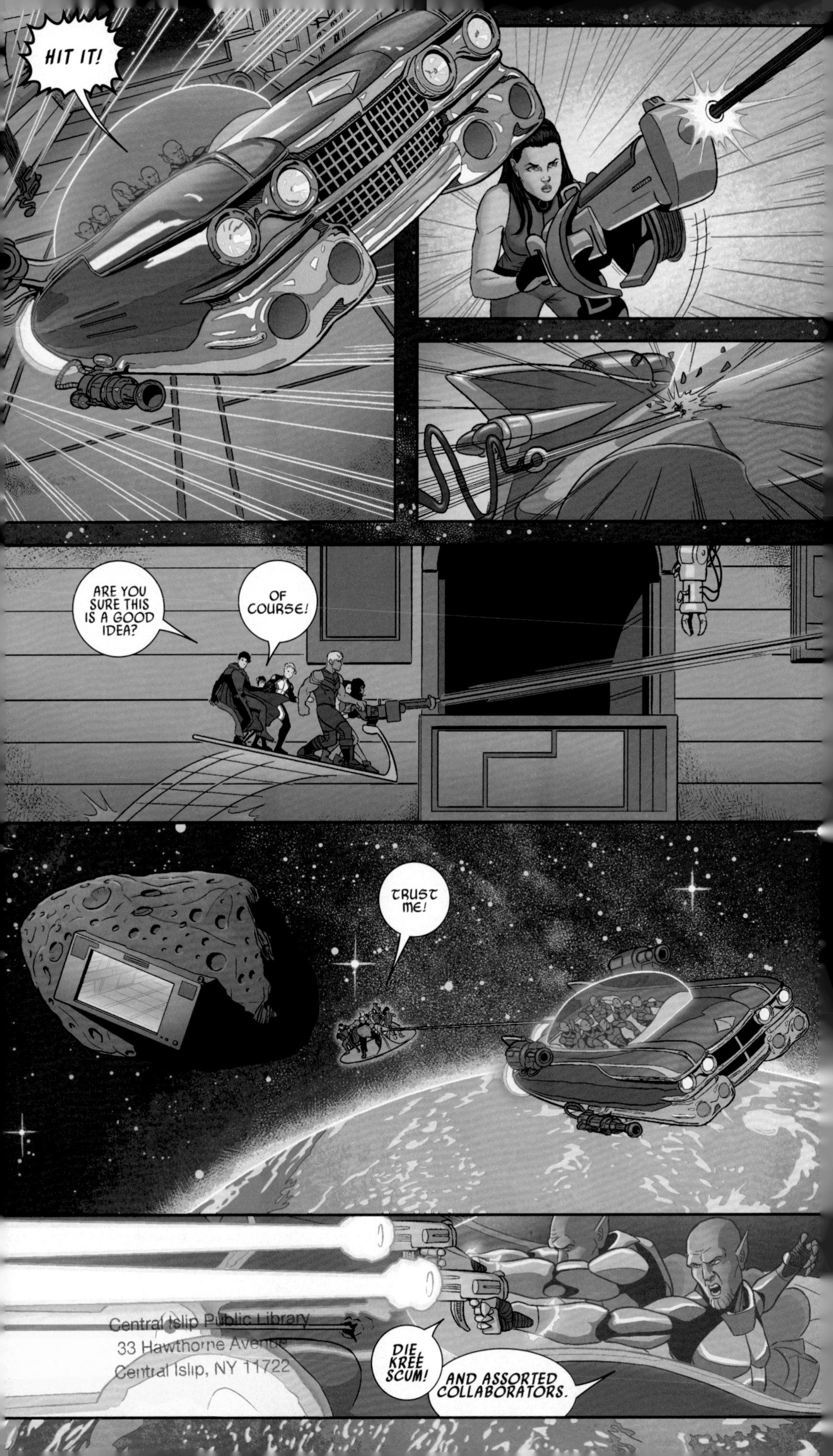
HIT IT!
ARE YOU SURE THIS IS A GOOD IDEA?
OF COURSE!
TRUST ME!
DIE, KREE SCUM!
AND ASSORTED COLLABORATORS.

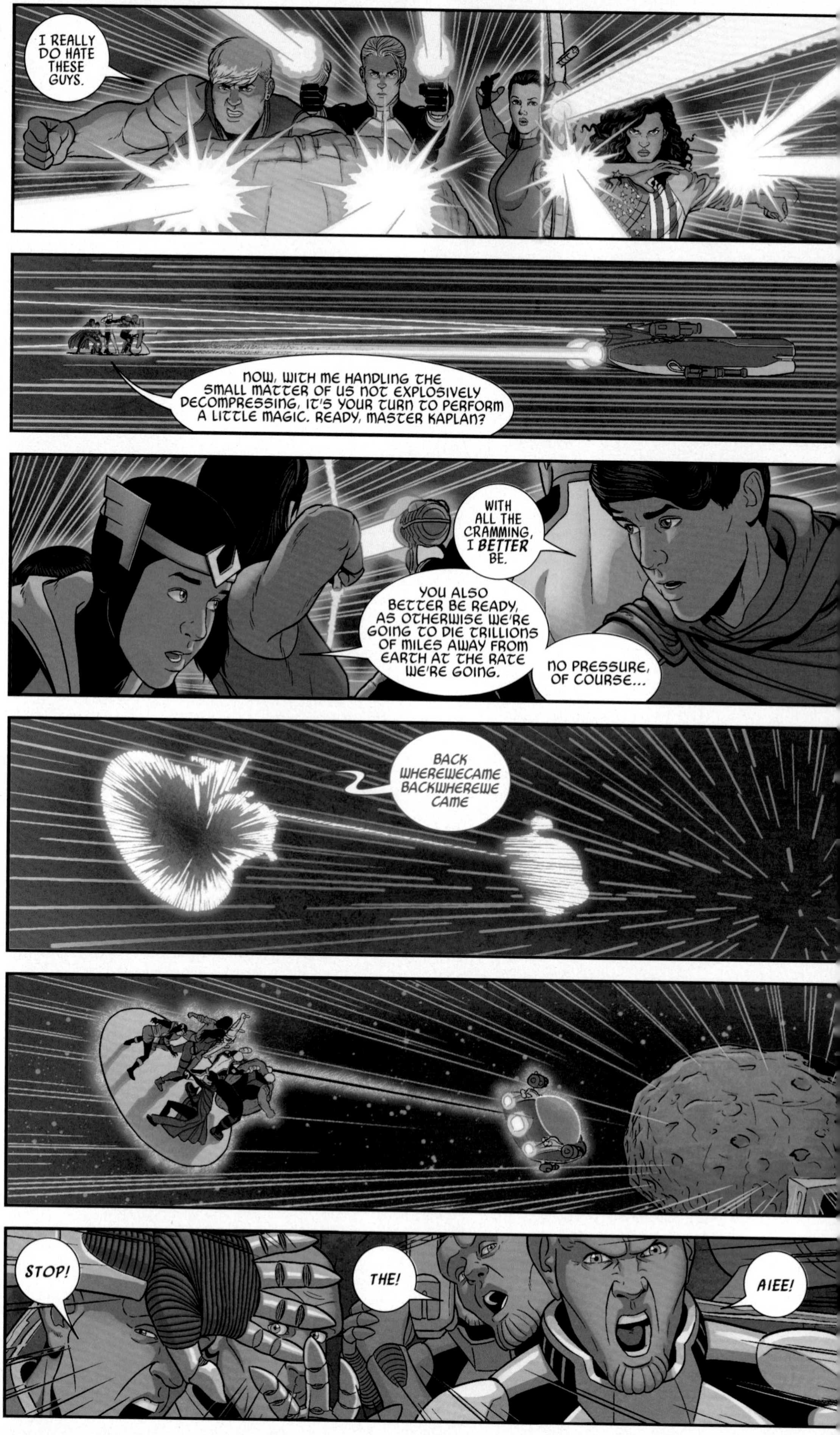
I REALLY DO HATE THESE GUYS.
NOW, WITH ME HANDLING THE SMALL MATTER OF US NOT EXPLOSIVELY DECOMPRESSING, IT'S YOUR TURN TO PERFORM A LITTLE MAGIC. READY, MASTER KAPLAN?
WITH ALL THE CRAMMING, I BETTER BE.
YOU ALSO BETTER BE READY, AS OTHERWISE WE'RE GOING TO DIE TRILLIONS OF MILES AWAY FROM EARTH AT THE RATE WE'RE GOING.
NO PRESSURE, OF COURSE...
BACK WHEREWECAME BACKWHEREWE CAME
STOP!
THE!
AIEE!

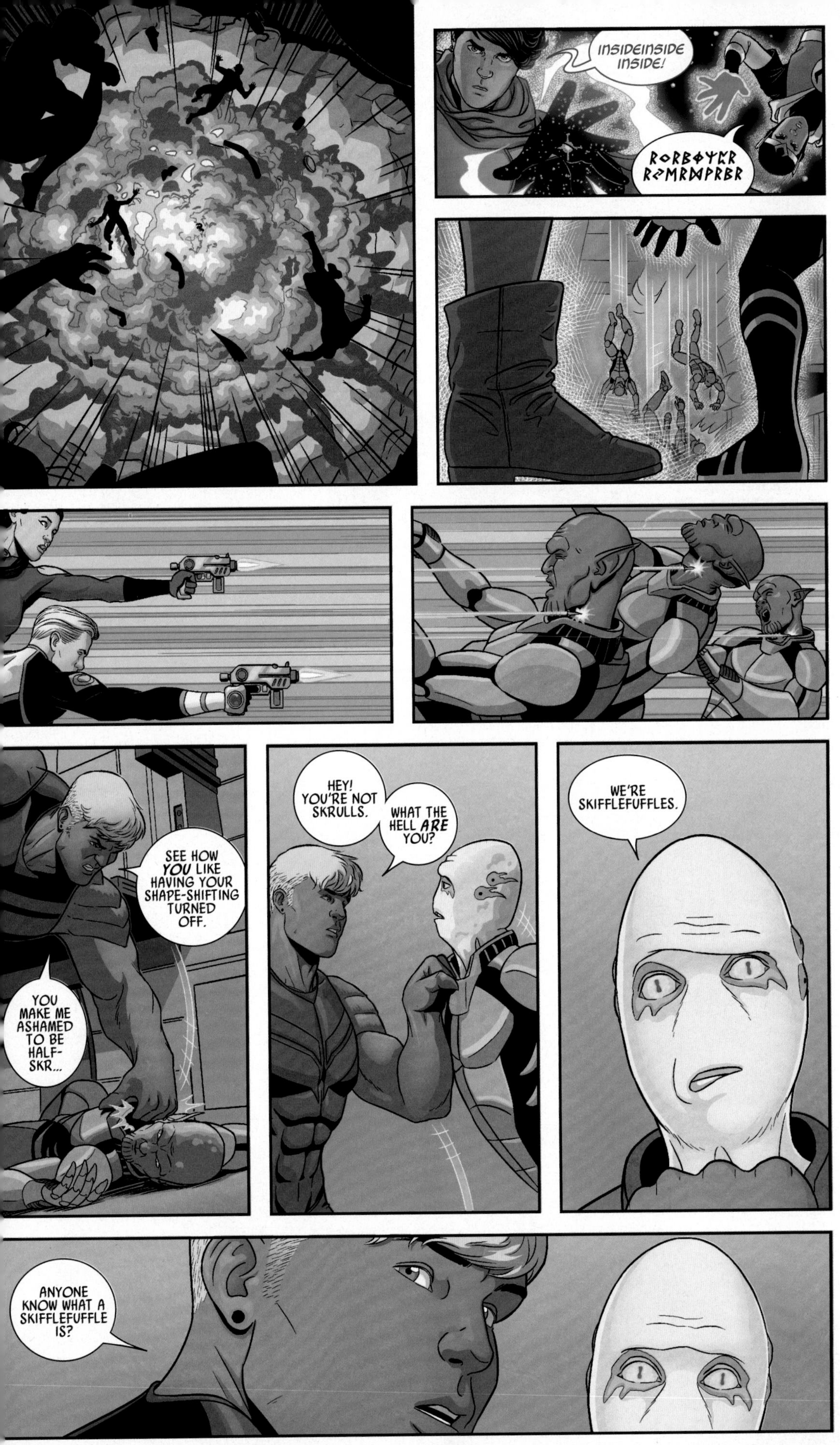
INSIDEINSIDE INSIDE!
SEE HOW YOU LIKE HAVING YOUR SHAPE-SHIFTING TURNED OFF.
YOU MAKE ME ASHAMED TO BE HALF-SKR...
HEY! YOU'RE NOT SKRULLS.
WHAT THE HELL ARE YOU?
WE'RE SKIFFLEFUFFLES.
ANYONE KNOW WHAT A SKIFFLEFUFFLE IS?

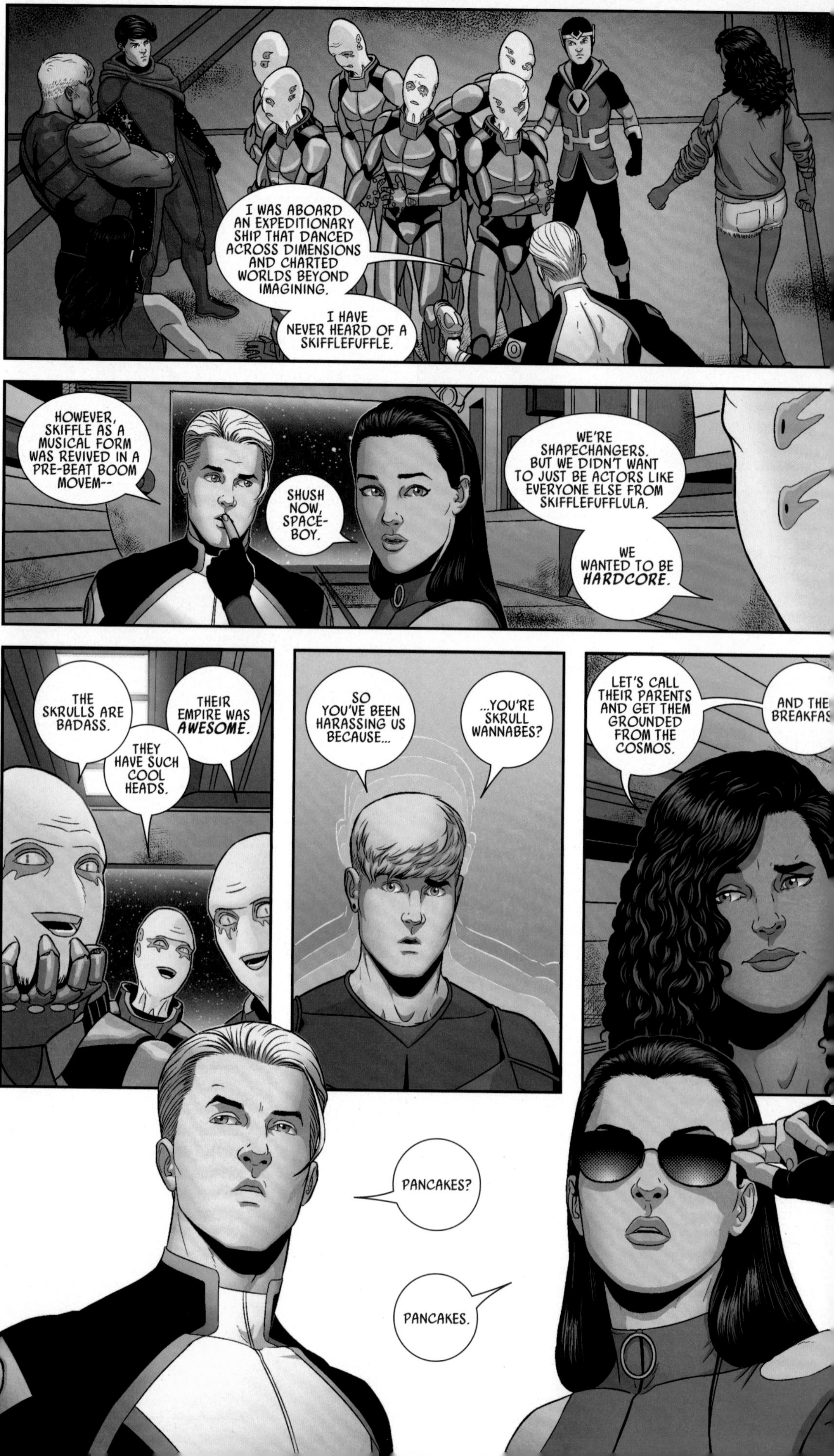
I WAS ABOARD AN EXPEDITIONARY SHIP THAT DANCED ACROSS DIMENSIONS AND CHARTED WORLDS BEYOND IMAGINING.
I HAVE NEVER HEARD OF A SKIFFLEFUFFLE.
HOWEVER, SKIFFLE AS A MUSICAL FORM WAS REVIVED IN A PRE-BEAT BOOM MOVEM--
SHUSH NOW, SPACE-BOY.
WE'RE SHAPECHANGERS. BUT WE DIDN'T WANT TO JUST BE ACTORS LIKE EVERYONE ELSE FROM SKIFFLEFUFFLULA.
WE WANTED TO BE HARDCORE.
THE SKRULLS ARE BADASS.
THEIR EMPIRE WAS AWESOME.
THEY HAVE SUCH COOL HEADS.
SO YOU'VE BEEN HARASSING US BECAUSE...
...YOU'RE SKRULL WANNABES?
LET'S CALL THEIR PARENTS AND GET THEM GROUNDED FROM THE COSMOS.
AND THE BREAKFAS
PANCAKES?
PANCAKES.

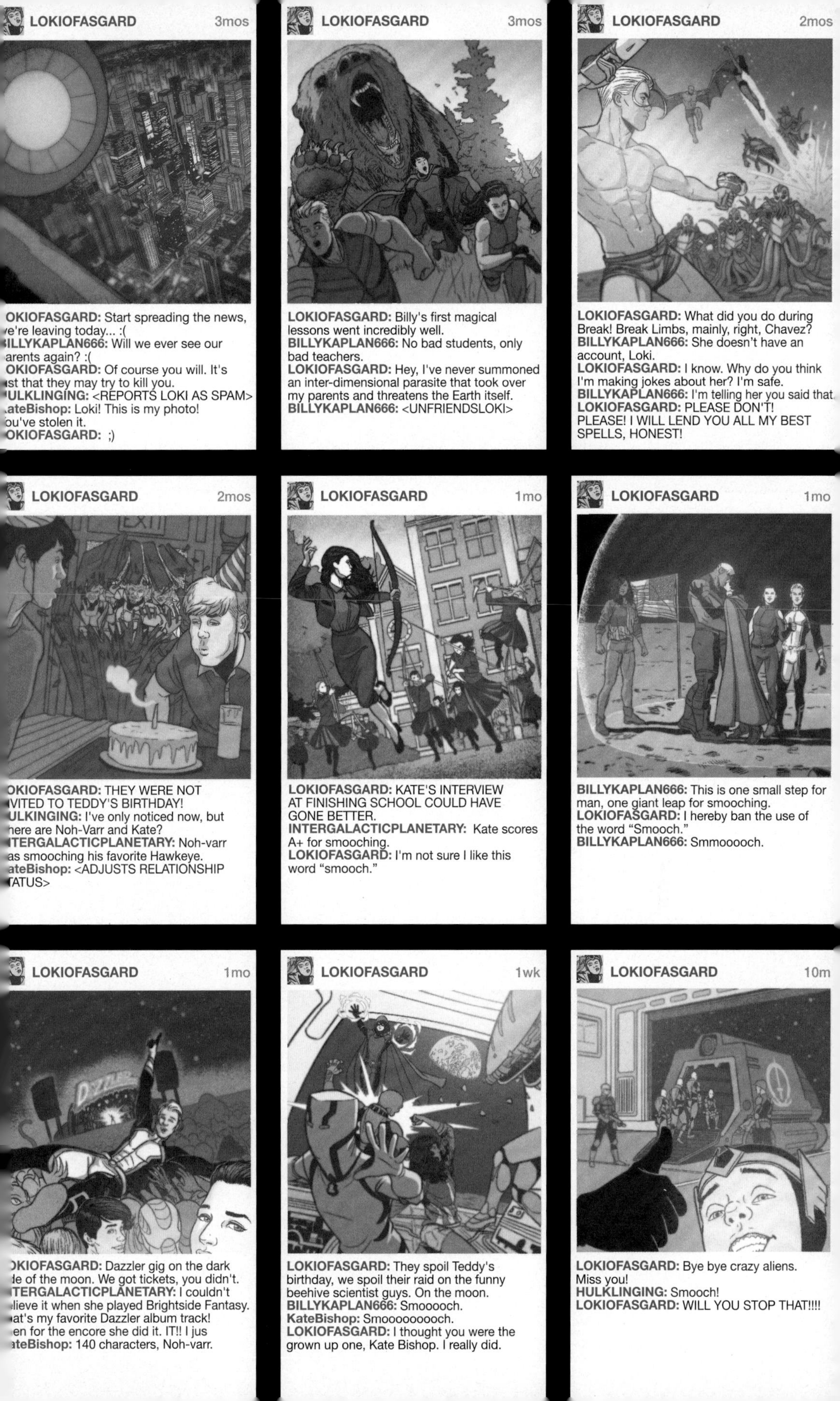
LOKIOFASGARD 3mos
OKIOFASGARD: Start spreading the news,
e're leaving today... :(
ILLYKAPLAN666: Will we ever see our
arents again? :(
OKIOFASGARD: Of course you will. It's
ist that they may try to kill you.
ULKLINGING: <REPORTS LOKI AS SPAM>
ateBishop: Loki! This is my photo!
ou've stolen it.
OKIOFASGARD: ;)
LOKIOFASGARD 3mos
LOKIOFASGARD: Billy's first magical lessons went incredibly well.
BILLYKAPLAN666: No bad students, only bad teachers.
LOKIOFASGARD: Hey, I've never summoned an inter-dimensional parasite that took over my parents and threatens the Earth itself.
BILLYKAPLAN666: <UNFRIENDSLOKI>
LOKIOFASGARD 2mos
LOKIOFASGARD: What did you do during Break! Break Limbs, mainly, right, Chavez?
BILLYKAPLAN666: She doesn't have an account, Loki.
LOKIOFASGARD: I know. Why do you think I'm making jokes about her? I'm safe.
BILLYKAPLAN666: I'm telling her you said that.
LOKIOFASGARD: PLEASE DON'T! PLEASE! I WILL LEND YOU ALL MY BEST SPELLS, HONEST!
LOKIOFASGARD 2mos
EXIT
OKIOFASGARD: THEY WERE NOT
VITED TO TEDDY'S BIRTHDAY!
ULKINGING: I've only noticed now, but
here are Noh-Varr and Kate?
TERGALACTICPLANETARY: Noh-varr
as smooching his favorite Hawkeye.
ateBishop: <ADJUSTS RELATIONSHIP
TATUS>
LOKIOFASGARD 1mo
LOKIOFASGARD: KATE'S INTERVIEW AT FINISHING SCHOOL COULD HAVE GONE BETTER.
INTERGALACTICPLANETARY: Kate scores A+ for smooching.
LOKIOFASGARD: I'm not sure I like this word "smooch."
LOKIOFASGARD 1mo
BILLYKAPLAN666: This is one small step for man, one giant leap for smooching.
LOKIOFASGARD: I hereby ban the use of the word "Smooch."
BILLYKAPLAN666: Smmooooch.
LOKIOFASGARD 1mo
DAZZLER
OKIOFASGARD: Dazzler gig on the dark
le of the moon. We got tickets, you didn't.
TERGALACTICPLANETARY: I couldn't
elieve it when she played Brightside Fantasy.
at's my favorite Dazzler album track!
en for the encore she did it. IT!! I jus
ateBishop: 140 characters, Noh-varr.
LOKIOFASGARD 1wk
LOKIOFASGARD: They spoil Teddy's birthday, we spoil their raid on the funny beehive scientist guys. On the moon.
BILLYKAPLAN666: Smooooch.
KateBishop: Smoooooooooch.
LOKIOFASGARD: I thought you were the grown up one, Kate Bishop. I really did.
LOKIOFASGARD 10m
LOKIOFASGARD: Bye bye crazy aliens. Miss you!
HULKLINGING: Smooch!
LOKIOFASGARD: WILL YOU STOP THAT!!!!

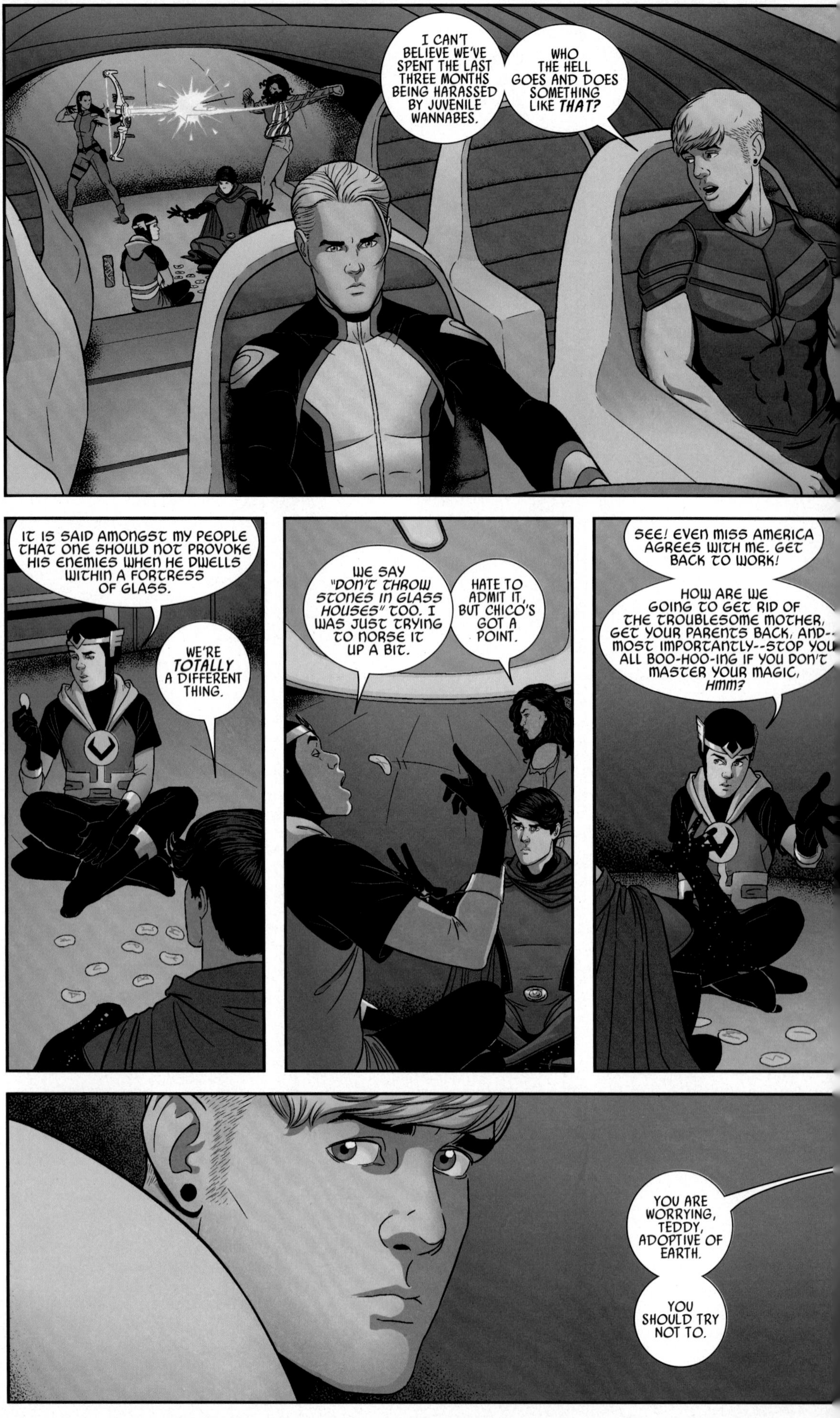
I CAN'T BELIEVE WE'VE SPENT THE LAST THREE MONTHS BEING HARASSED BY JUVENILE WANNABES.
WHO THE HELL GOES AND DOES SOMETHING LIKE THAT?
IT IS SAID AMONGST MY PEOPLE THAT ONE SHOULD NOT PROVOKE HIS ENEMIES WHEN HE DWELLS WITHIN A FORTRESS OF GLASS.
WE'RE TOTALLY A DIFFERENT THING.
WE SAY "DON'T THROW STONES IN GLASS HOUSES" TOO. I WAS JUST TRYING TO NORSE IT UP A BIT.
HATE TO ADMIT IT, BUT CHICO'S GOT A POINT.
SEE! EVEN MISS AMERICA AGREES WITH ME. GET BACK TO WORK!
HOW ARE WE GOING TO GET RID OF THE TROUBLESOME MOTHER, GET YOUR PARENTS BACK, AND--MOST IMPORTANTLY--STOP YOU ALL BOO-HOO-ING IF YOU DON'T MASTER YOUR MAGIC, HMM?
YOU ARE WORRYING, TEDDY, ADOPTIVE OF EARTH.
YOU SHOULD TRY NOT TO.

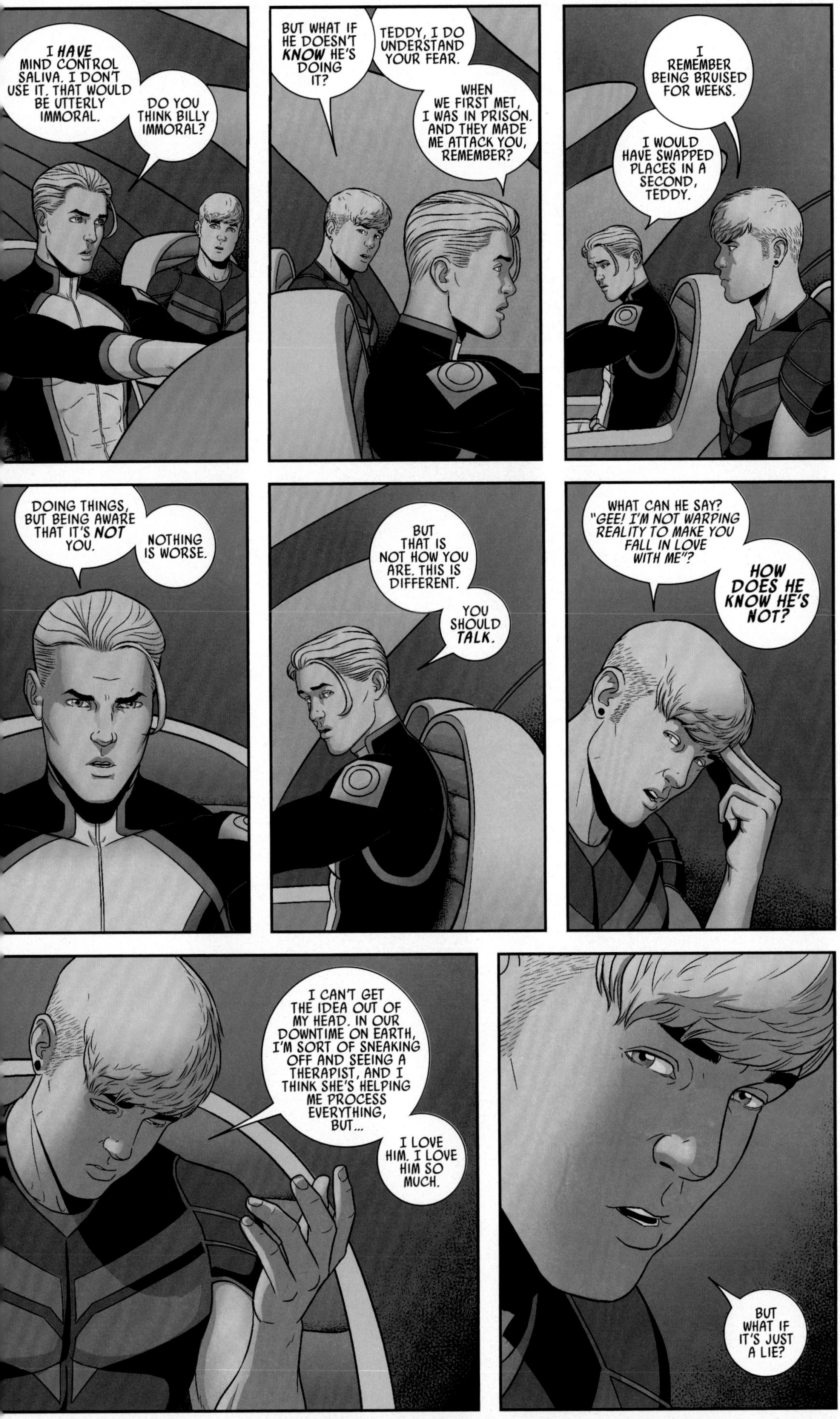

I HAVE MIND CONTROL SALIVA. I DON'T USE IT. THAT WOULD BE UTTERLY IMMORAL.
DO YOU THINK BILLY IMMORAL?
BUT WHAT IF HE DOESN'T KNOW HE'S DOING IT?
TEDDY, I DO UNDERSTAND YOUR FEAR.
WHEN WE FIRST MET, I WAS IN PRISON. AND THEY MADE ME ATTACK YOU, REMEMBER?
I REMEMBER BEING BRUISED FOR WEEKS.
I WOULD HAVE SWAPPED PLACES IN A SECOND, TEDDY.
DOING THINGS, BUT BEING AWARE THAT IT'S NOT YOU.
NOTHING IS WORSE.
BUT THAT IS NOT HOW YOU ARE. THIS IS DIFFERENT.
YOU SHOULD TALK.
WHAT CAN HE SAY? "GEE! I'M NOT WARPING REALITY TO MAKE YOU FALL IN LOVE WITH ME"?
HOW DOES HE KNOW HE'S NOT?
I CAN'T GET THE IDEA OUT OF MY HEAD. IN OUR DOWNTIME ON EARTH, I'M SORT OF SNEAKING OFF AND SEEING A THERAPIST, AND I THINK SHE'S HELPING ME PROCESS EVERYTHING, BUT...
I LOVE HIM. I LOVE HIM SO MUCH.
BUT WHAT IF IT'S JUST A LIE?

YOU ARE BOTH GOOD PEOPLE. TO HAVE SUCH LOVE IS PRECIOUS. TRUST ME. I KNOW WHAT IT'S LIKE TO LOVE. IF IT WAS TAKEN, ITS GHOST WOULD LINGER AND TORMENT YOU...

YOU WILL FIND A WAY. HAVE FAITH IN THIS. IT IS LIKE THE SUPREMES SAY, YOU CAN'T--

THANKS, NOH-VARR.

HMM. KATE. TEDDY REMINDS ME.

HAVE I MENTIONED I HAVE MIND CONTROL SALIVA?

IT'S OKAY.

MANY PARTS OF MY BODY ARE MIND CONTROL.

THIS IS TRUE.

CONVERSATIONS ABOUT SALIVA ARE HENCE OUT OF BOUNDS UNTIL I HAVE BREAKFAST BEFORE ME!

CAN'T THIS SPACESHIP GO ANY FASTER? BREAKFAST! GIVE ME BREAKFAST!

"THE NORSE GOD OF MISCHIEF CRAVES THE CONGRESS OF BREAKFAST MEAT!"

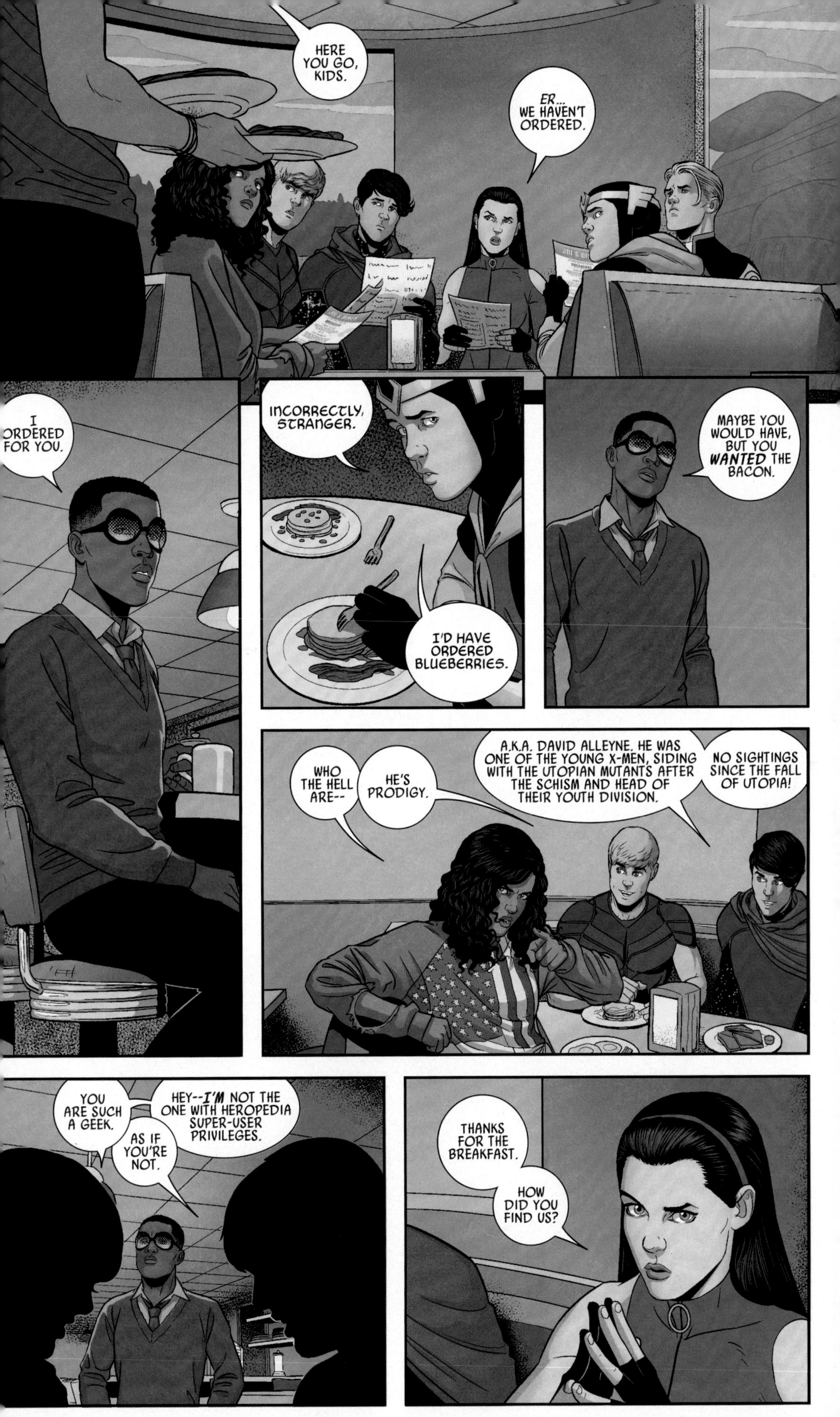
HERE YOU GO, KIDS.
ER... WE HAVEN'T ORDERED.
I ORDERED FOR YOU.
INCORRECTLY, STRANGER.
I'D HAVE ORDERED BLUEBERRIES.
MAYBE YOU WOULD HAVE, BUT YOU WANTED THE BACON.
WHO THE HELL ARE--
HE'S PRODIGY.
A.K.A. DAVID ALLEYNE. HE WAS ONE OF THE YOUNG X-MEN, SIDING WITH THE UTOPIAN MUTANTS AFTER THE SCHISM AND HEAD OF THEIR YOUTH DIVISION.
NO SIGHTINGS SINCE THE FALL OF UTOPIA!
YOU ARE SUCH A GEEK.
HEY--I'M NOT THE ONE WITH HEROPEDIA SUPER-USER PRIVILEGES.
AS IF YOU'RE NOT.
THANKS FOR THE BREAKFAST.
HOW DID YOU FIND US?

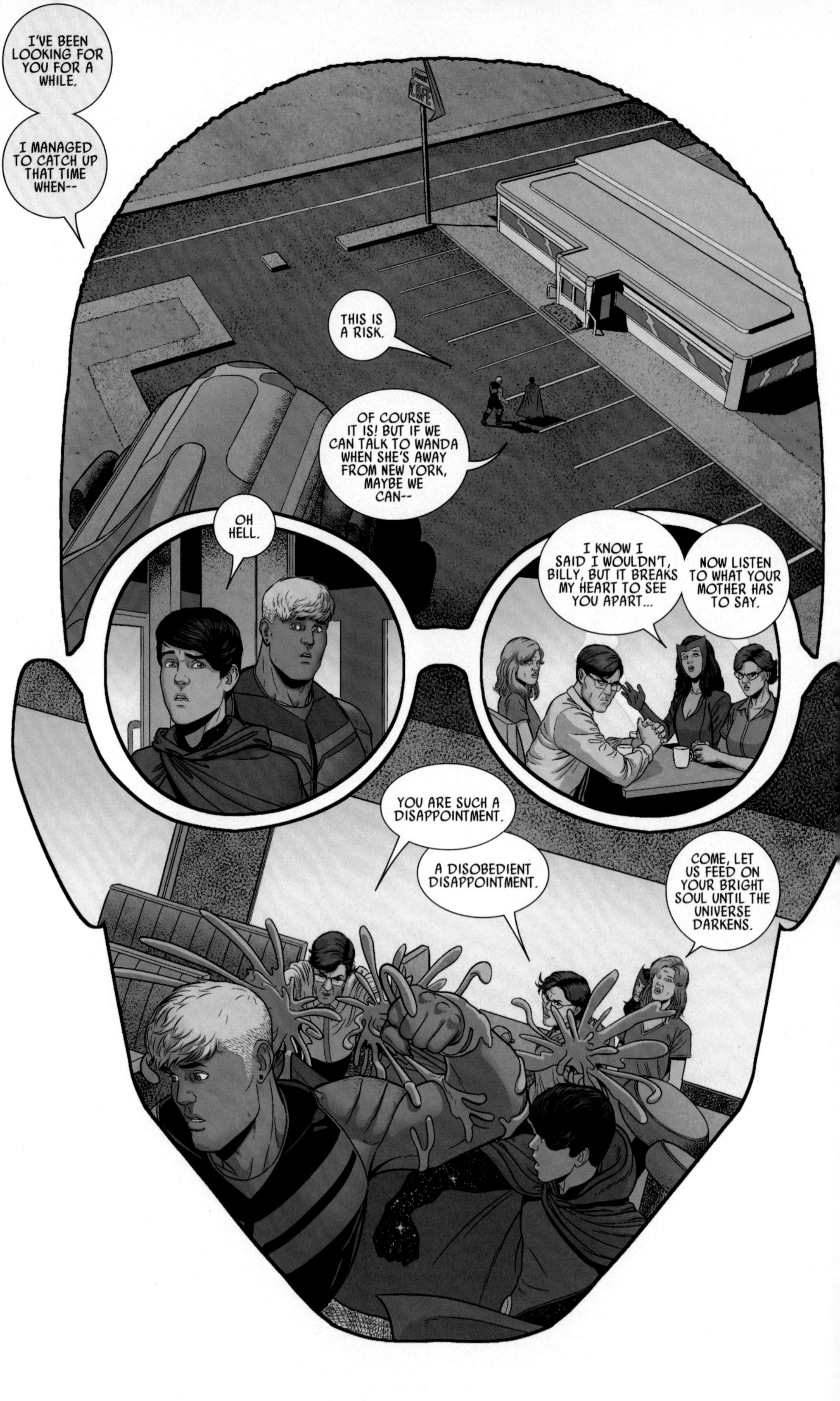

I'VE BEEN LOOKING FOR YOU FOR A WHILE.
I MANAGED TO CATCH UP THAT TIME WHEN--
CAFE
THIS IS A RISK.
OF COURSE IT IS! BUT IF WE CAN TALK TO WANDA WHEN SHE'S AWAY FROM NEW YORK, MAYBE WE CAN--
OH HELL.
I KNOW I SAID I WOULDN'T, BILLY, BUT IT BREAKS MY HEART TO SEE YOU APART...
NOW LISTEN TO WHAT YOUR MOTHER HAS TO SAY.
YOU ARE SUCH A DISAPPOINTMENT.
A DISOBEDIENT DISAPPOINTMENT.
COME, LET US FEED ON YOUR BRIGHT SOUL UNTIL THE UNIVERSE DARKENS.

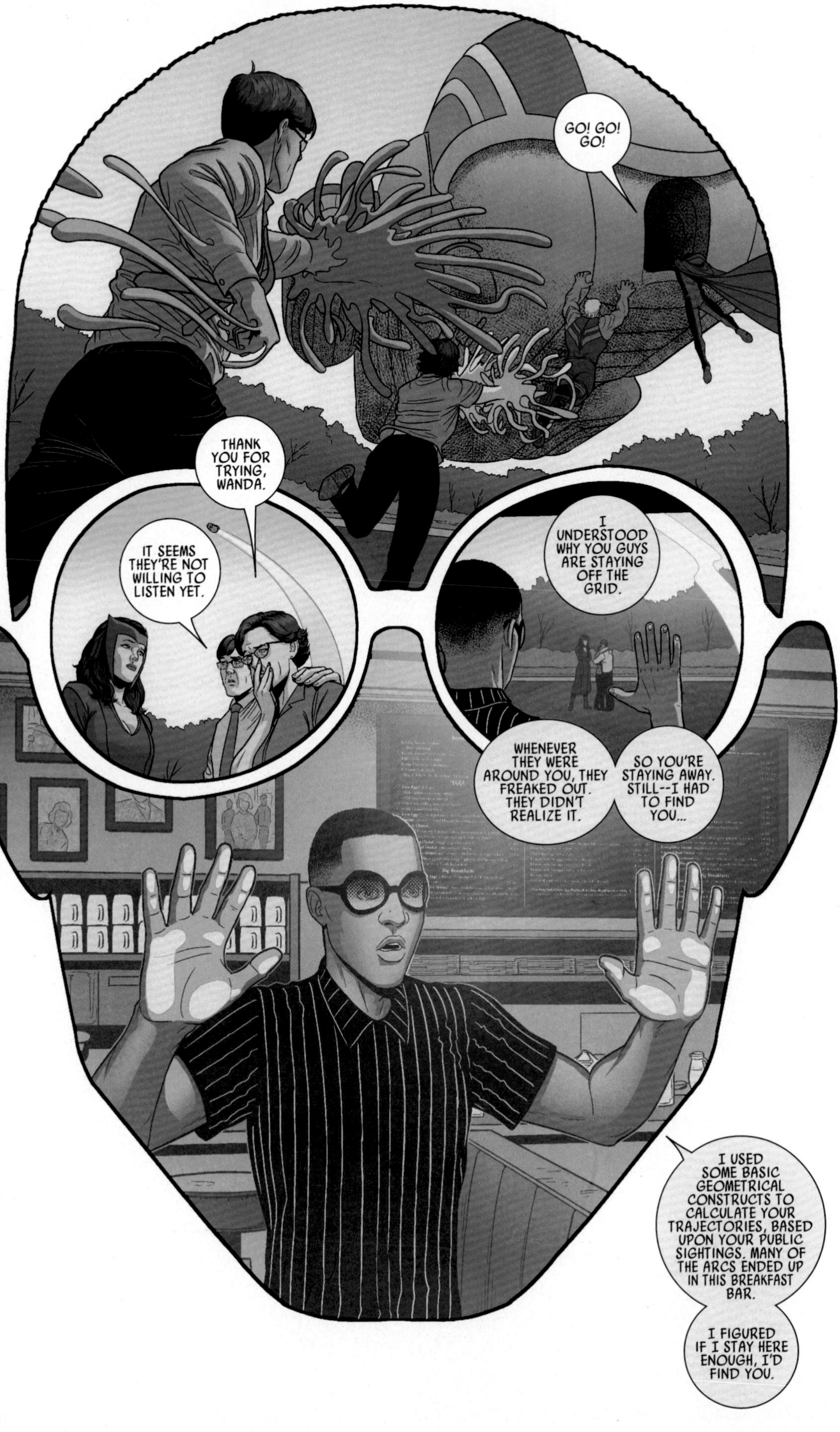
GO! GO! GO!
THANK YOU FOR TRYING, WANDA.
IT SEEMS THEY'RE NOT WILLING TO LISTEN YET.
I UNDERSTOOD WHY YOU GUYS ARE STAYING OFF THE GRID.
WHENEVER THEY WERE AROUND YOU, THEY FREAKED OUT. THEY DIDN'T REALIZE IT.
SO YOU'RE STAYING AWAY. STILL--I HAD TO FIND YOU...
I USED SOME BASIC GEOMETRICAL CONSTRUCTS TO CALCULATE YOUR TRAJECTORIES, BASED UPON YOUR PUBLIC SIGHTINGS. MANY OF THE ARCS ENDED UP IN THIS BREAKFAST BAR.
I FIGURED IF I STAY HERE ENOUGH, I'D FIND YOU.

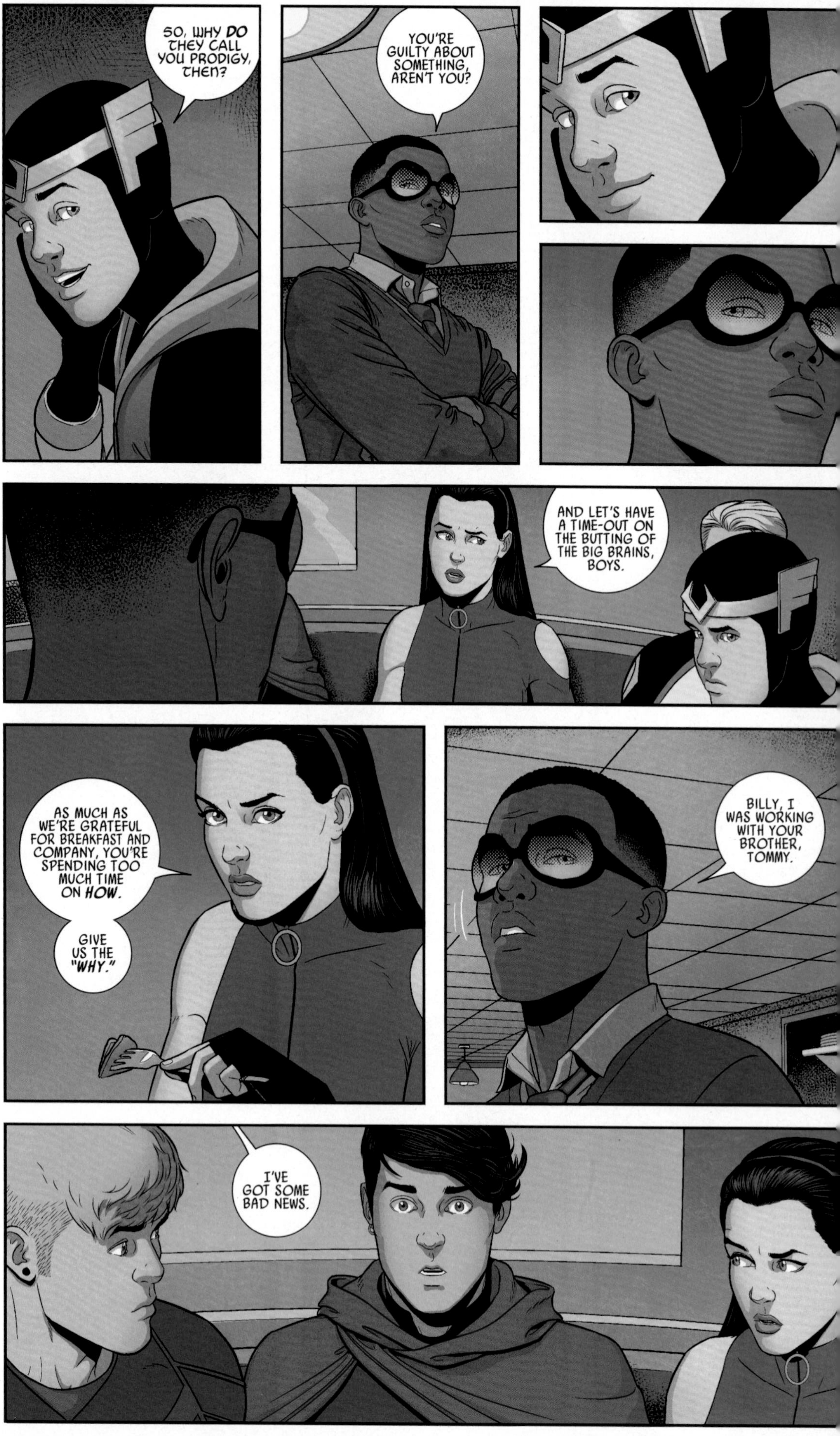
SO, WHY DO THEY CALL YOU PRODIGY, THEN?
YOU'RE GUILTY ABOUT SOMETHING, AREN'T YOU?
AND LET'S HAVE A TIME-OUT ON THE BUTTING OF THE BIG BRAINS, BOYS.
AS MUCH AS WE'RE GRATEFUL FOR BREAKFAST AND COMPANY, YOU'RE SPENDING TOO MUCH TIME ON HOW.
GIVE US THE "WHY."
BILLY, I WAS WORKING WITH YOUR BROTHER, TOMMY.
I'VE GOT SOME BAD NEWS.

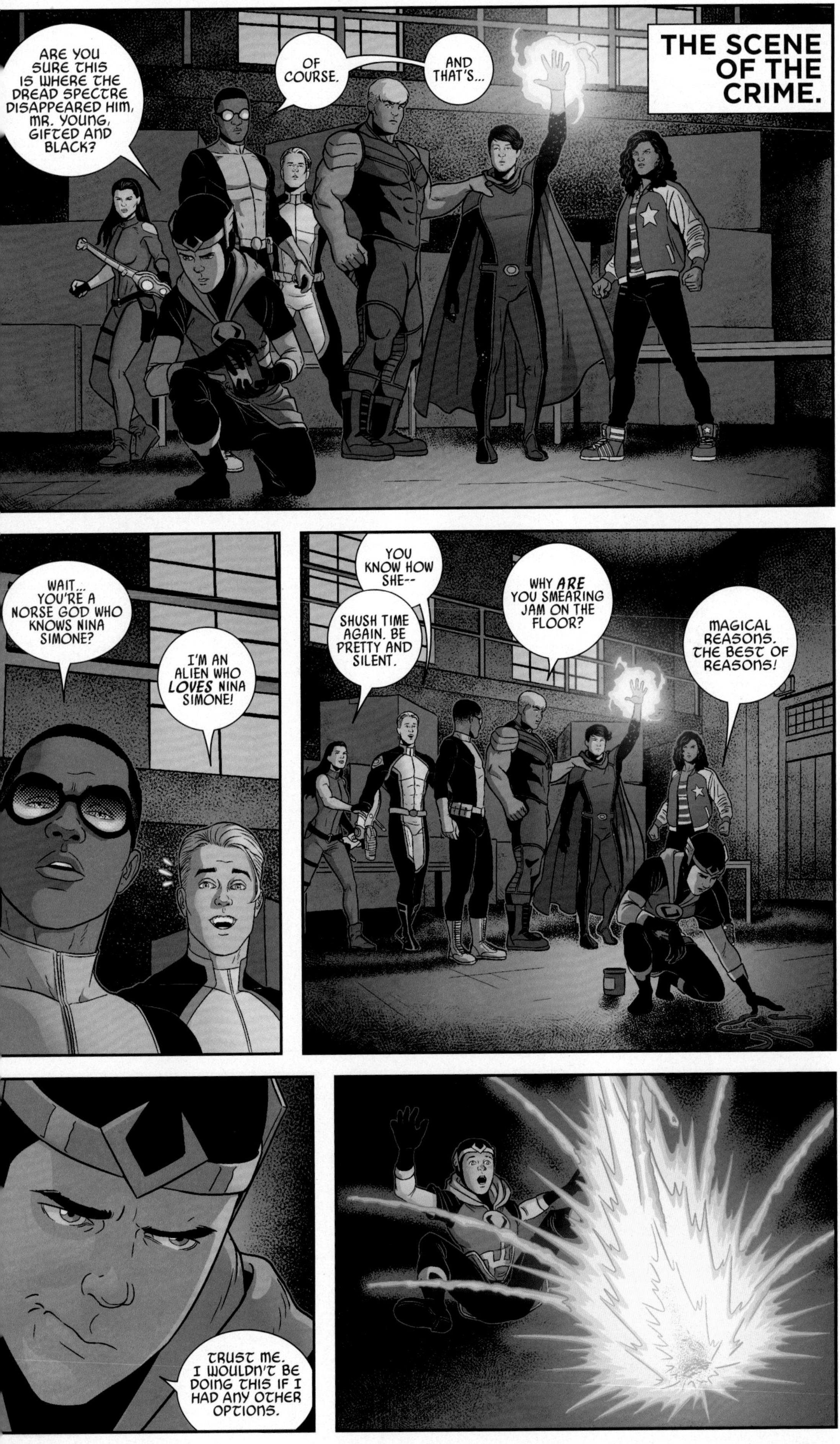
THE SCENE OF THE CRIME.
ARE YOU SURE THIS IS WHERE THE DREAD SPECTRE DISAPPEARED HIM, MR. YOUNG, GIFTED AND BLACK?
OF COURSE.
AND THAT'S...
WAIT... YOU'RE A NORSE GOD WHO KNOWS NINA SIMONE?
I'M AN ALIEN WHO LOVES NINA SIMONE!
YOU KNOW HOW SHE--
SHUSH TIME AGAIN. BE PRETTY AND SILENT.
WHY ARE YOU SMEARING JAM ON THE FLOOR?
MAGICAL REASONS. THE BEST OF REASONS!
TRUST ME. I WOULDN'T BE DOING THIS IF I HAD ANY OTHER OPTIONS.

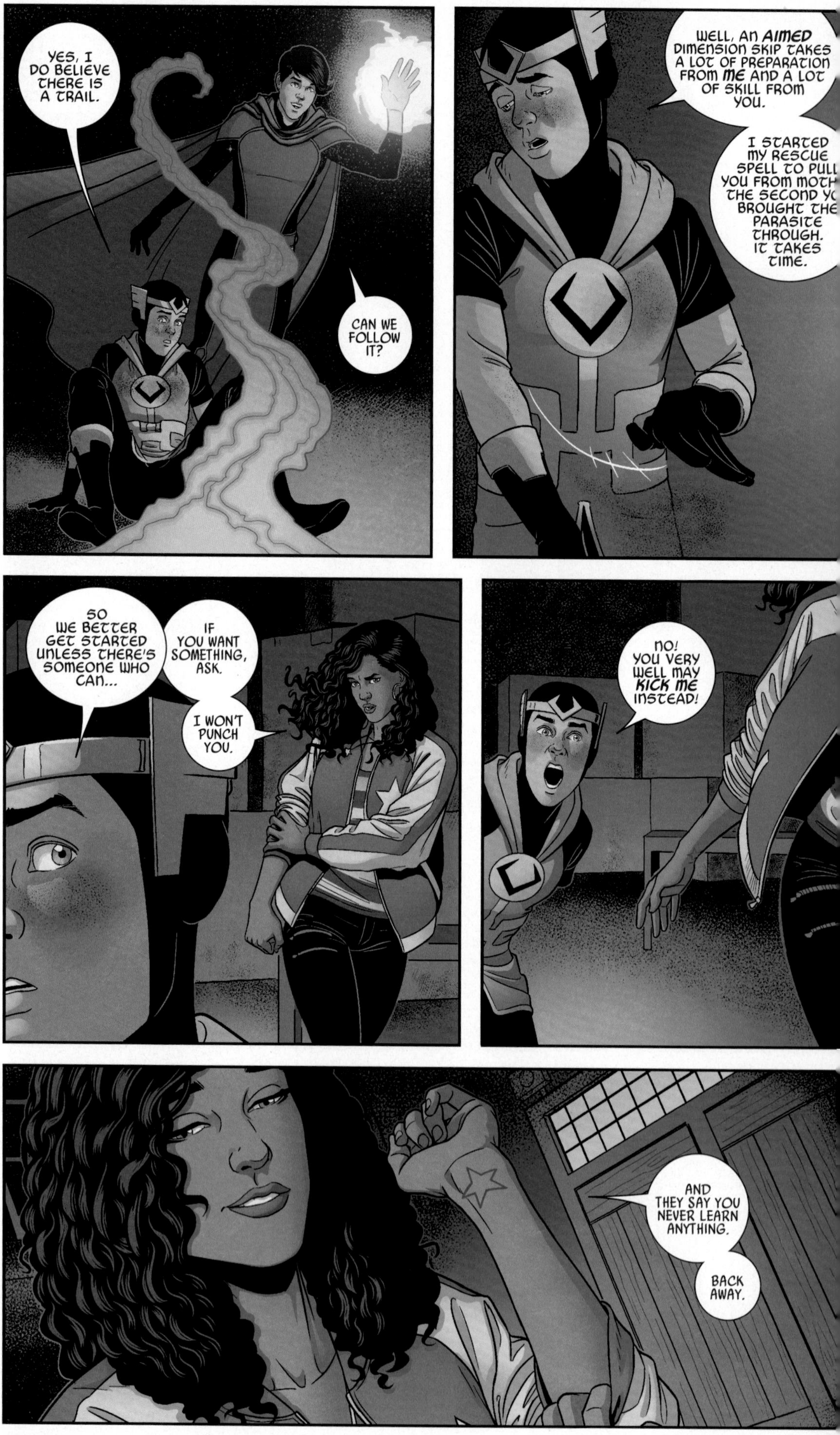
YES, I DO BELIEVE THERE IS A TRAIL.
CAN WE FOLLOW IT?
WELL, AN AIMED DIMENSION SKIP TAKES A LOT OF PREPARATION FROM ME AND A LOT OF SKILL FROM YOU.
I STARTED MY RESCUE SPELL TO PULL YOU FROM MOTH THE SECOND YO BROUGHT THE PARASITE THROUGH. IT TAKES TIME.
SO WE BETTER GET STARTED UNLESS THERE'S SOMEONE WHO CAN...
IF YOU WANT SOMETHING, ASK.
I WON'T PUNCH YOU.
NO! YOU VERY WELL MAY KICK ME INSTEAD!
AND THEY SAY YOU NEVER LEARN ANYTHING.
BACK AWAY.

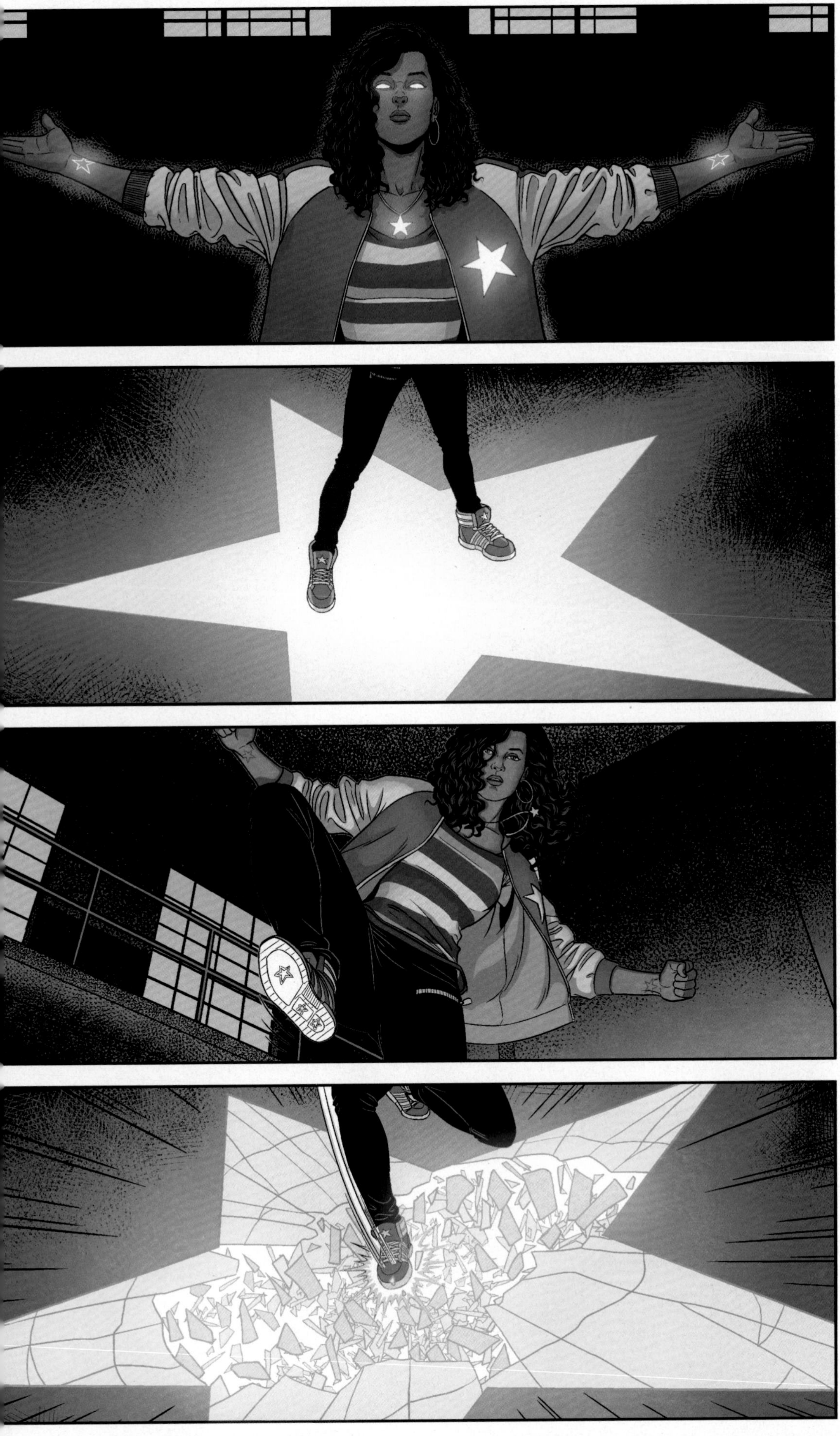

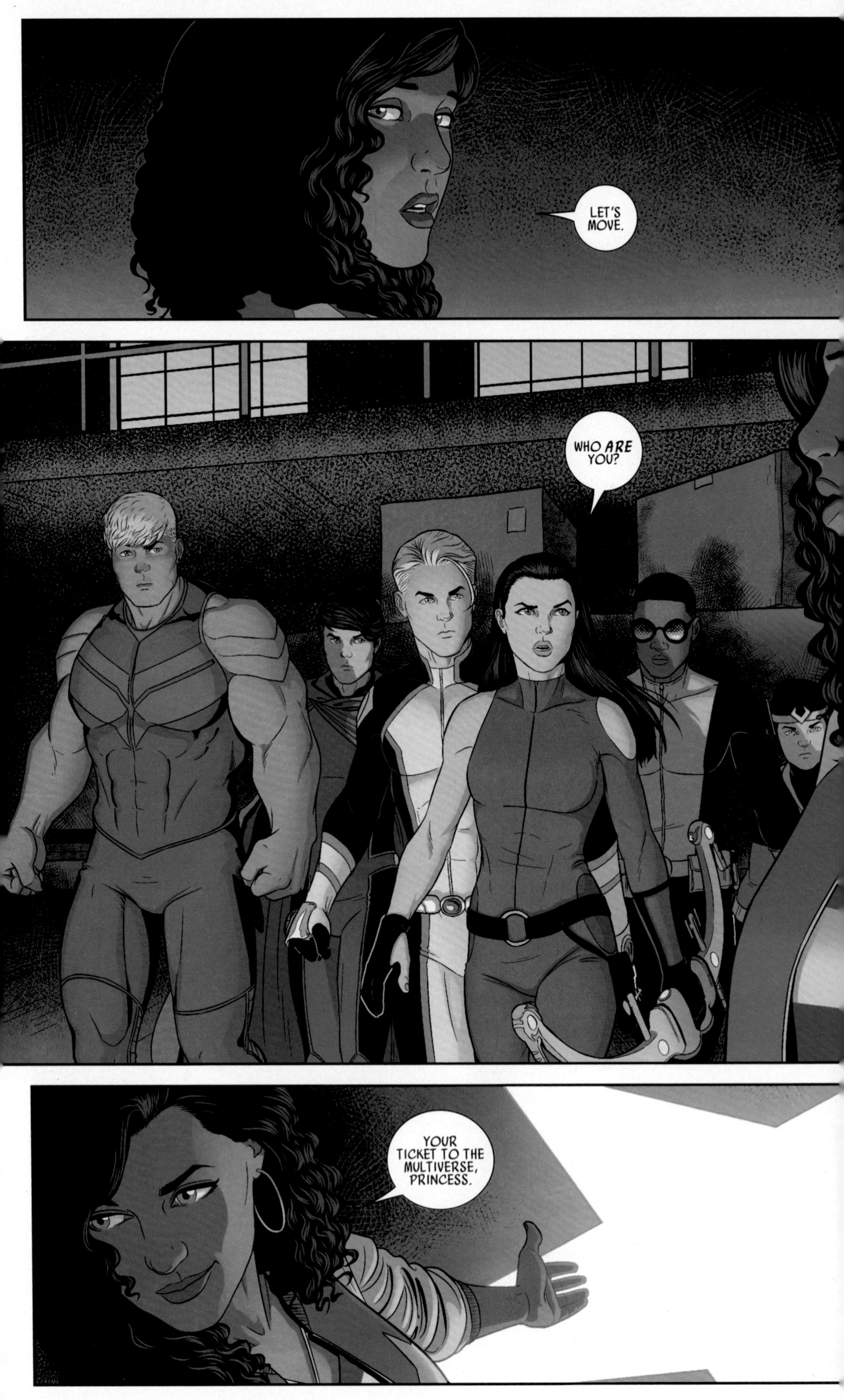
LET'S MOVE.
WHO ARE YOU?
YOUR TICKET TO THE MULTIVERSE, PRINCESS.

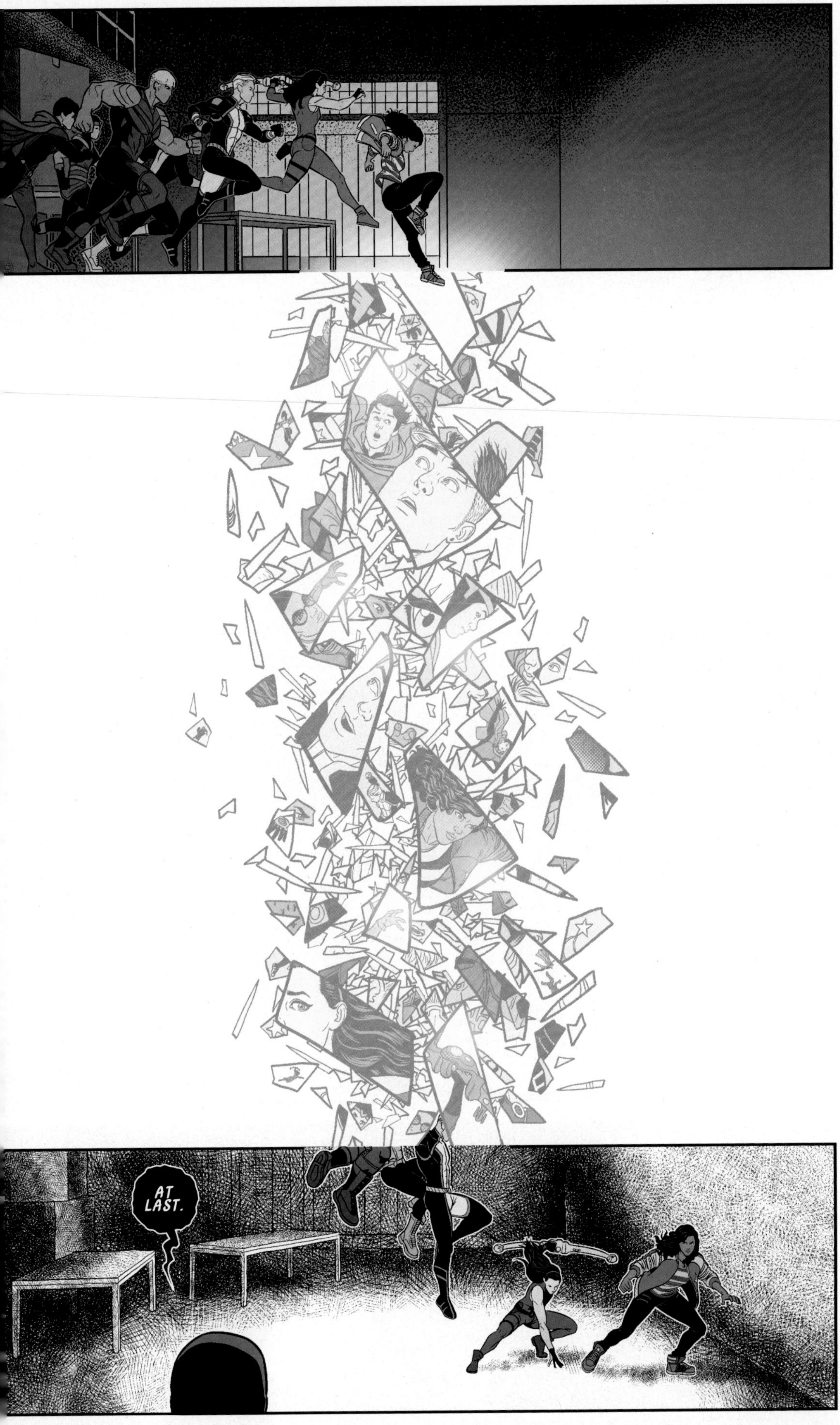
AT LAST.

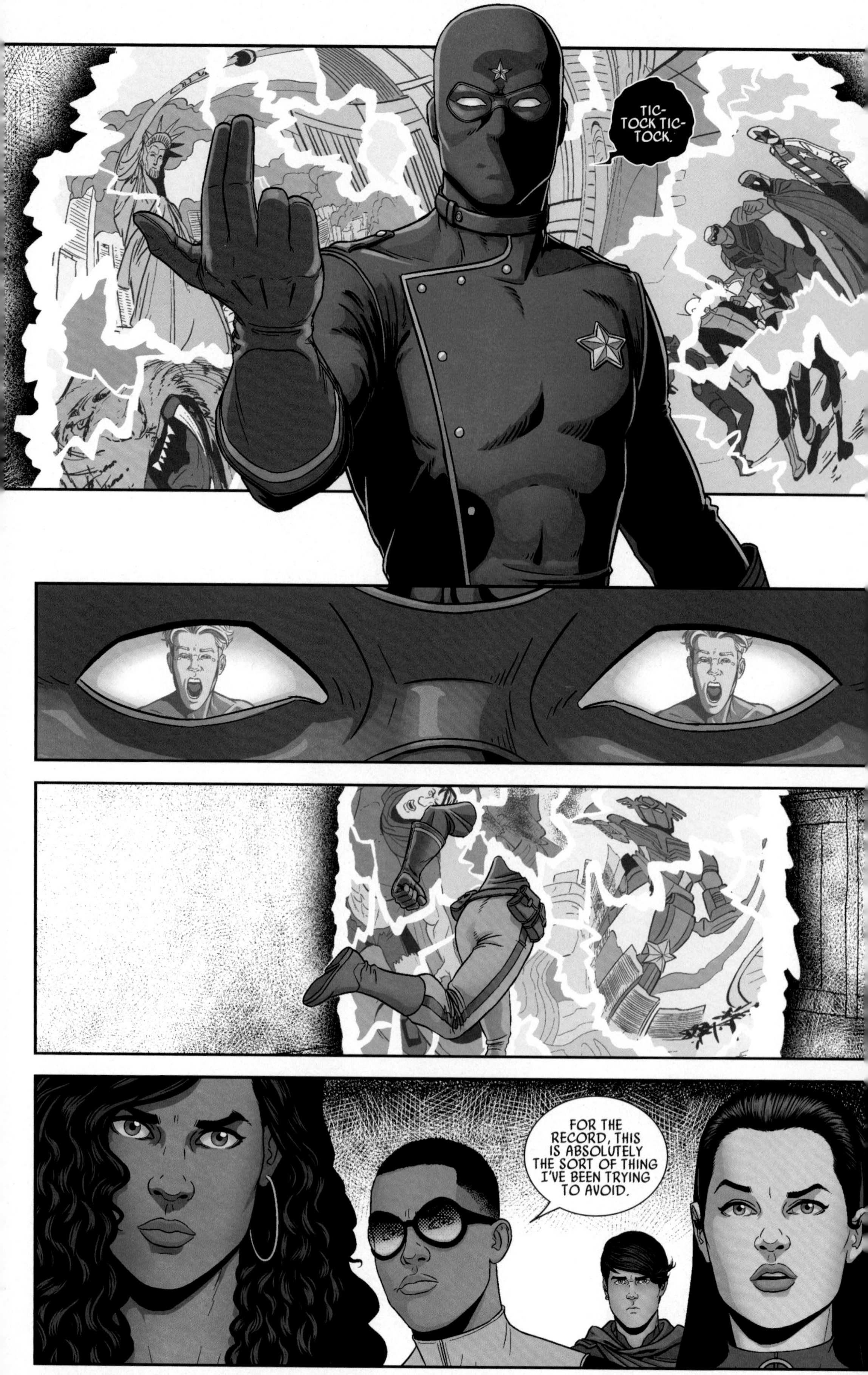
TIC-TOCK TIC-TOCK.
FOR THE RECORD, THIS IS ABSOLUTELY THE SORT OF THING I'VE BEEN TRYING TO AVOID.

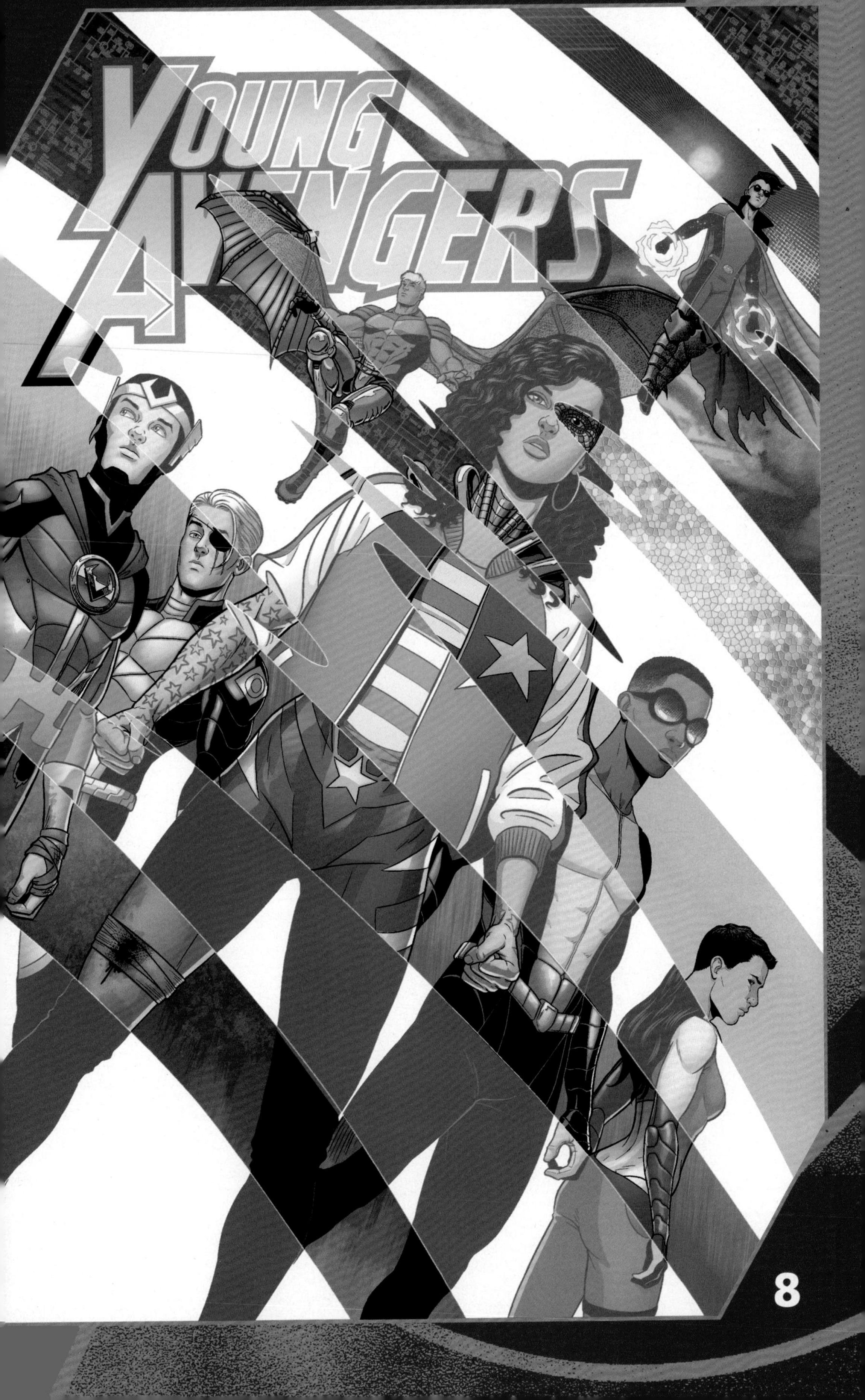
YOUNG AVENGERS
8

Kate Bishop's Interdimensional Journal. Week Five.

A couple of weeks ag[o] I wrote, "I hope we g[et] home in time for m[y] birthday." I was jokin[g]

I write it again, this time wi[th] all seriousness: I hope we g[et] home in time for my birthd[ay]

Let's go one further: I hope we get home at all.

We've seen astounding sights that catch my breath and will haunt me for life.

MayFly dimensions full of horro[r] craving to be more than a tin[y] fragment of time.

Desperate dimensions f[ull] of fears, all time runni[ng] out. The interndimension[s] hungering after what w[e] were lucky enough to be born into.

It's awful for everyone. Even Chavez is exhausted. Barely anyone's sleeping, and when they do, what they dream of makes them wish they hadn't.

"Gaze not down the rabbit hole, in ca[se] you become a rabbit," as Loki said. Everyo[ne] rolled their eyes. And then there wa[s] the dimension with the *rabbits*.

Oh God. I hav[e] nightmares about rabbit[s]

I've had bad times. We all have.

But this is the hardest thing we've ever had to do.

These days...

Everyone just wishes they would *end.*

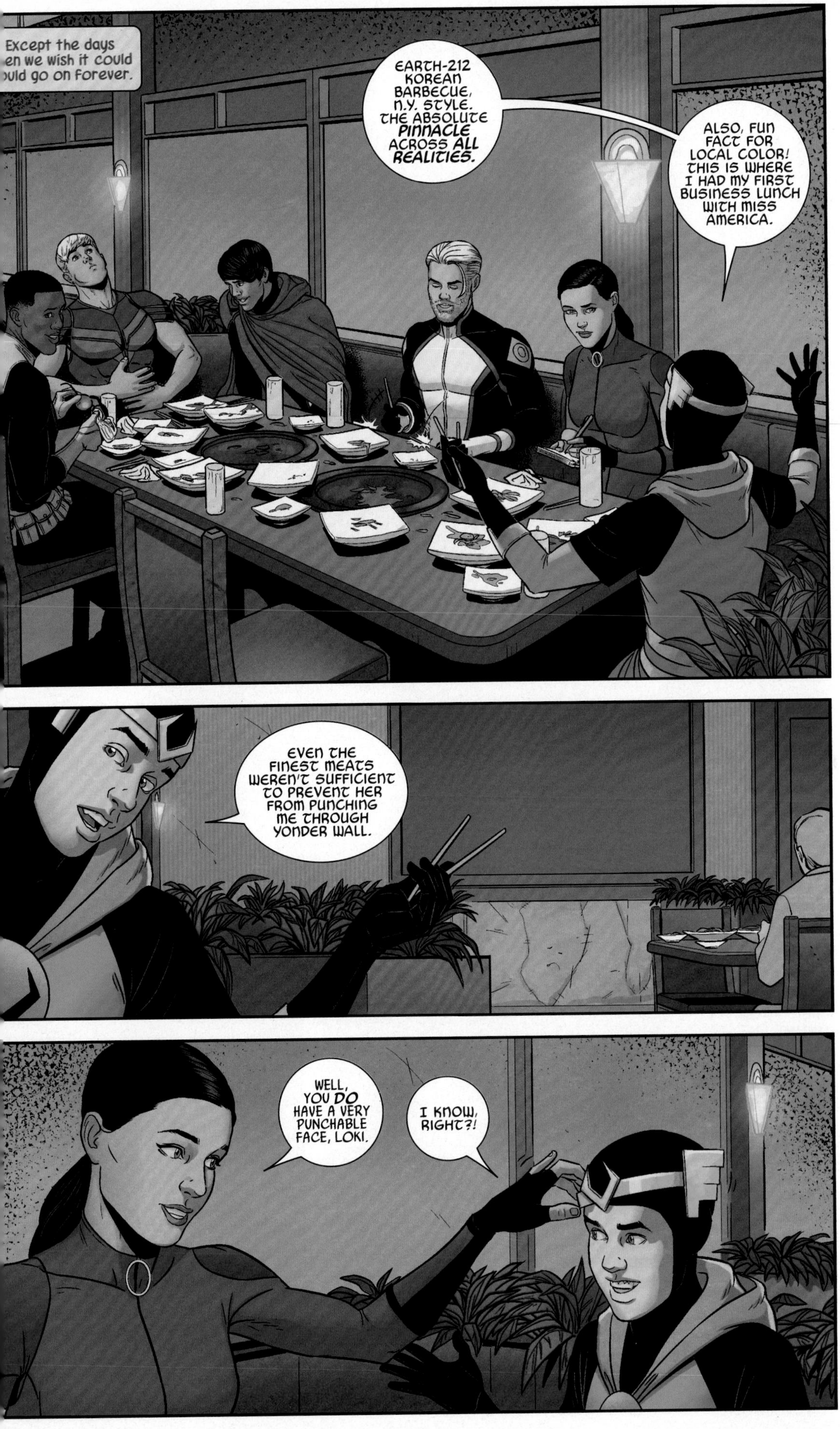

Except the days
en we wish it could
ould go on forever.
EARTH-212 KOREAN BARBECUE, N.Y. STYLE. THE ABSOLUTE PINNACLE ACROSS ALL REALITIES.
ALSO, FUN FACT FOR LOCAL COLOR! THIS IS WHERE I HAD MY FIRST BUSINESS LUNCH WITH MISS AMERICA.
EVEN THE FINEST MEATS WEREN'T SUFFICIENT TO PREVENT HER FROM PUNCHING ME THROUGH YONDER WALL.
WELL, YOU DO HAVE A VERY PUNCHABLE FACE, LOKI.
I KNOW, RIGHT?!

SO, HOW LONG ARE YOU GOING TO GROW THAT ...BEARD, NOH-VARR?

AS LONG AS IT FEELS RIGHT. IT IS APPROPRIATE.

I HAVE DISCOVERE THE JOY C COUNTRY. GI PARSONS I MY HERO.

I HAVE ONE HOPE FOR THIS MISSION.

THAT WE COME TO A DIMENSION WHERE HE STILL LIVES.

AND THAT WE CATCH UP WITH THIS PATRIOT MONSTER AND RESCUE TOMMY, RIGHT?

OF COURSE.

I ALSO HAVE HOPES OF MEETING JOHNNY CASH.

YOU! YOU'RE NOT ALLOWED IN HERE!

YOU--

YEAH I KNO

WALL HAS PATCHED UP GREAT.

SORRY.

I'VE FOUND THE PATRIOT'S TRAIL.

PAY THE LADY. LET'S MOVE.

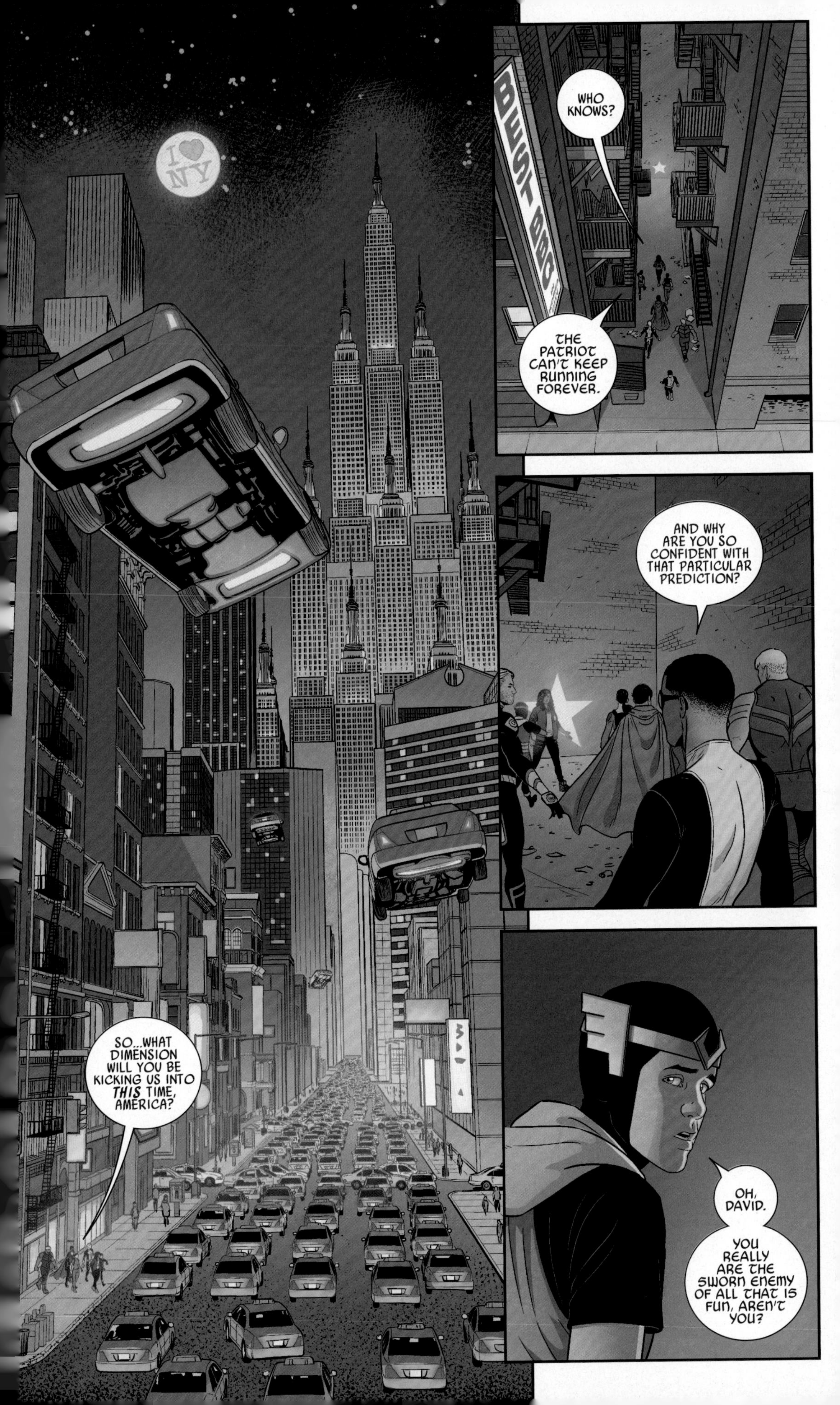
SO...WHAT DIMENSION WILL YOU BE KICKING US INTO THIS TIME, AMERICA?
BEST BBQ
WHO KNOWS?
THE PATRIOT CAN'T KEEP RUNNING FOREVER.
AND WHY ARE YOU SO CONFIDENT WITH THAT PARTICULAR PREDICTION?
OH, DAVID.
YOU REALLY ARE THE SWORN ENEMY OF ALL THAT IS FUN, AREN'T YOU?

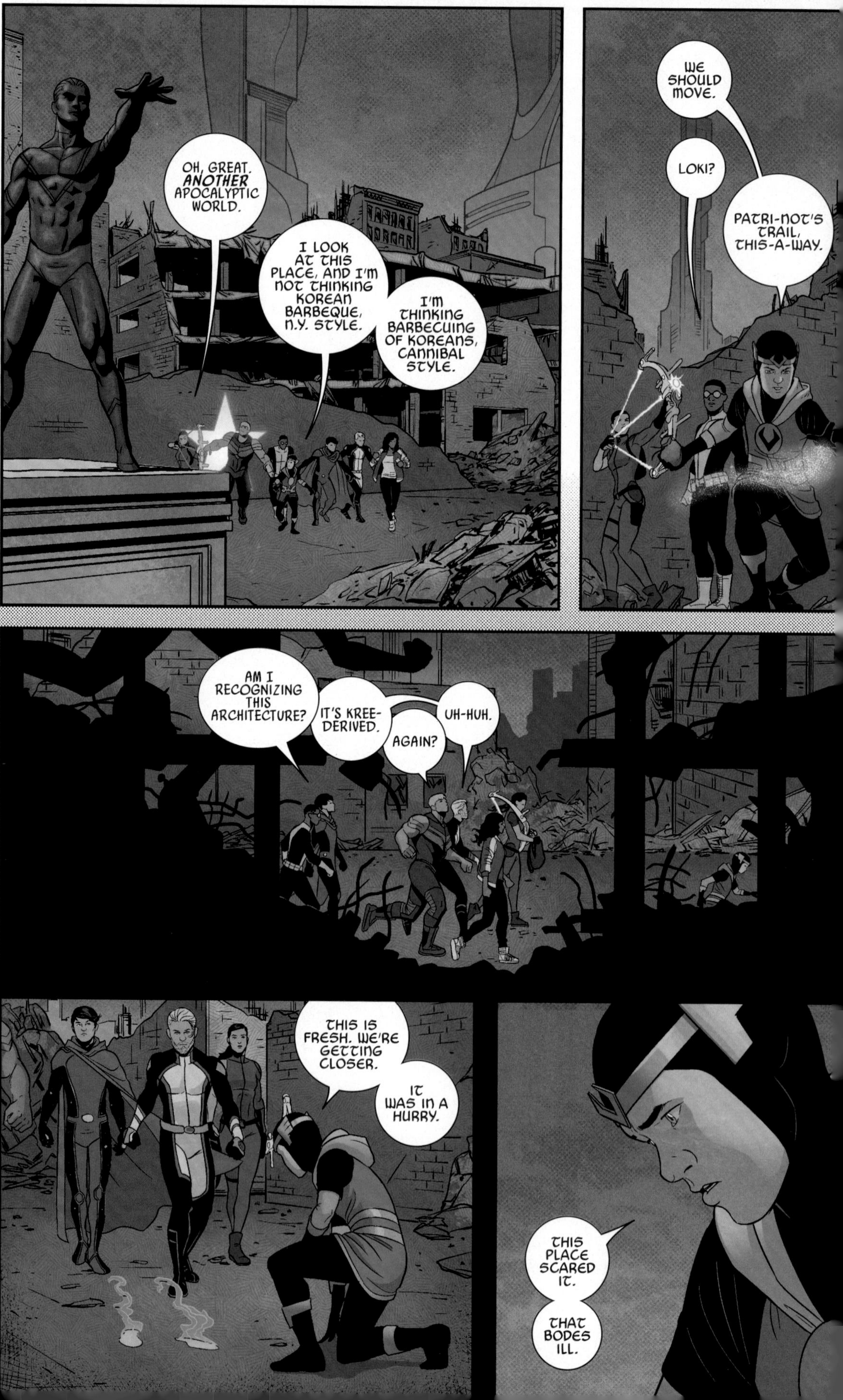
OH, GREAT. ANOTHER APOCALYPTIC WORLD.
I LOOK AT THIS PLACE, AND I'M NOT THINKING KOREAN BARBEQUE, N.Y. STYLE.
I'M THINKING BARBECUING OF KOREANS, CANNIBAL STYLE.
WE SHOULD MOVE.
LOKI?
PATRI-NOT'S TRAIL, THIS-A-WAY.
AM I RECOGNIZING THIS ARCHITECTURE?
IT'S KREE-DERIVED.
AGAIN?
UH-HUH.
THIS IS FRESH. WE'RE GETTING CLOSER.
IT WAS IN A HURRY.
THIS PLACE SCARED IT.
THAT BODES ILL.

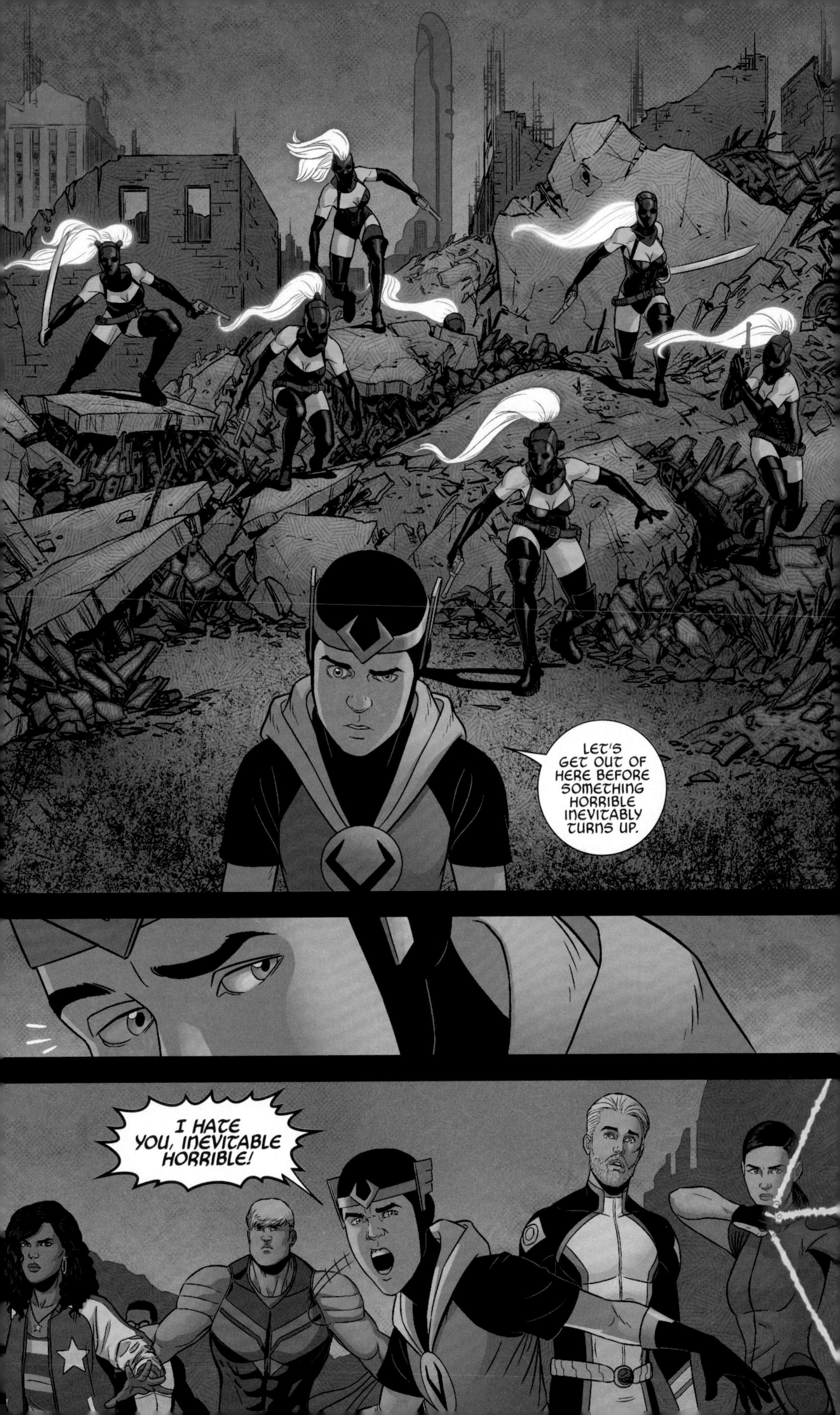
LET'S GET OUT OF HERE BEFORE SOMETHING HORRIBLE INEVITABLY TURNS UP.
I HATE YOU, INEVITABLE HORRIBLE!

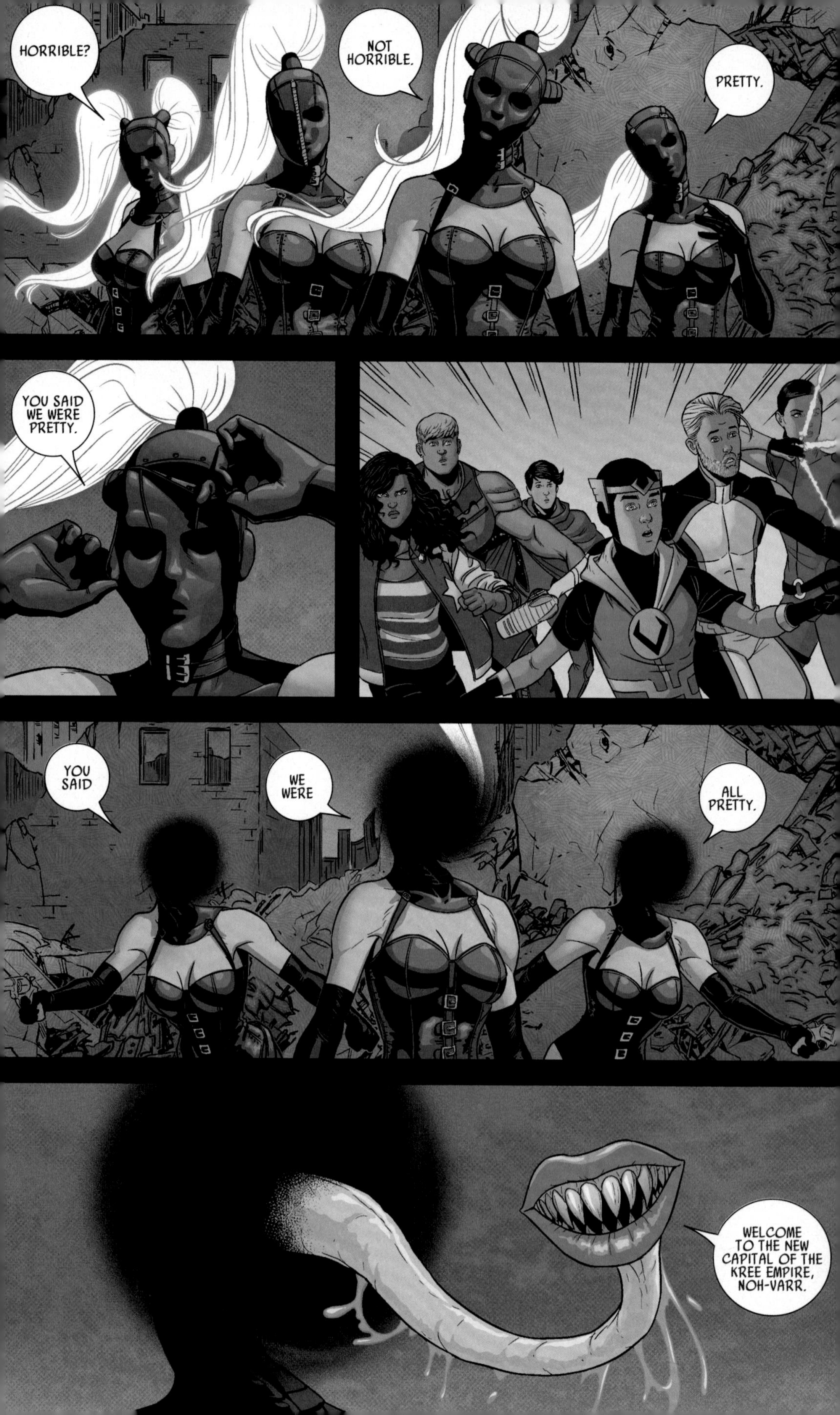
HORRIBLE?
NOT HORRIBLE.
PRETTY.
YOU SAID WE WERE PRETTY.
YOU SAID
WE WERE
ALL PRETTY.
WELCOME TO THE NEW CAPITAL OF THE KREE EMPIRE, NOH-VARR.

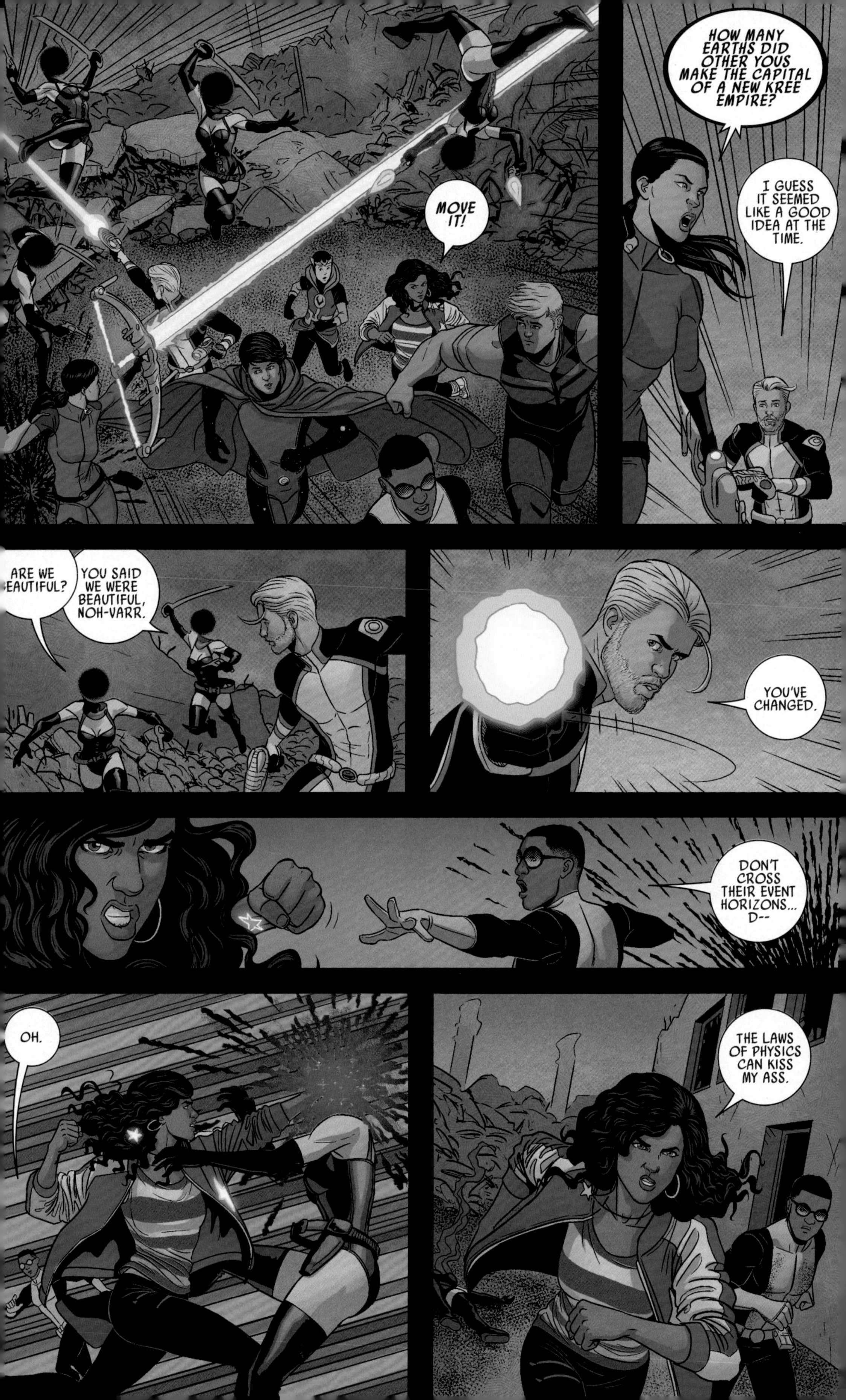
MOVE IT!
HOW MANY EARTHS DID OTHER YOUS MAKE THE CAPITAL OF A NEW KREE EMPIRE?
I GUESS IT SEEMED LIKE A GOOD IDEA AT THE TIME.
ARE WE BEAUTIFUL?
YOU SAID WE WERE BEAUTIFUL, NOH-VARR.
YOU'VE CHANGED.
DON'T CROSS THEIR EVENT HORIZONS... D--
OH.
THE LAWS OF PHYSICS CAN KISS MY ASS.

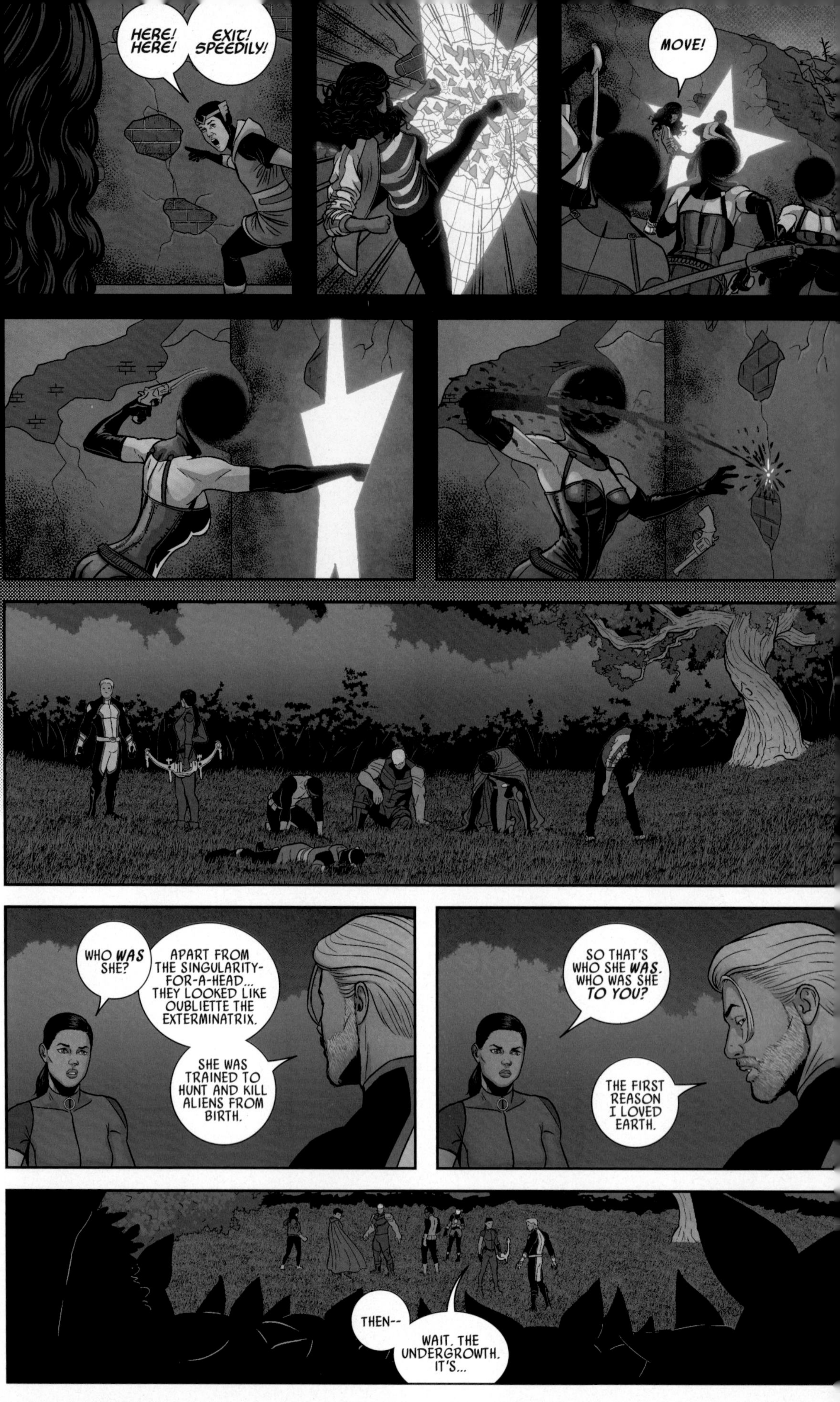
HERE! HERE!
EXIT! SPEEDILY!
MOVE!
WHO WAS SHE?
APART FROM THE SINGULARITY-FOR-A-HEAD... THEY LOOKED LIKE OUBLIETTE THE EXTERMINATRIX.
SHE WAS TRAINED TO HUNT AND KILL ALIENS FROM BIRTH.
SO THAT'S WHO SHE WAS. WHO WAS SHE TO YOU?
THE FIRST REASON I LOVED EARTH.
THEN--
WAIT. THE UNDERGROWTH. IT'S...

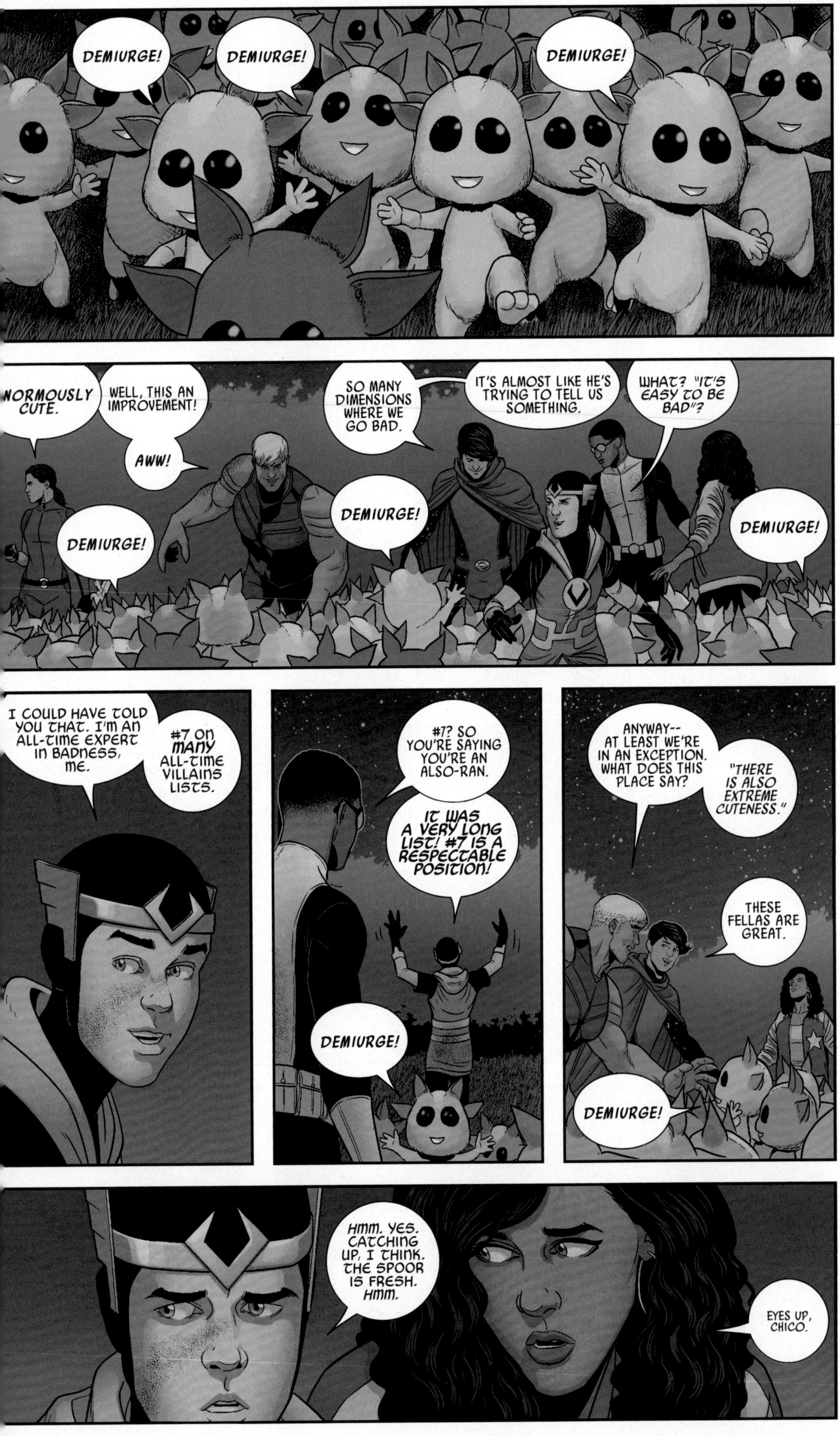
DEMIURGE!
DEMIURGE!
DEMIURGE!
NORMOUSLY CUTE.
WELL, THIS AN IMPROVEMENT!
AWW!
SO MANY DIMENSIONS WHERE WE GO BAD.
IT'S ALMOST LIKE HE'S TRYING TO TELL US SOMETHING.
WHAT? "IT'S EASY TO BE BAD"?
DEMIURGE!
DEMIURGE!
DEMIURGE!
I COULD HAVE TOLD YOU THAT. I'M AN ALL-TIME EXPERT IN BADNESS, ME.
#7 ON MANY ALL-TIME VILLAINS LISTS.
#7? SO YOU'RE SAYING YOU'RE AN ALSO-RAN.
IT WAS A VERY LONG LIST! #7 IS A RESPECTABLE POSITION!
DEMIURGE!
ANYWAY-- AT LEAST WE'RE IN AN EXCEPTION. WHAT DOES THIS PLACE SAY?
"THERE IS ALSO EXTREME CUTENESS."
THESE FELLAS ARE GREAT.
DEMIURGE!
HMM. YES. CATCHING UP, I THINK. THE SPOOR IS FRESH. HMM.
EYES UP, CHICO.

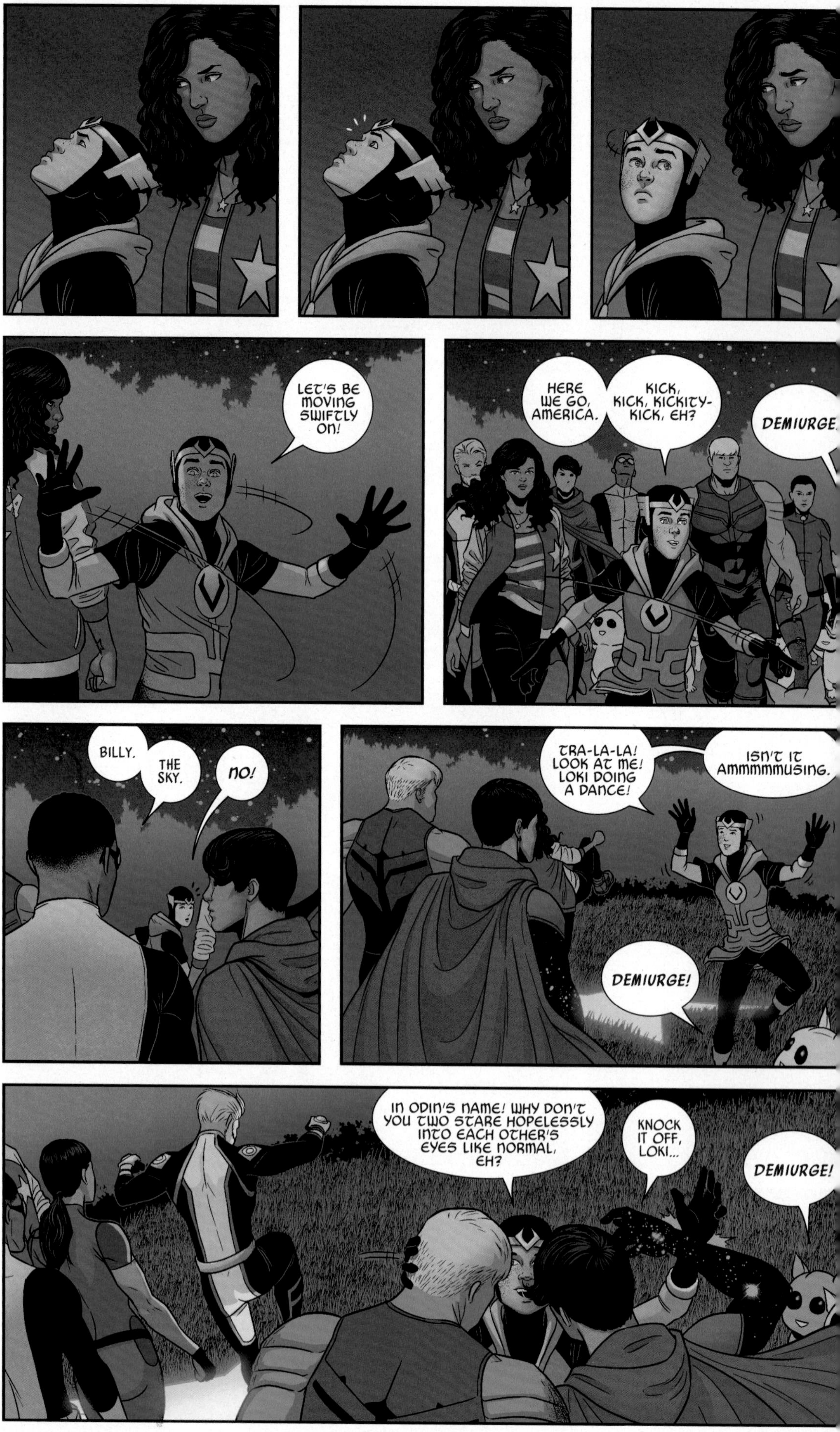
LET'S BE MOVING SWIFTLY ON!
HERE WE GO, AMERICA.
KICK, KICK, KICKITY-KICK, EH?
DEMIURGE.
BILLY.
THE SKY.
NO!
TRA-LA-LA! LOOK AT ME! LOKI DOING A DANCE!
ISN'T IT AMMMMMUSING.
DEMIURGE!
IN ODIN'S NAME! WHY DON'T YOU TWO STARE HOPELESSLY INTO EACH OTHER'S EYES LIKE NORMAL, EH?
KNOCK IT OFF, LOKI...
DEMIURGE!

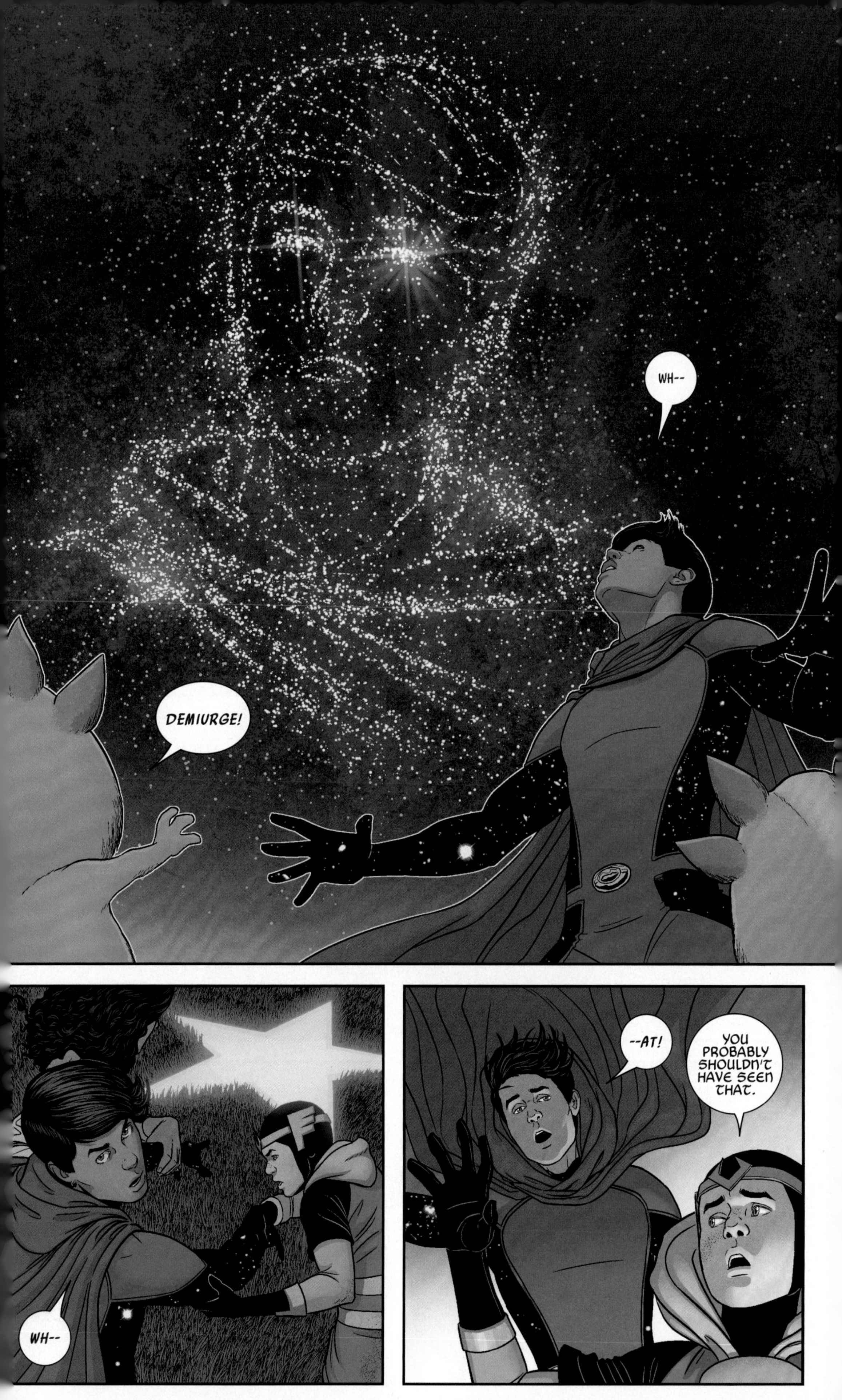
WH--
DEMIURGE!
WH--
--AT!
YOU PROBABLY SHOULDN'T HAVE SEEN THAT.

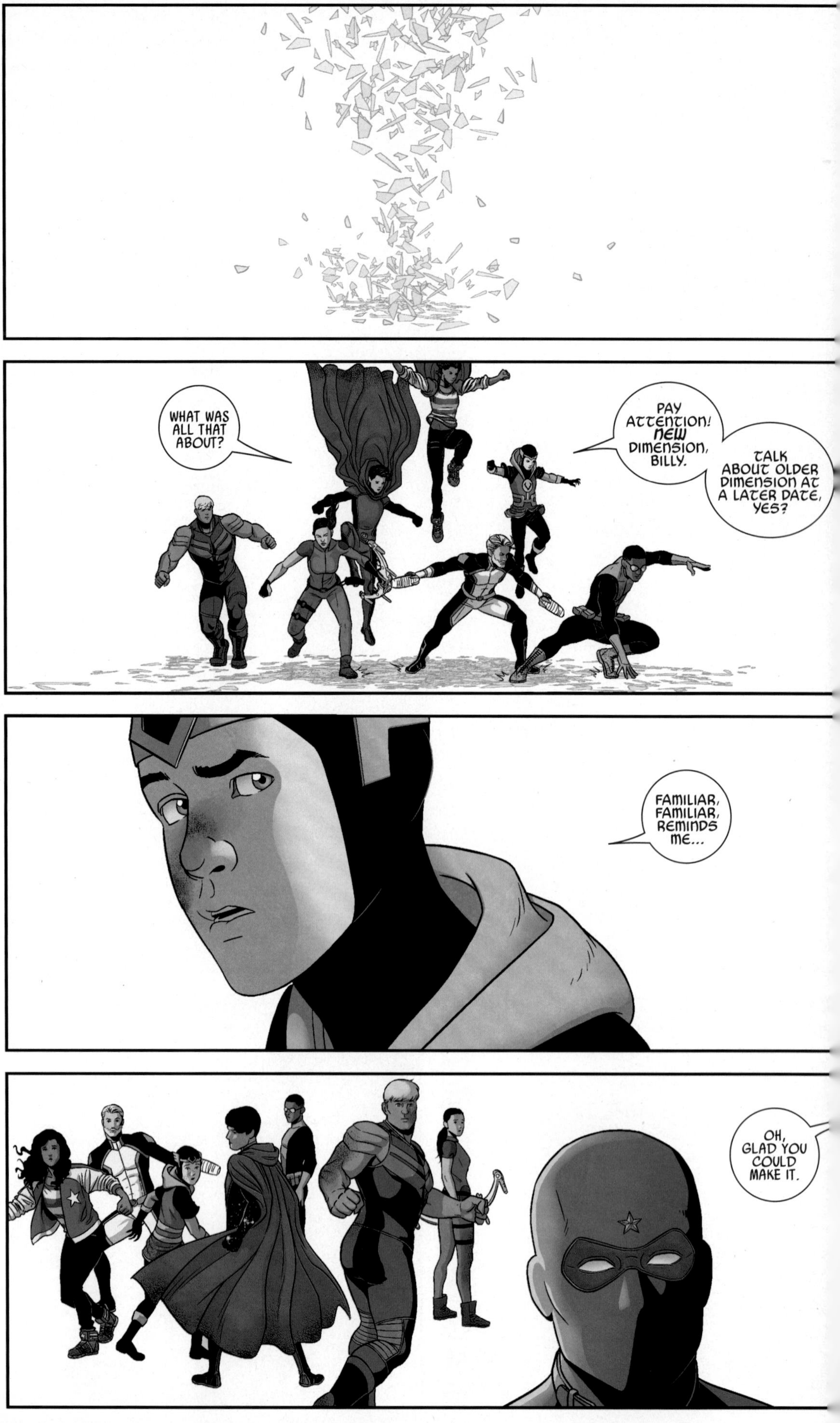
WHAT WAS ALL THAT ABOUT?
PAY ATTENTION! NEW DIMENSION, BILLY.
TALK ABOUT OLDER DIMENSION AT A LATER DATE, YES?
FAMILIAR, FAMILIAR, REMINDS ME...
OH, GLAD YOU COULD MAKE IT.

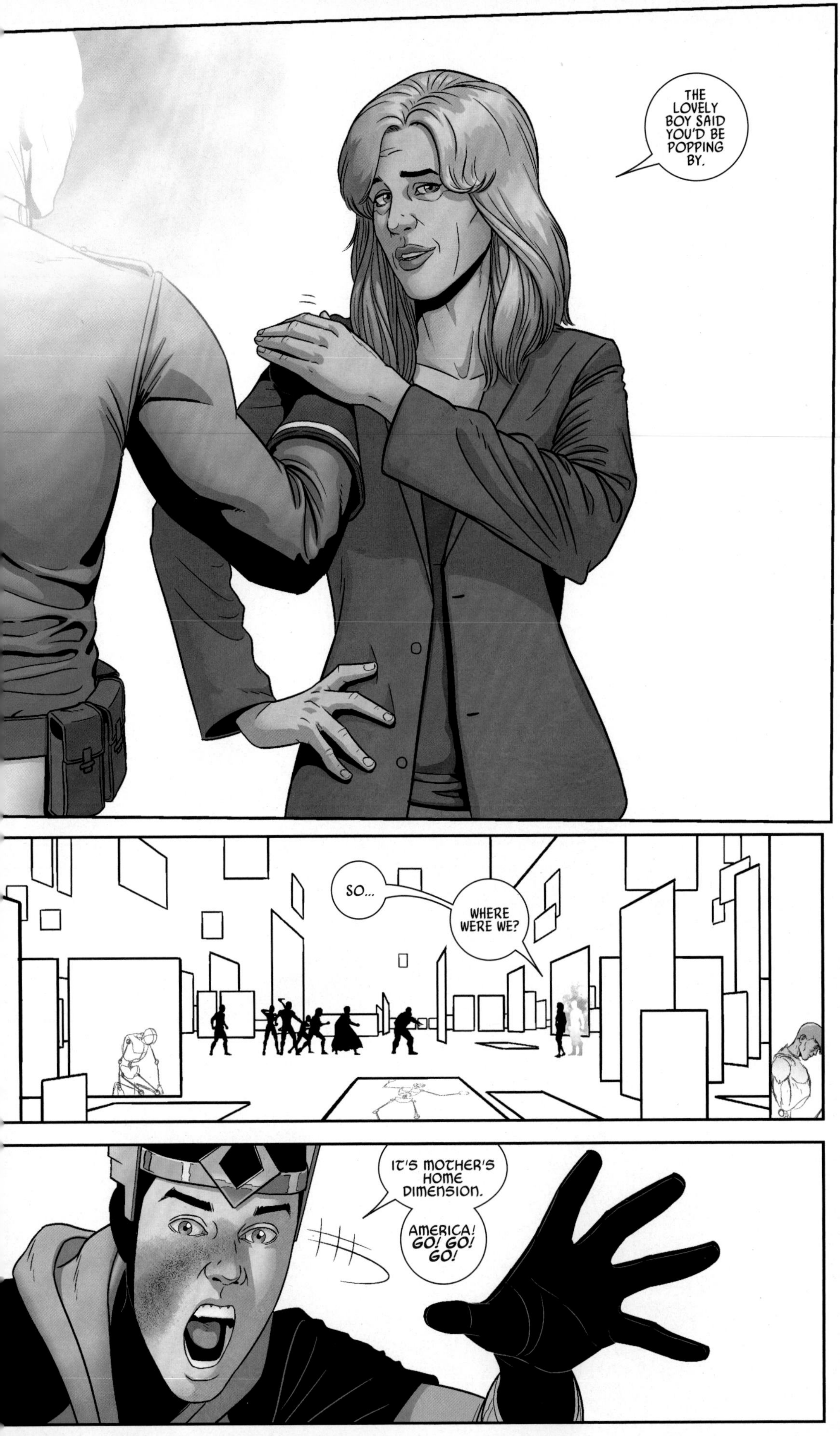
THE LOVELY BOY SAID YOU'D BE POPPING BY.
SO...
WHERE WERE WE?
IT'S MOTHER'S HOME DIMENSION.
AMERICA! GO! GO! GO!

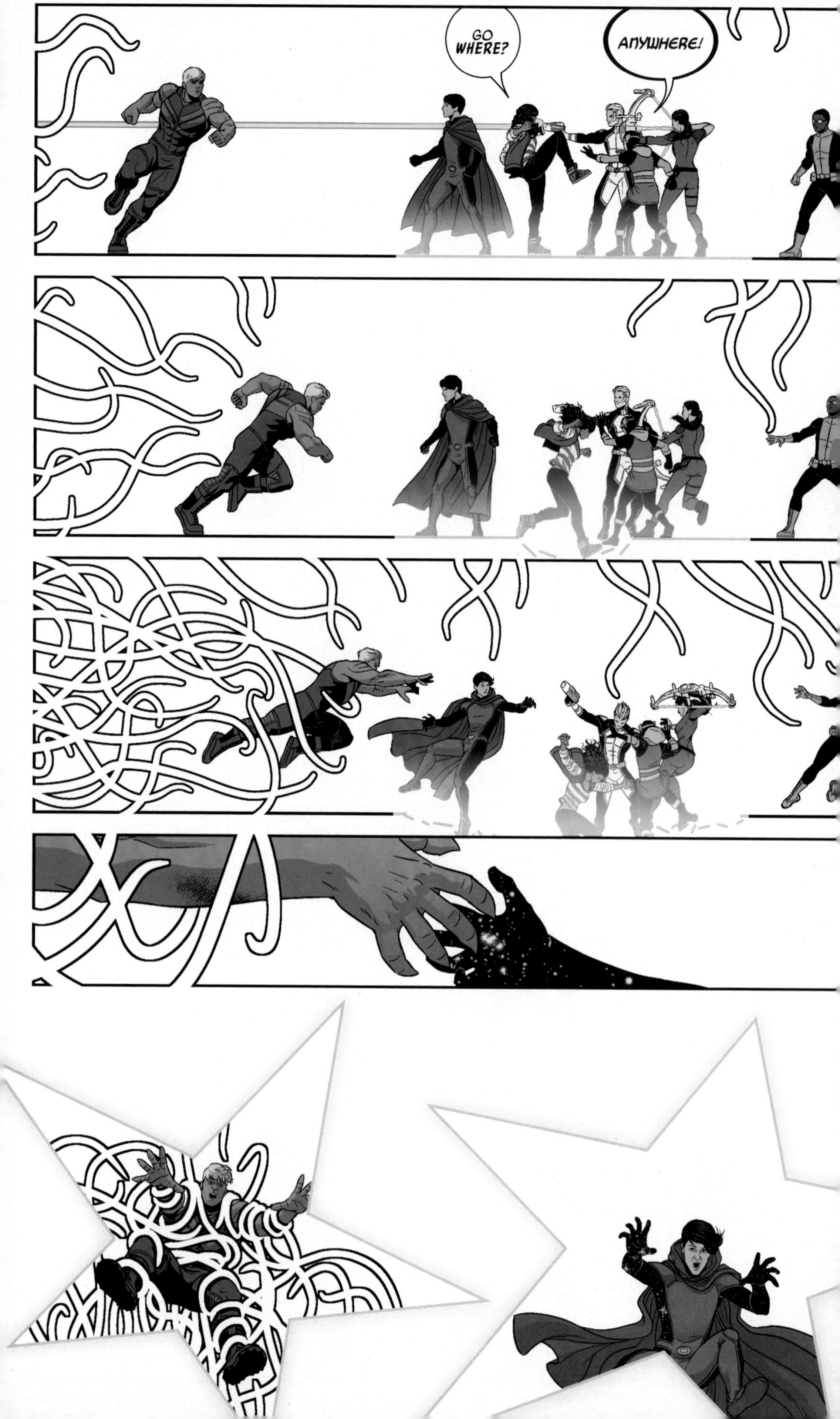
GO WHERE?
ANYWHERE!

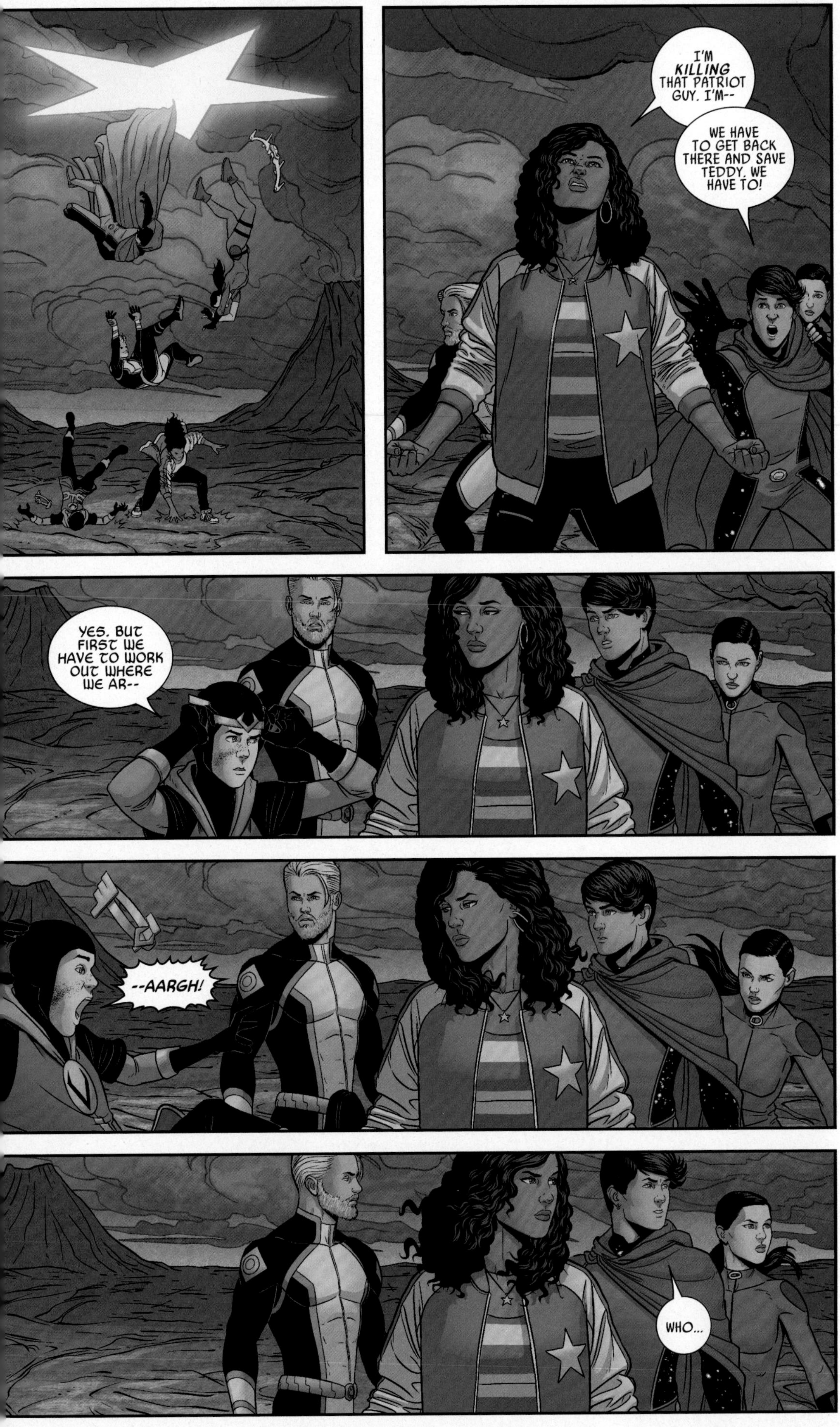
I'M KILLING THAT PATRIOT GUY. I'M--
WE HAVE TO GET BACK THERE AND SAVE TEDDY. WE HAVE TO!
YES. BUT FIRST WE HAVE TO WORK OUT WHERE WE AR--
--AARGH!
WHO...

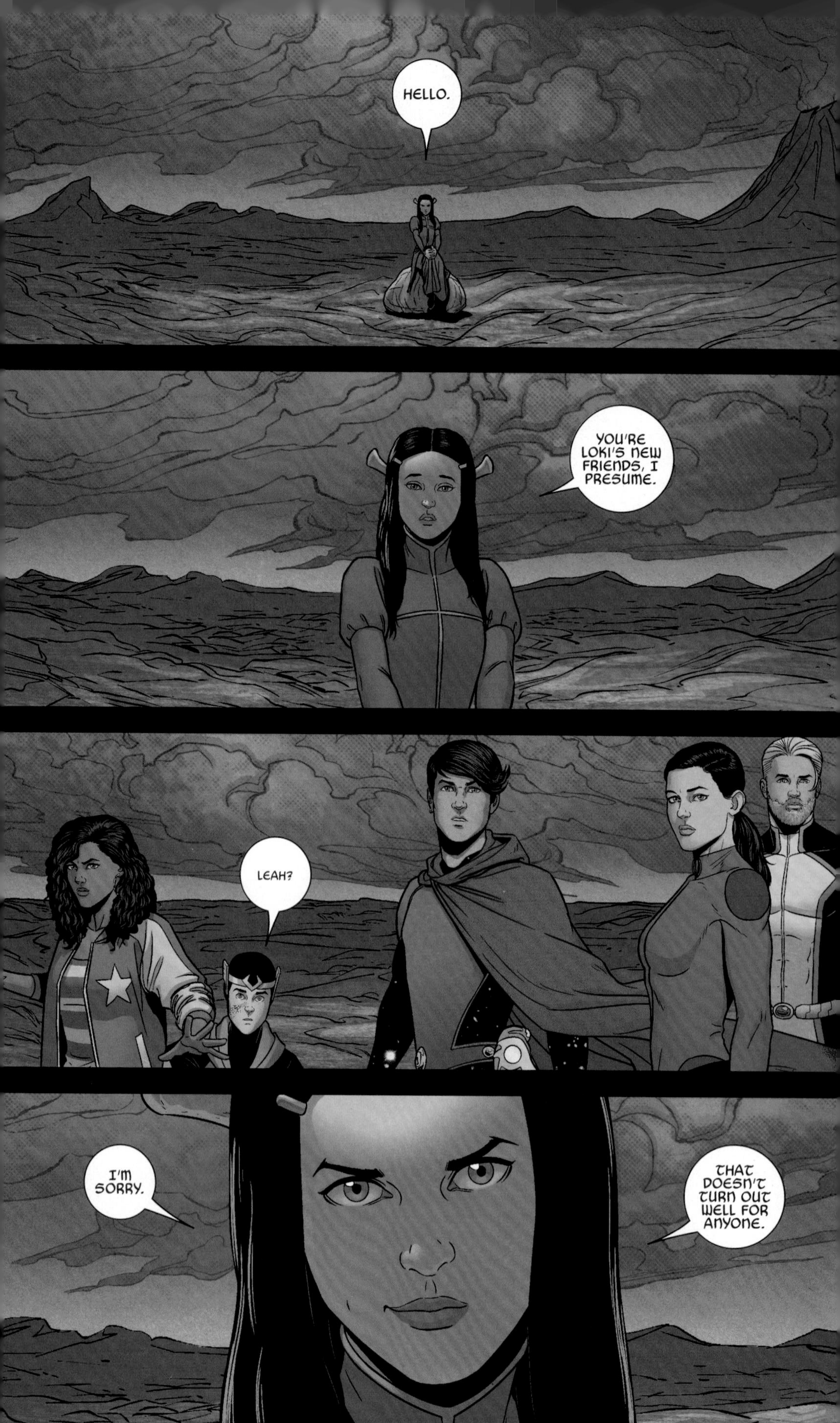
HELLO.
YOU'RE LOKI'S NEW FRIENDS, I PRESUME.
LEAH?
I'M SORRY.
THAT DOESN'T TURN OUT WELL FOR ANYONE.

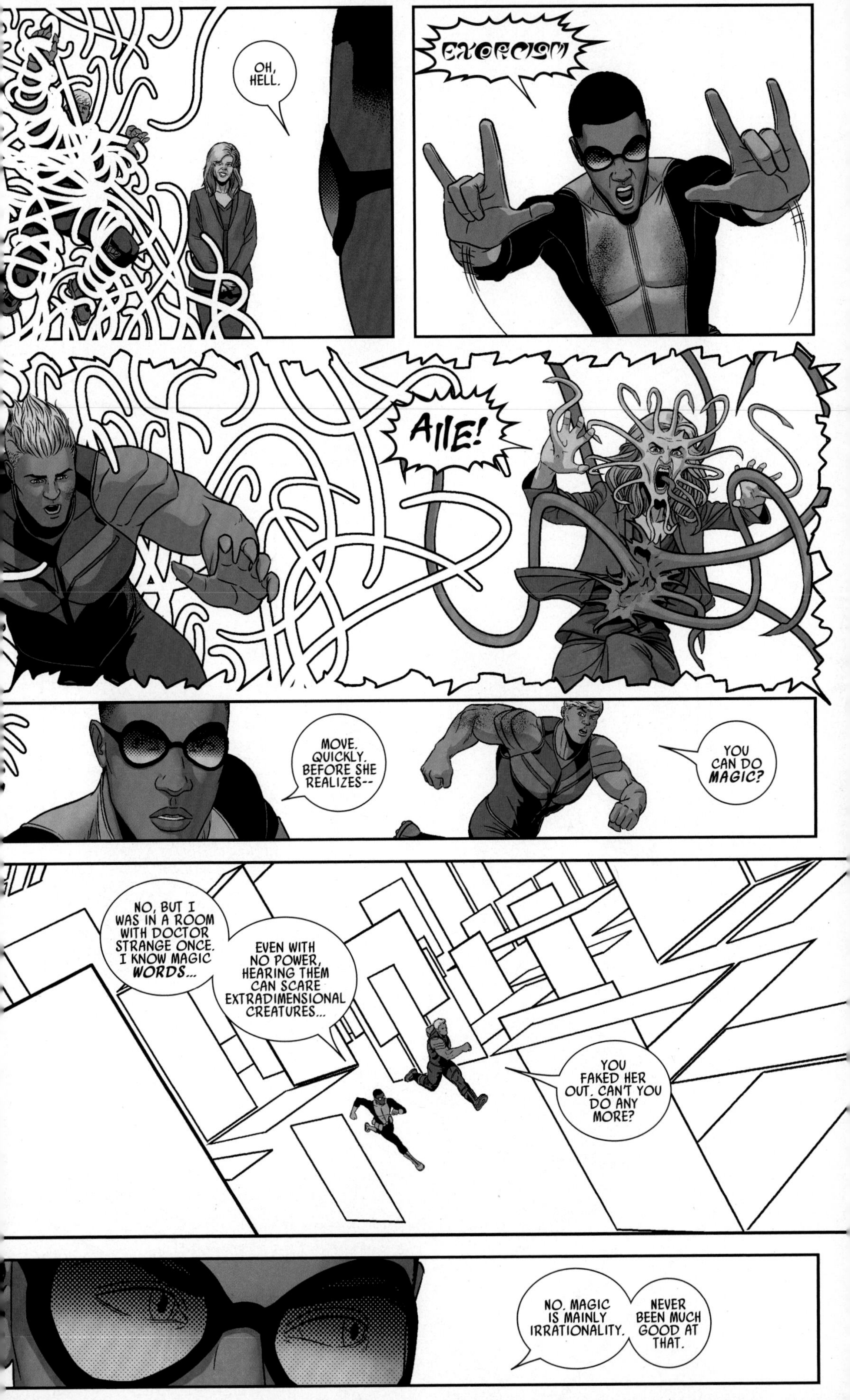
OH, HELL.
EXORCISM
AIIE!
MOVE. QUICKLY. BEFORE SHE REALIZES--
YOU CAN DO *MAGIC?*
NO, BUT I WAS IN A ROOM WITH DOCTOR STRANGE ONCE. I KNOW MAGIC *WORDS...*
EVEN WITH NO POWER, HEARING THEM CAN SCARE EXTRADIMENSIONAL CREATURES...
YOU FAKED HER OUT. CAN'T YOU DO ANY MORE?
NO. MAGIC IS MAINLY IRRATIONALITY.
NEVER BEEN MUCH GOOD AT THAT.

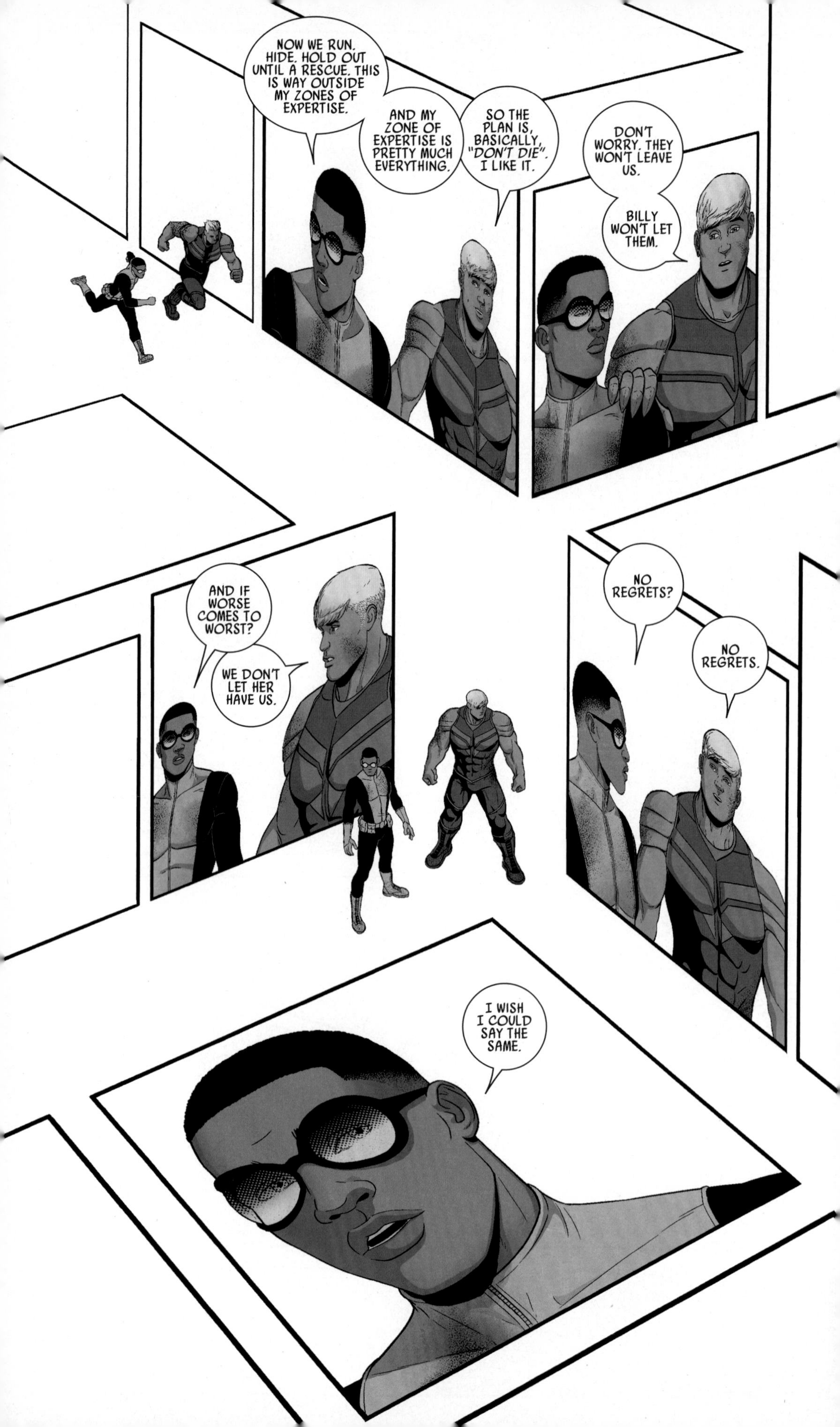
NOW WE RUN. HIDE. HOLD OUT UNTIL A RESCUE. THIS IS WAY OUTSIDE MY ZONES OF EXPERTISE.
AND MY ZONE OF EXPERTISE IS PRETTY MUCH EVERYTHING.
SO THE PLAN IS, BASICALLY, "DON'T DIE". I LIKE IT.
DON'T WORRY. THEY WON'T LEAVE US.
BILLY WON'T LET THEM.
AND IF WORSE COMES TO WORST?
WE DON'T LET HER HAVE US.
NO REGRETS?
NO REGRETS.
I WISH I COULD SAY THE SAME.

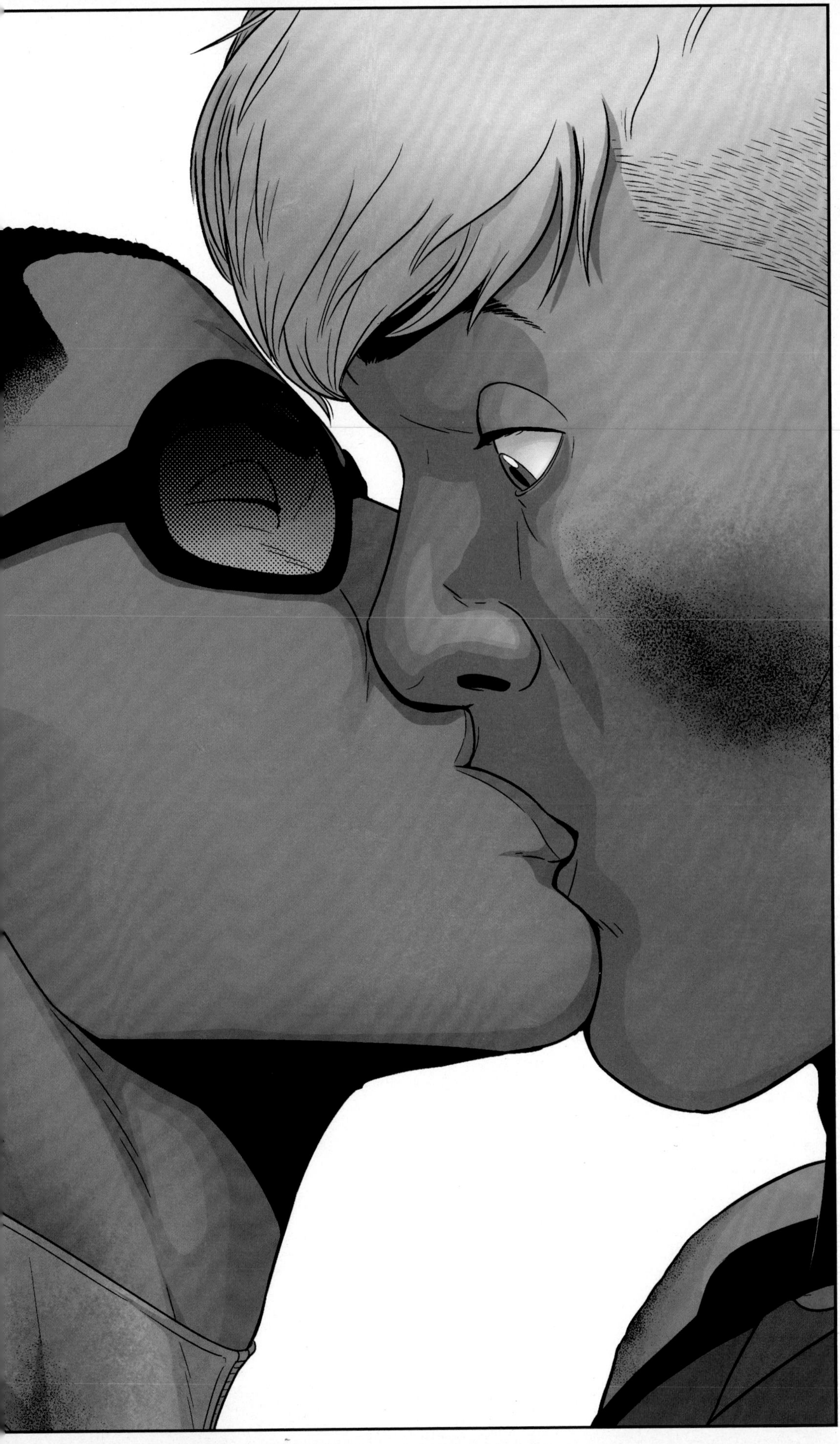

YOUNG AVENGERS

THE KISS AND THE MAKE UP

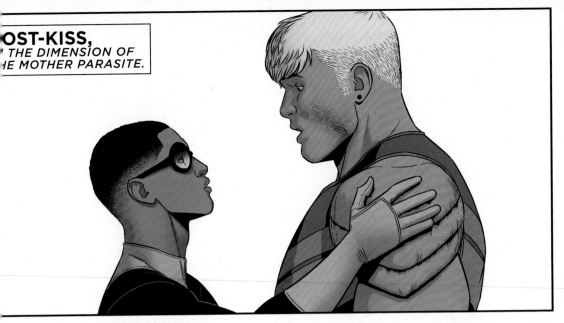

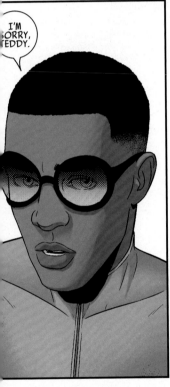

OST-KISS,
THE DIMENSION OF
IE MOTHER PARASITE.
I'M
SORRY,
TEDDY.
...WHAT?
WE SHOULD GET MOVING AGAIN, BEFORE WE DIE.
OF EMBARRASSMENT.
DAVID?!

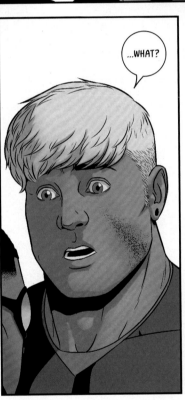

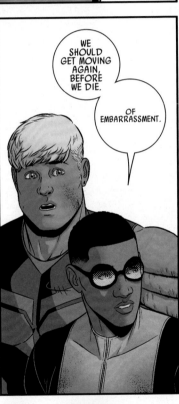

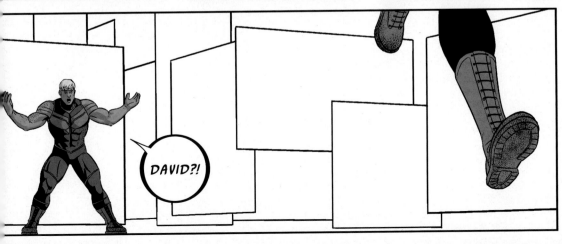

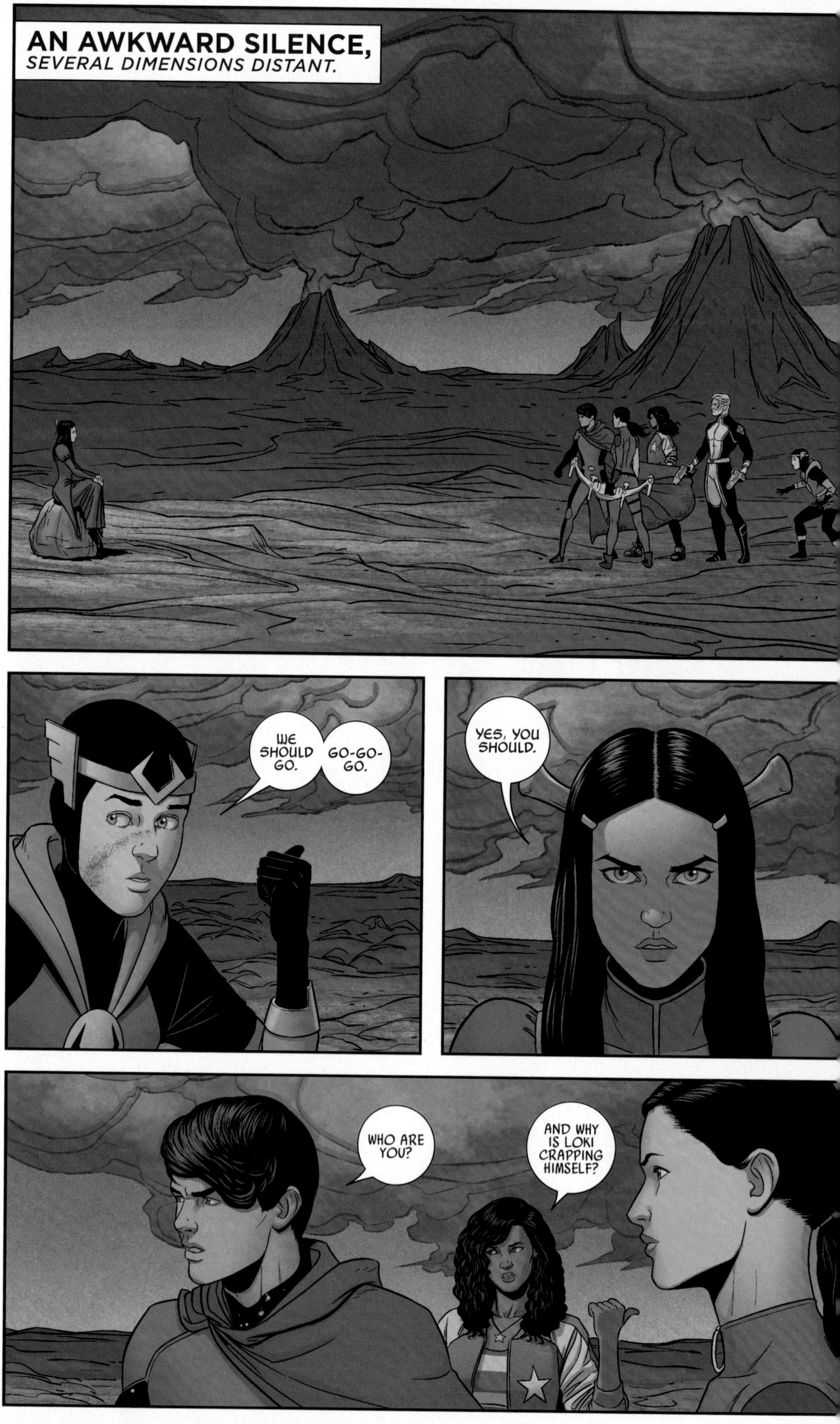

AN AWKWARD SILENCE,
SEVERAL DIMENSIONS DISTANT.
WE SHOULD GO.
GO-GO-GO.
YES, YOU SHOULD.
WHO ARE YOU?
AND WHY IS LOKI CRAPPING HIMSELF?

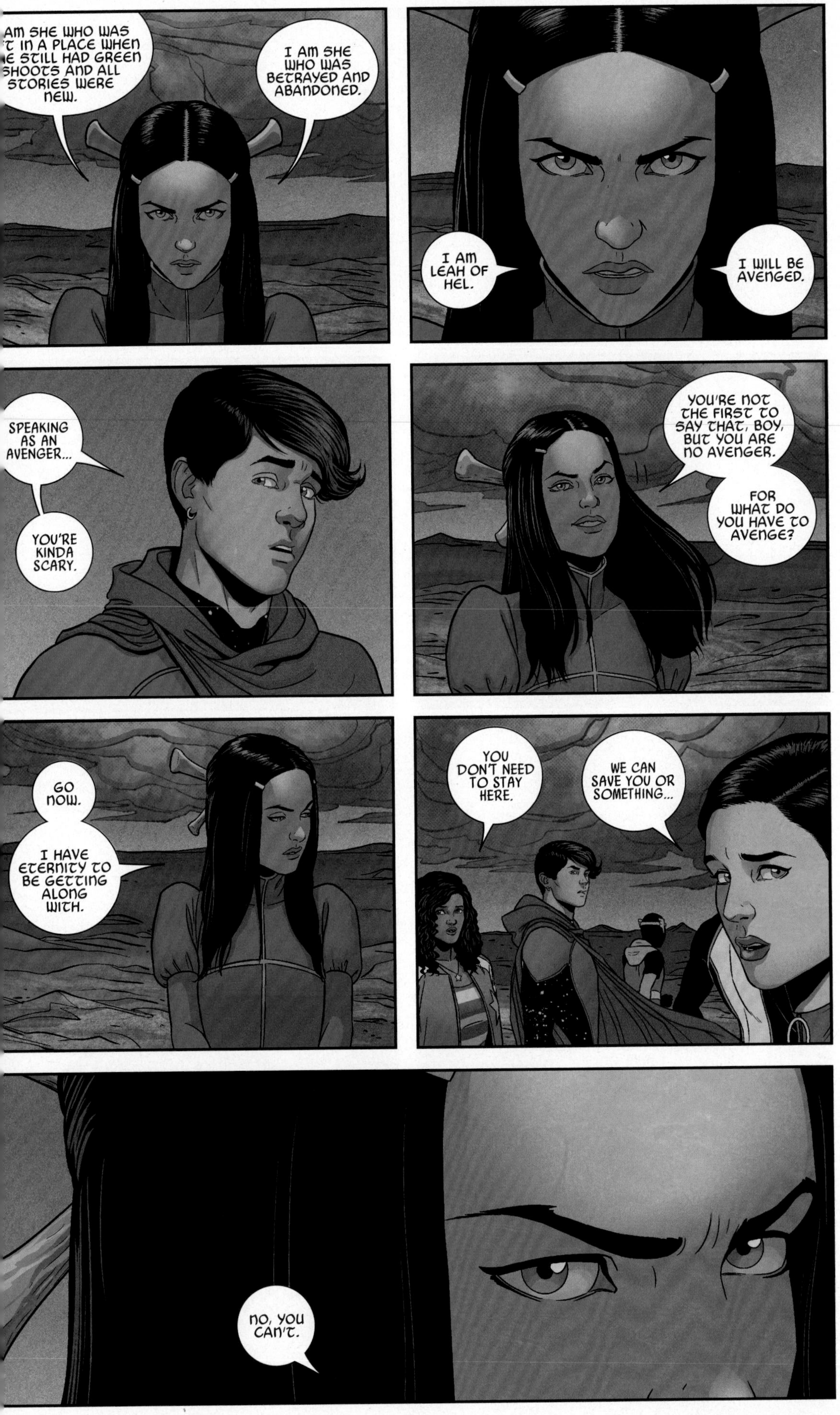

AM SHE WHO WAS IN A PLACE WHEN STILL HAD GREEN SHOOTS AND ALL STORIES WERE NEW.
I AM SHE WHO WAS BETRAYED AND ABANDONED.
I AM LEAH OF HEL.
I WILL BE AVENGED.
SPEAKING AS AN AVENGER...
YOU'RE KINDA SCARY.
YOU'RE NOT THE FIRST TO SAY THAT, BOY, BUT YOU ARE NO AVENGER.
FOR WHAT DO YOU HAVE TO AVENGE?
GO NOW.
I HAVE ETERNITY TO BE GETTING ALONG WITH.
YOU DON'T NEED TO STAY HERE.
WE CAN SAVE YOU OR SOMETHING...
NO, YOU CAN'T.

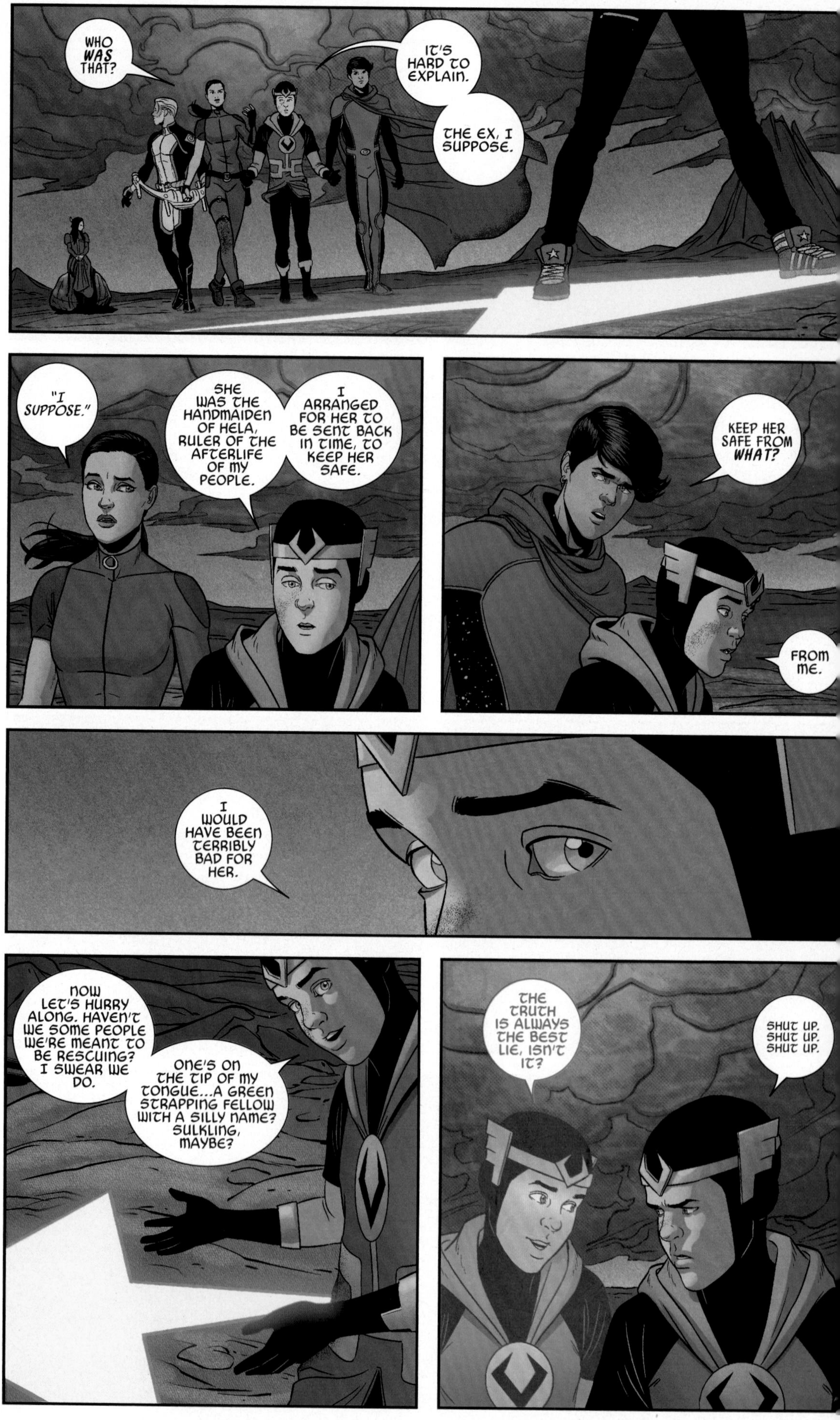
WHO WAS THAT?
IT'S HARD TO EXPLAIN.
THE EX, I SUPPOSE.
"I SUPPOSE."
SHE WAS THE HANDMAIDEN OF HELA, RULER OF THE AFTERLIFE OF MY PEOPLE.
I ARRANGED FOR HER TO BE SENT BACK IN TIME, TO KEEP HER SAFE.
KEEP HER SAFE FROM WHAT?
FROM ME.
I WOULD HAVE BEEN TERRIBLY BAD FOR HER.
NOW LET'S HURRY ALONG. HAVEN'T WE SOME PEOPLE WE'RE MEANT TO BE RESCUING? I SWEAR WE DO.
ONE'S ON THE TIP OF MY TONGUE...A GREEN STRAPPING FELLOW WITH A SILLY NAME? SULKLING, MAYBE?
THE TRUTH IS ALWAYS THE BEST LIE, ISN'T IT?
SHUT UP. SHUT UP. SHUT UP.

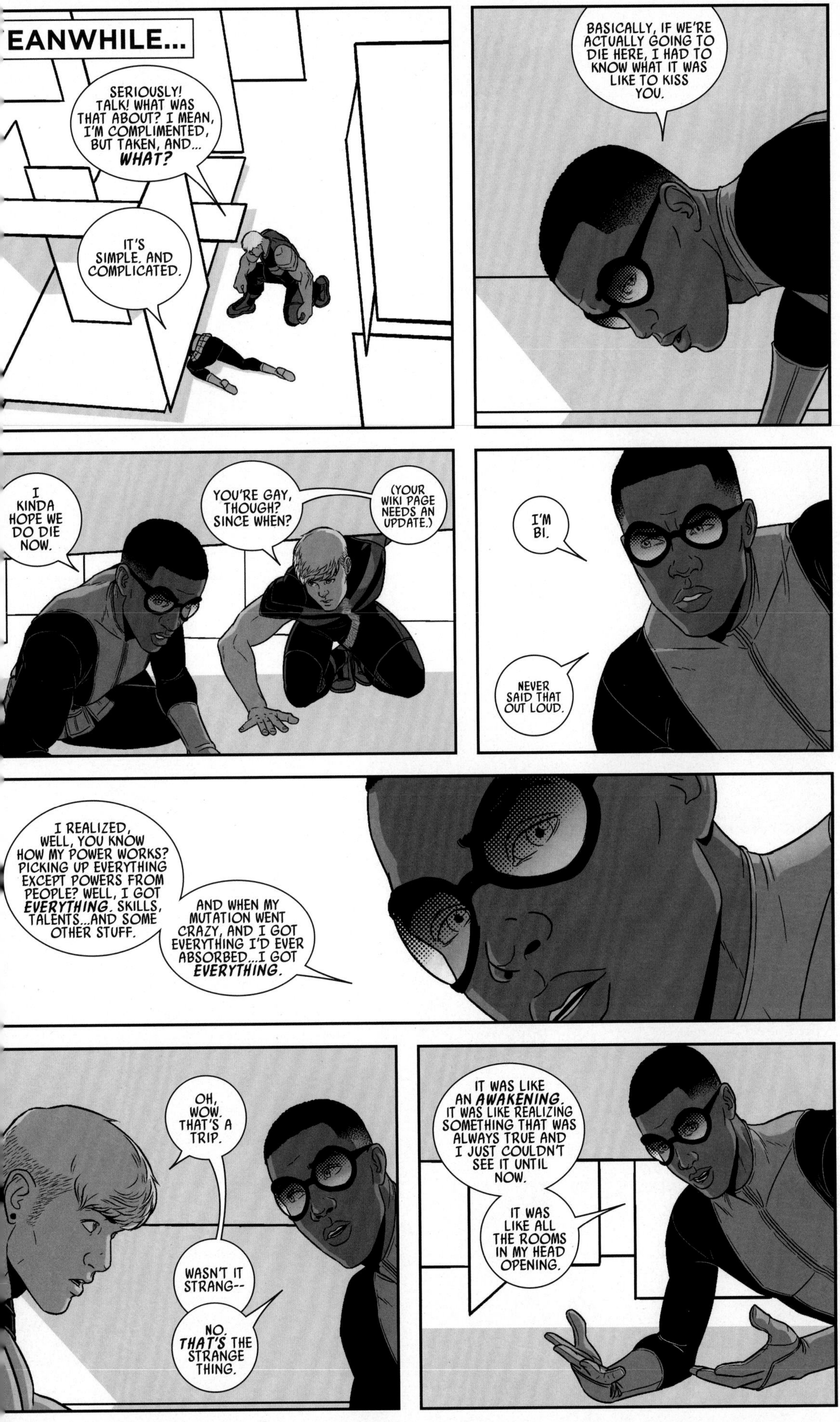
EANWHILE...
SERIOUSLY! TALK! WHAT WAS THAT ABOUT? I MEAN, I'M COMPLIMENTED, BUT TAKEN, AND... WHAT?
IT'S SIMPLE. AND COMPLICATED.
BASICALLY, IF WE'RE ACTUALLY GOING TO DIE HERE, I HAD TO KNOW WHAT IT WAS LIKE TO KISS YOU.
I KINDA HOPE WE DO DIE NOW.
YOU'RE GAY, THOUGH? SINCE WHEN?
(YOUR WIKI PAGE NEEDS AN UPDATE.)
I'M BI.
NEVER SAID THAT OUT LOUD.
I REALIZED, WELL, YOU KNOW HOW MY POWER WORKS? PICKING UP EVERYTHING EXCEPT POWERS FROM PEOPLE? WELL, I GOT EVERYTHING. SKILLS, TALENTS...AND SOME OTHER STUFF.
AND WHEN MY MUTATION WENT CRAZY, AND I GOT EVERYTHING I'D EVER ABSORBED...I GOT EVERYTHING.
OH, WOW. THAT'S A TRIP.
WASN'T IT STRANG--
NO. THAT'S THE STRANGE THING.
IT WAS LIKE AN AWAKENING. IT WAS LIKE REALIZING SOMETHING THAT WAS ALWAYS TRUE AND I JUST COULDN'T SEE IT UNTIL NOW.
IT WAS LIKE ALL THE ROOMS IN MY HEAD OPENING.

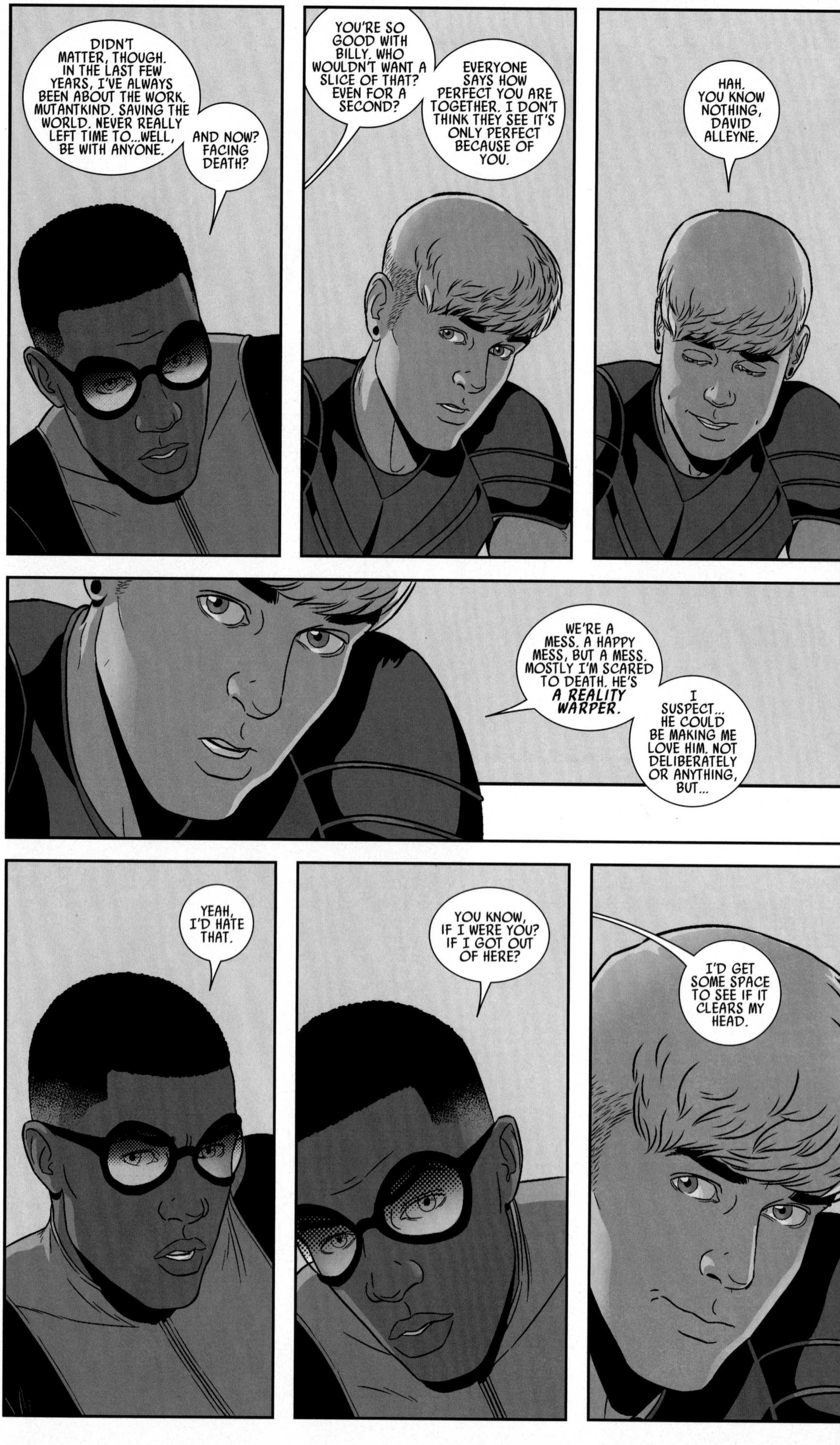
DIDN'T MATTER, THOUGH. IN THE LAST FEW YEARS, I'VE ALWAYS BEEN ABOUT THE WORK. MUTANTKIND. SAVING THE WORLD. NEVER REALLY LEFT TIME TO...WELL, BE WITH ANYONE.
AND NOW? FACING DEATH?
YOU'RE SO GOOD WITH BILLY. WHO WOULDN'T WANT A SLICE OF THAT? EVEN FOR A SECOND?
EVERYONE SAYS HOW PERFECT YOU ARE TOGETHER. I DON'T THINK THEY SEE IT'S ONLY PERFECT BECAUSE OF YOU.
HAH. YOU KNOW NOTHING, DAVID ALLEYNE.
WE'RE A MESS. A HAPPY MESS, BUT A MESS. MOSTLY I'M SCARED TO DEATH. HE'S *A REALITY WARPER.*
I SUSPECT... HE COULD BE MAKING ME LOVE HIM. NOT DELIBERATELY OR ANYTHING, BUT...
YEAH, I'D HATE THAT.
YOU KNOW, IF I WERE YOU? IF I GOT OUT OF HERE?
I'D GET SOME SPACE TO SEE IF IT CLEARS MY HEAD.

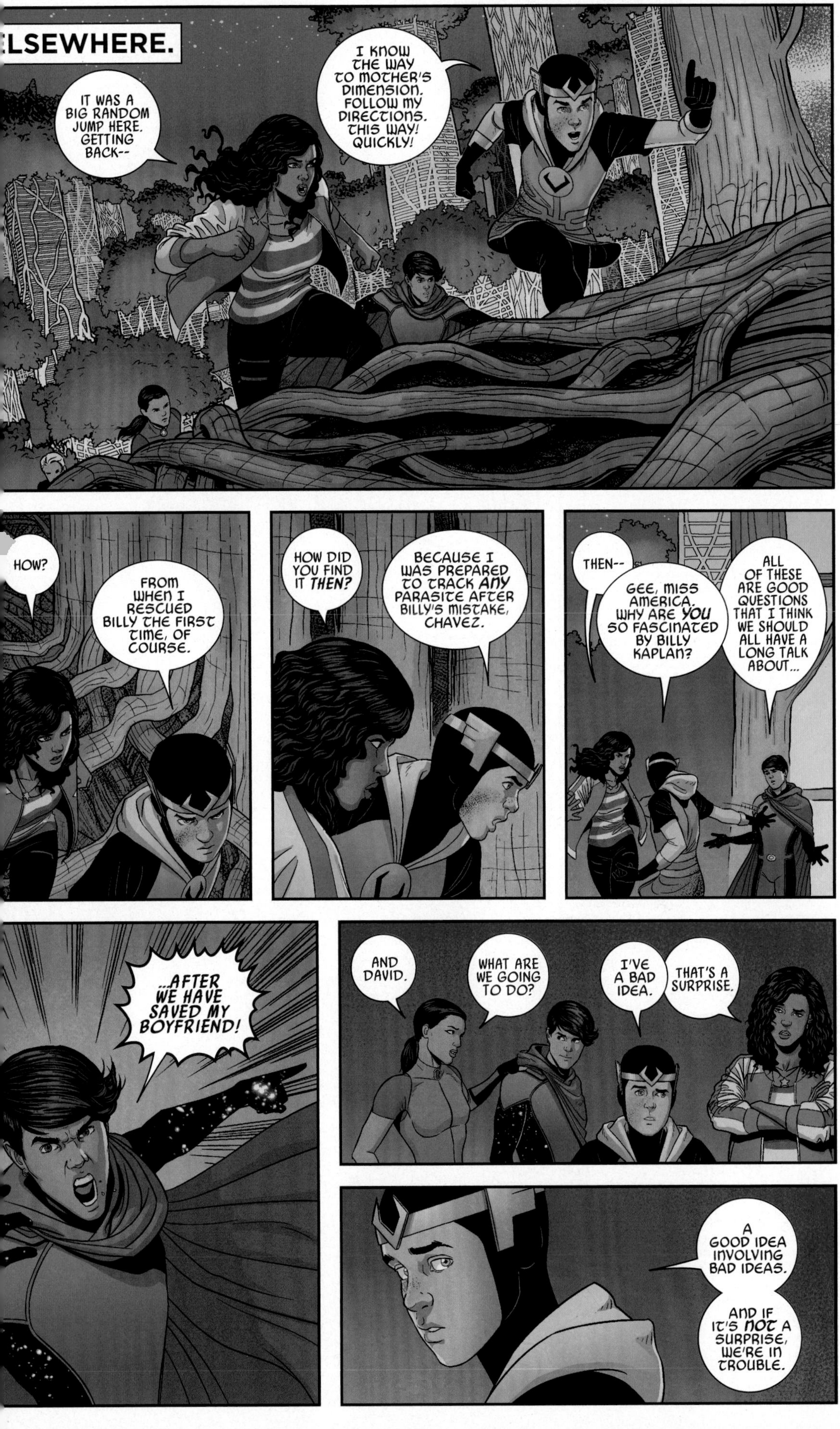
ELSEWHERE.
IT WAS A BIG RANDOM JUMP HERE. GETTING BACK--
I KNOW THE WAY TO MOTHER'S DIMENSION. FOLLOW MY DIRECTIONS. THIS WAY! QUICKLY!
HOW?
FROM WHEN I RESCUED BILLY THE FIRST TIME, OF COURSE.
HOW DID YOU FIND IT THEN?
BECAUSE I WAS PREPARED TO TRACK ANY PARASITE AFTER BILLY'S MISTAKE, CHAVEZ.
THEN--
GEE, MISS AMERICA. WHY ARE YOU SO FASCINATED BY BILLY KAPLAN?
ALL OF THESE ARE GOOD QUESTIONS THAT I THINK WE SHOULD ALL HAVE A LONG TALK ABOUT...
...AFTER WE HAVE SAVED MY BOYFRIEND!
AND DAVID.
WHAT ARE WE GOING TO DO?
I'VE A BAD IDEA.
THAT'S A SURPRISE.
A GOOD IDEA INVOLVING BAD IDEAS.
AND IF IT'S NOT A SURPRISE, WE'RE IN TROUBLE.

FINALLY!

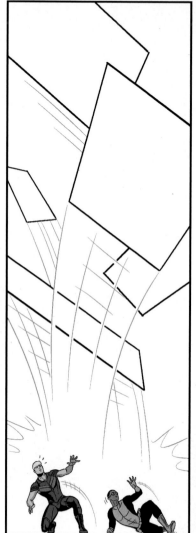

TEDDY. I DON'T BELIEVE YOU'VE INTRODUCED ME TO YOUR FRIEND.

BUT DON'T WORRY.

WE DO HAVE THE REST OF TIME FOR THAT.

HI, MRS. ALTMAN!

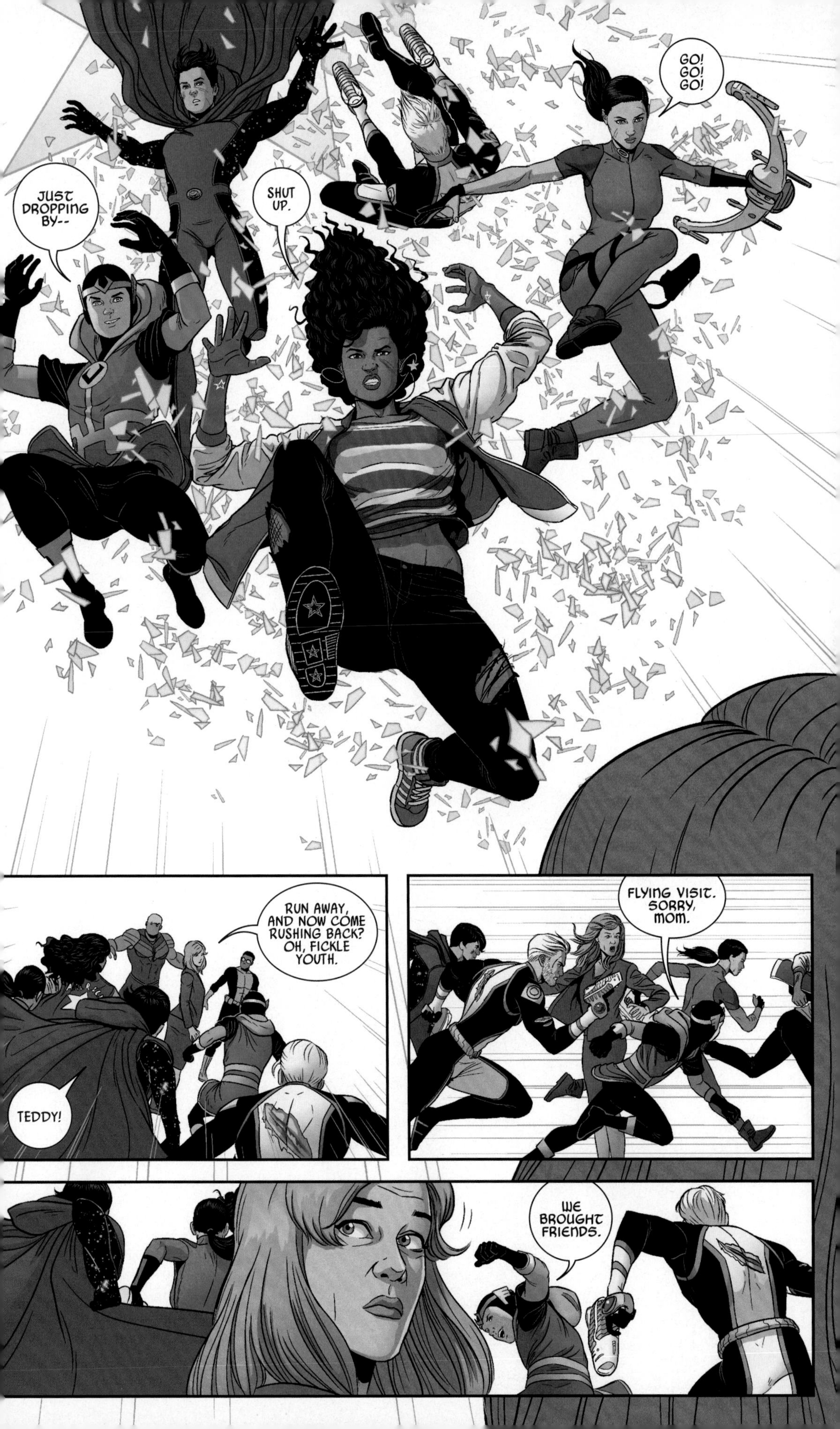
GO! GO! GO!
JUST DROPPING BY--
SHUT UP.
RUN AWAY, AND NOW COME RUSHING BACK? OH, FICKLE YOUTH.
TEDDY!
FLYING VISIT. SORRY, MOM.
WE BROUGHT FRIENDS.

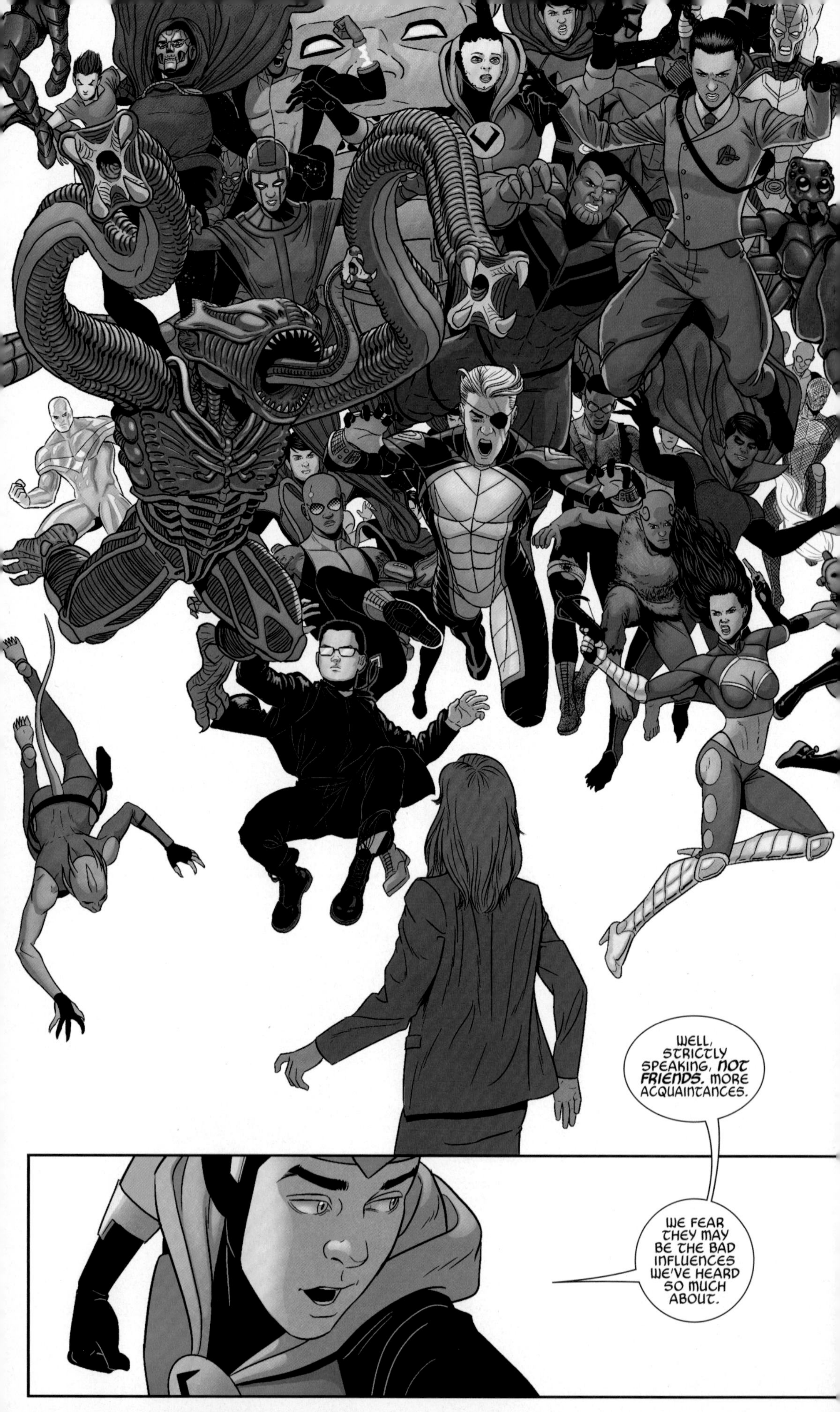
WELL, STRICTLY SPEAKING, NOT FRIENDS. MORE ACQUAINTANCES.
WE FEAR THEY MAY BE THE BAD INFLUENCES WE'VE HEARD SO MUCH ABOUT.

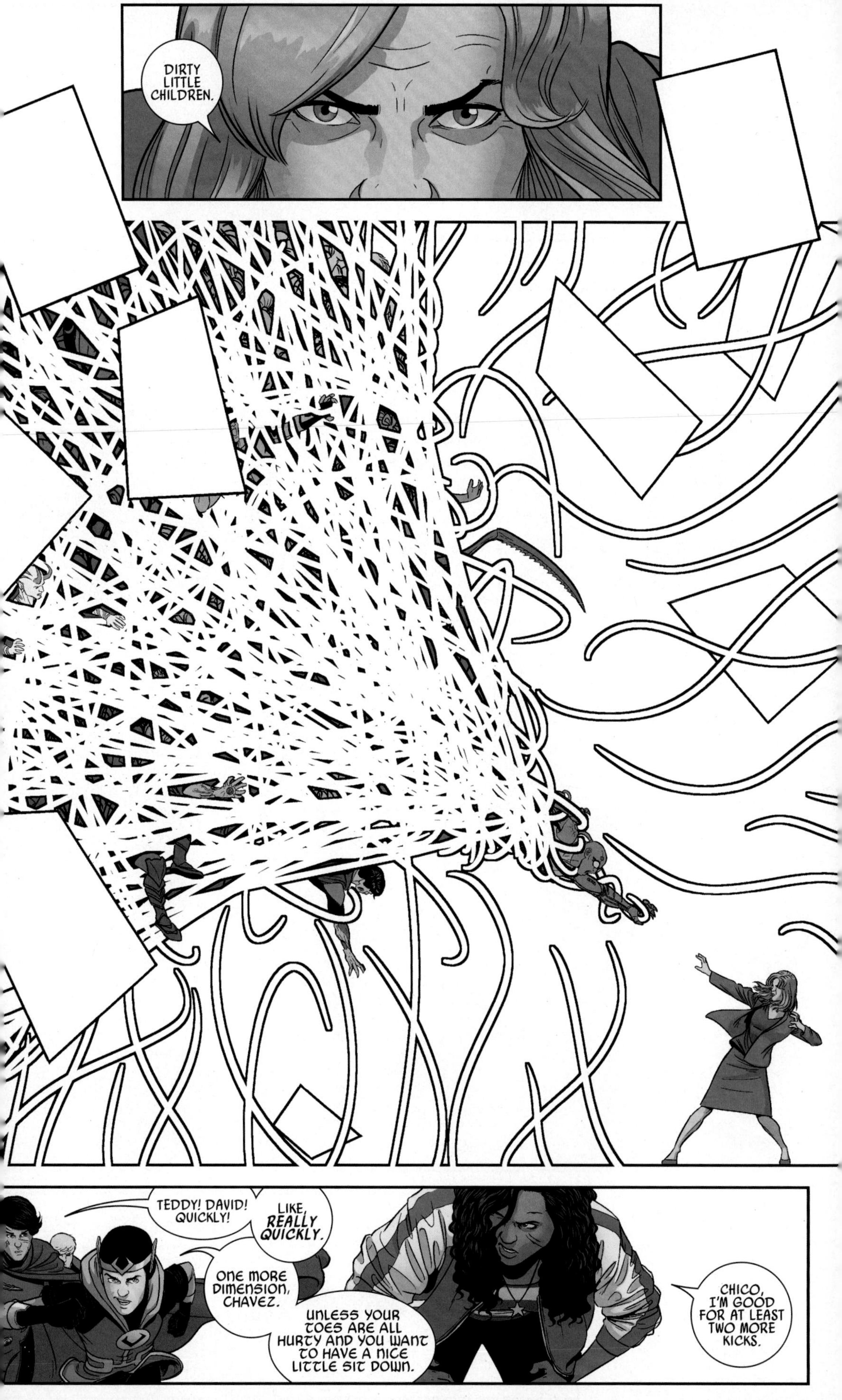
DIRTY LITTLE CHILDREN.
TEDDY! DAVID! QUICKLY!
LIKE, REALLY QUICKLY.
ONE MORE DIMENSION, CHAVEZ.
UNLESS YOUR TOES ARE ALL HURTY AND YOU WANT TO HAVE A NICE LITTLE SIT DOWN.
CHICO, I'M GOOD FOR AT LEAST TWO MORE KICKS.

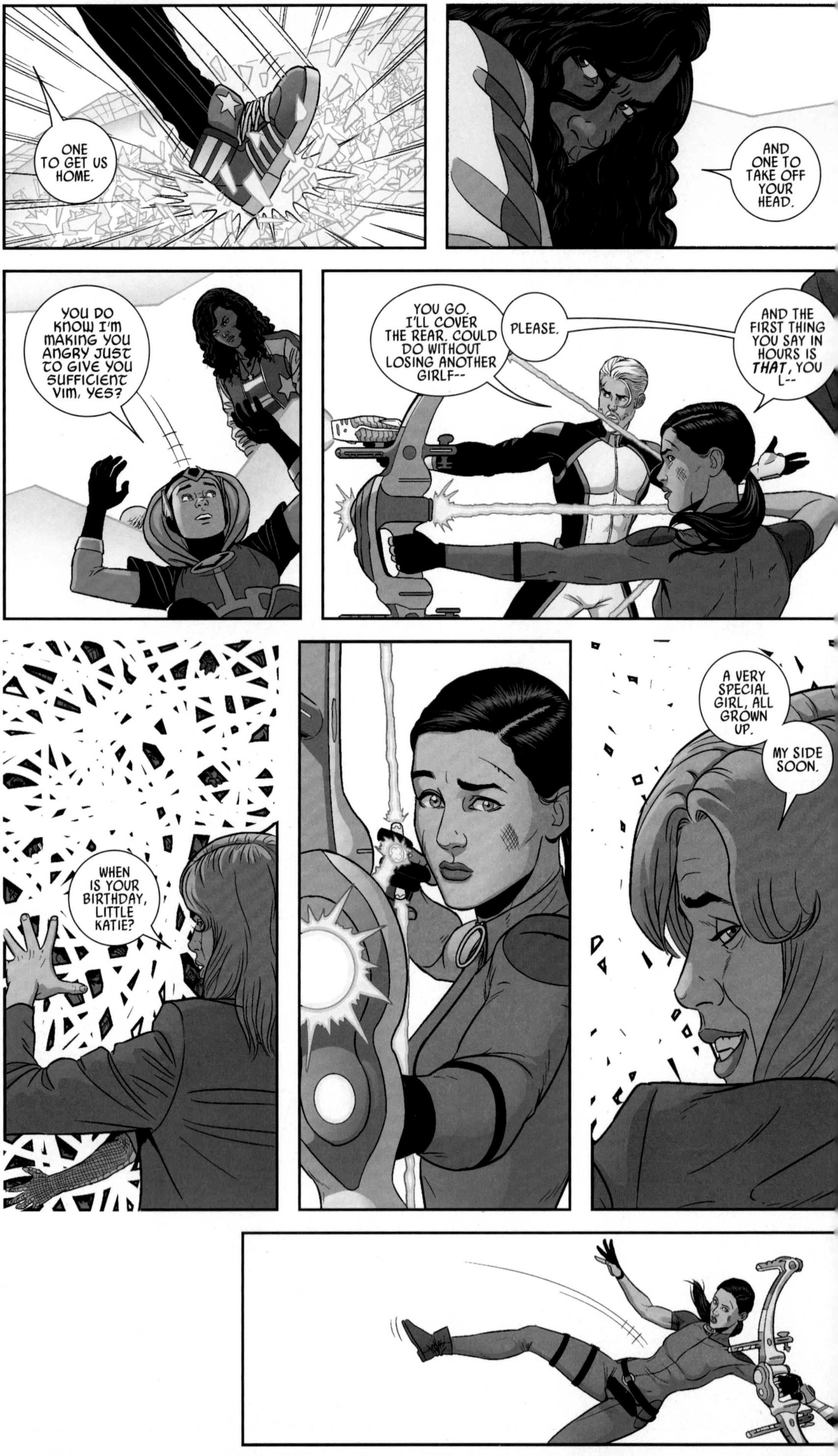
ONE TO GET US HOME.
AND ONE TO TAKE OFF YOUR HEAD.
YOU DO KNOW I'M MAKING YOU ANGRY JUST TO GIVE YOU SUFFICIENT VIM, YES?
YOU GO. I'LL COVER THE REAR. COULD DO WITHOUT LOSING ANOTHER GIRLF--
PLEASE.
AND THE FIRST THING YOU SAY IN HOURS IS *THAT*, YOU L--
WHEN IS YOUR BIRTHDAY, LITTLE KATIE?
A VERY SPECIAL GIRL, ALL GROWN UP.
MY SIDE SOON.

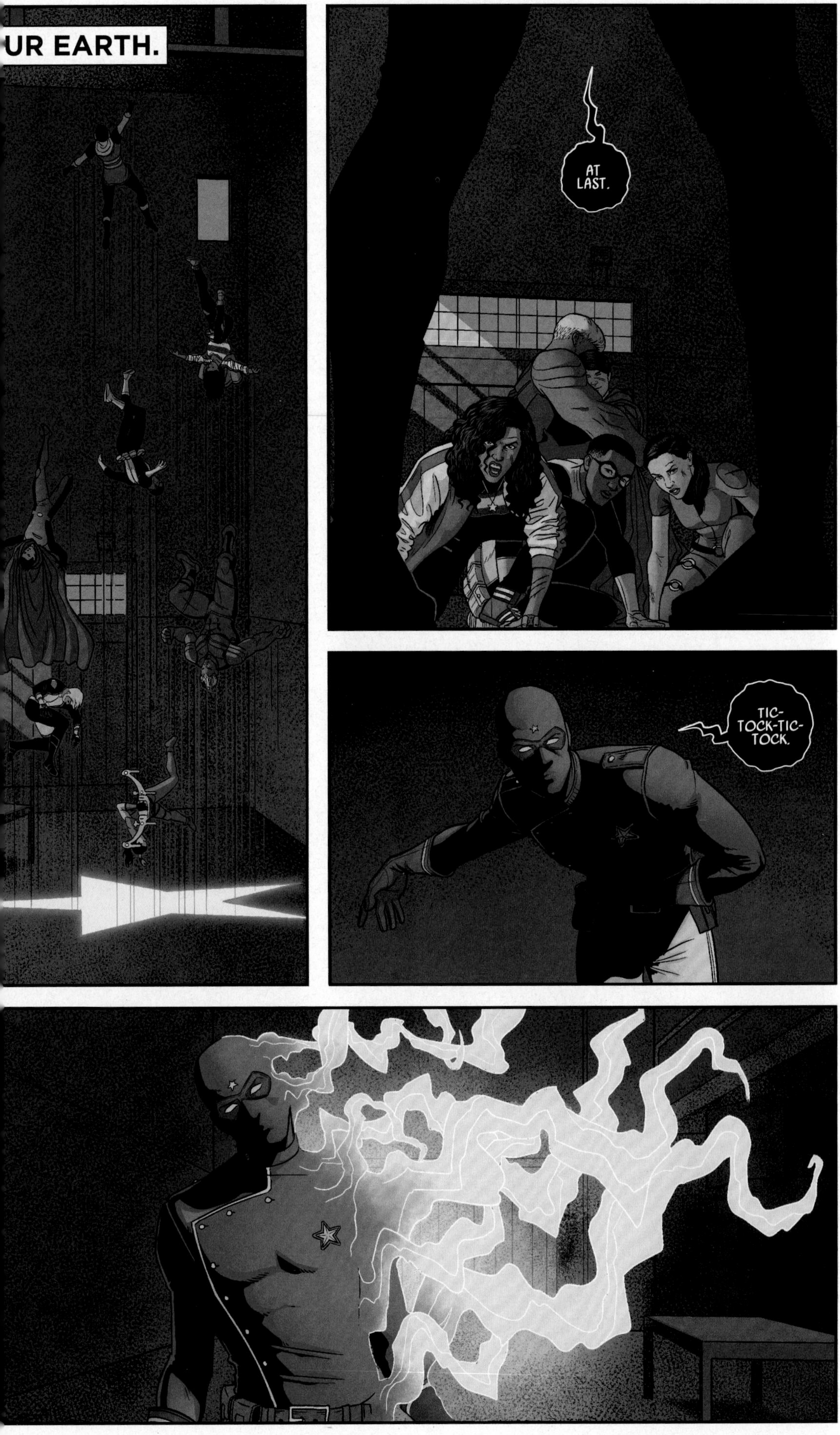
UR EARTH.
AT LAST.
TIC-TOCK-TIC-TOCK.

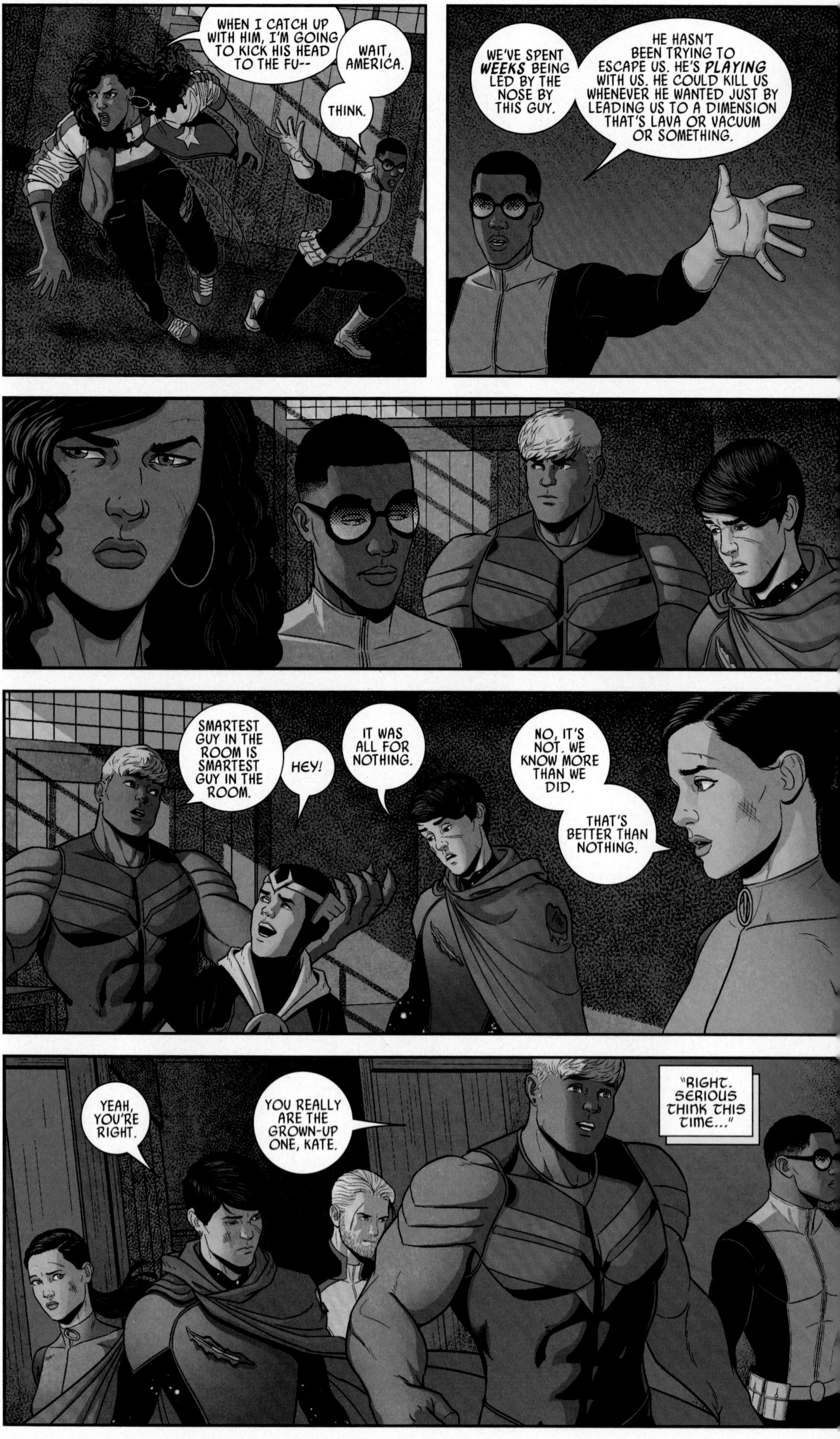
WHEN I CATCH UP WITH HIM, I'M GOING TO KICK HIS HEAD TO THE FU--
WAIT, AMERICA.
THINK.
WE'VE SPENT *WEEKS* BEING LED BY THE NOSE BY THIS GUY.
HE HASN'T BEEN TRYING TO ESCAPE US. HE'S *PLAYING* WITH US. HE COULD KILL US WHENEVER HE WANTED JUST BY LEADING US TO A DIMENSION THAT'S LAVA OR VACUUM OR SOMETHING.
SMARTEST GUY IN THE ROOM IS SMARTEST GUY IN THE ROOM.
HEY!
IT WAS ALL FOR NOTHING.
NO, IT'S NOT. WE KNOW MORE THAN WE DID.
THAT'S BETTER THAN NOTHING.
YEAH, YOU'RE RIGHT.
YOU REALLY ARE THE GROWN-UP ONE, KATE.
"RIGHT. SERIOUS THINK THIS TIME..."

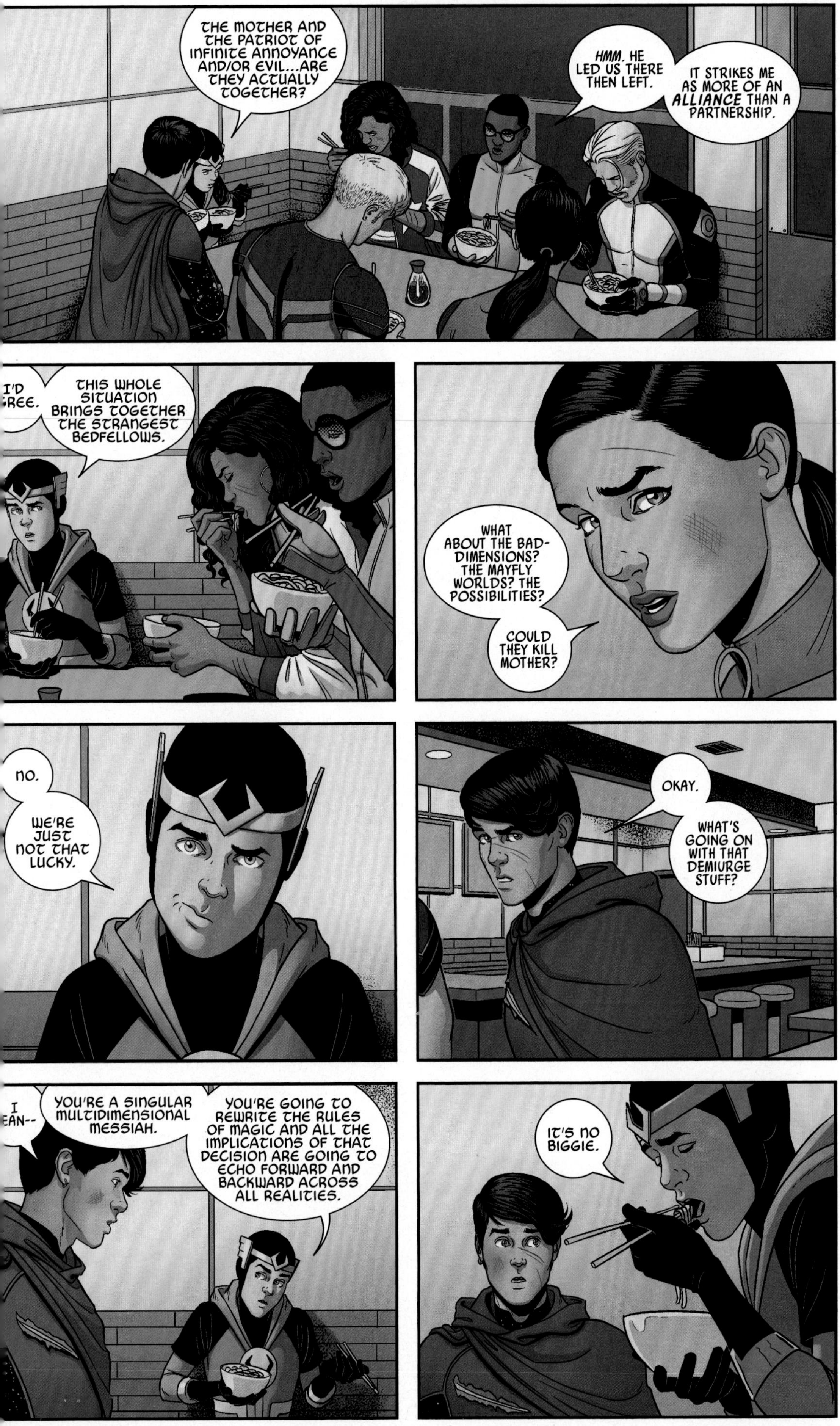
THE MOTHER AND THE PATRIOT OF INFINITE ANNOYANCE AND/OR EVIL...ARE THEY ACTUALLY TOGETHER?
HMM. HE LED US THERE THEN LEFT.
IT STRIKES ME AS MORE OF AN ALLIANCE THAN A PARTNERSHIP.
I'D GREE.
THIS WHOLE SITUATION BRINGS TOGETHER THE STRANGEST BEDFELLOWS.
WHAT ABOUT THE BAD-DIMENSIONS? THE MAYFLY WORLDS? THE POSSIBILITIES?
COULD THEY KILL MOTHER?
NO.
WE'RE JUST NOT THAT LUCKY.
OKAY.
WHAT'S GOING ON WITH THAT DEMIURGE STUFF?
I EAN--
YOU'RE A SINGULAR MULTIDIMENSIONAL MESSIAH.
YOU'RE GOING TO REWRITE THE RULES OF MAGIC AND ALL THE IMPLICATIONS OF THAT DECISION ARE GOING TO ECHO FORWARD AND BACKWARD ACROSS ALL REALITIES.
IT'S NO BIGGIE.

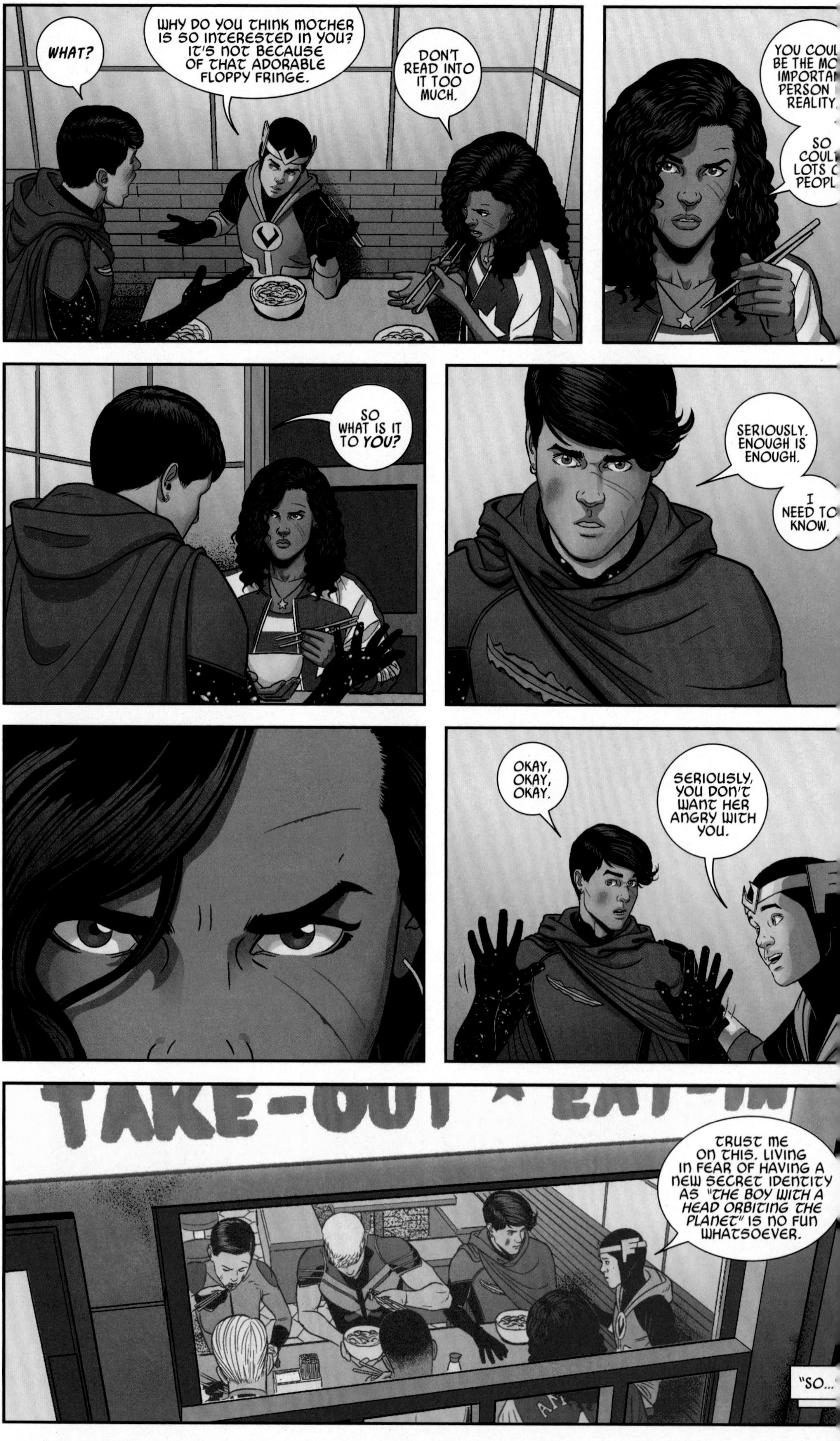
WHAT?
WHY DO YOU THINK MOTHER IS SO INTERESTED IN YOU? IT'S NOT BECAUSE OF THAT ADORABLE FLOPPY FRINGE.
DON'T READ INTO IT TOO MUCH.
YOU COUL BE THE MO IMPORTAN PERSON REALITY.
SO COUL LOTS O PEOPL
SO WHAT IS IT TO YOU?
SERIOUSLY. ENOUGH IS ENOUGH.
I NEED TO KNOW.
OKAY, OKAY, OKAY.
SERIOUSLY, YOU DON'T WANT HER ANGRY WITH YOU.
TAKE-OUT
TRUST ME ON THIS. LIVING IN FEAR OF HAVING A NEW SECRET IDENTITY AS "THE BOY WITH A HEAD ORBITING THE PLANET" IS NO FUN WHATSOEVER.
"SO...

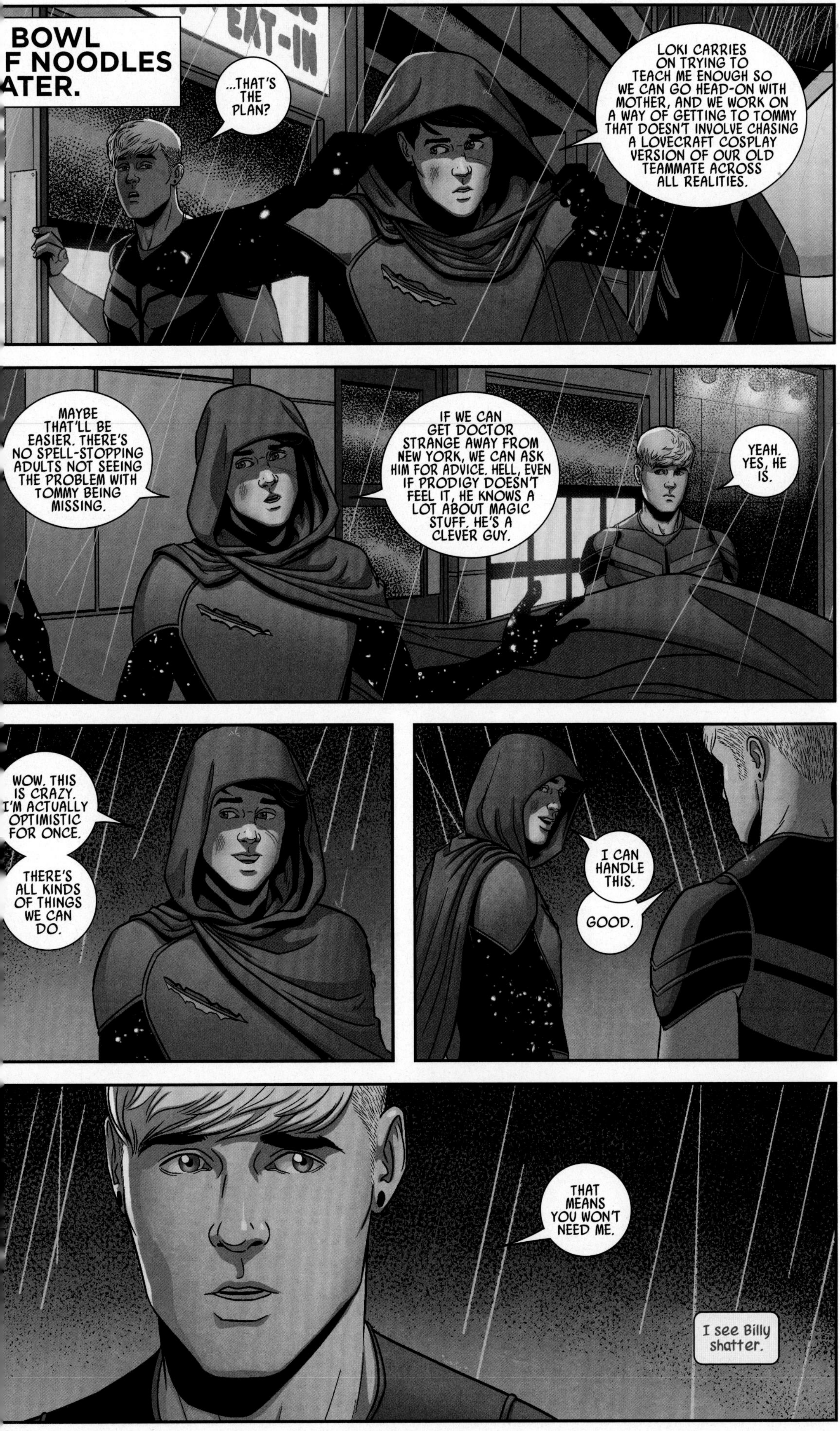
BOWL
F NOODLES
ATER.
...THAT'S THE PLAN?
LOKI CARRIES ON TRYING TO TEACH ME ENOUGH SO WE CAN GO HEAD-ON WITH MOTHER, AND WE WORK ON A WAY OF GETTING TO TOMMY THAT DOESN'T INVOLVE CHASING A LOVECRAFT COSPLAY VERSION OF OUR OLD TEAMMATE ACROSS ALL REALITIES.
MAYBE THAT'LL BE EASIER. THERE'S NO SPELL-STOPPING ADULTS NOT SEEING THE PROBLEM WITH TOMMY BEING MISSING.
IF WE CAN GET DOCTOR STRANGE AWAY FROM NEW YORK, WE CAN ASK HIM FOR ADVICE. HELL, EVEN IF PRODIGY DOESN'T FEEL IT, HE KNOWS A LOT ABOUT MAGIC STUFF. HE'S A CLEVER GUY.
YEAH. YES, HE IS.
WOW. THIS IS CRAZY. I'M ACTUALLY OPTIMISTIC FOR ONCE.
THERE'S ALL KINDS OF THINGS WE CAN DO.
I CAN HANDLE THIS.
GOOD.
THAT MEANS YOU WON'T NEED ME.
I see Billy shatter.

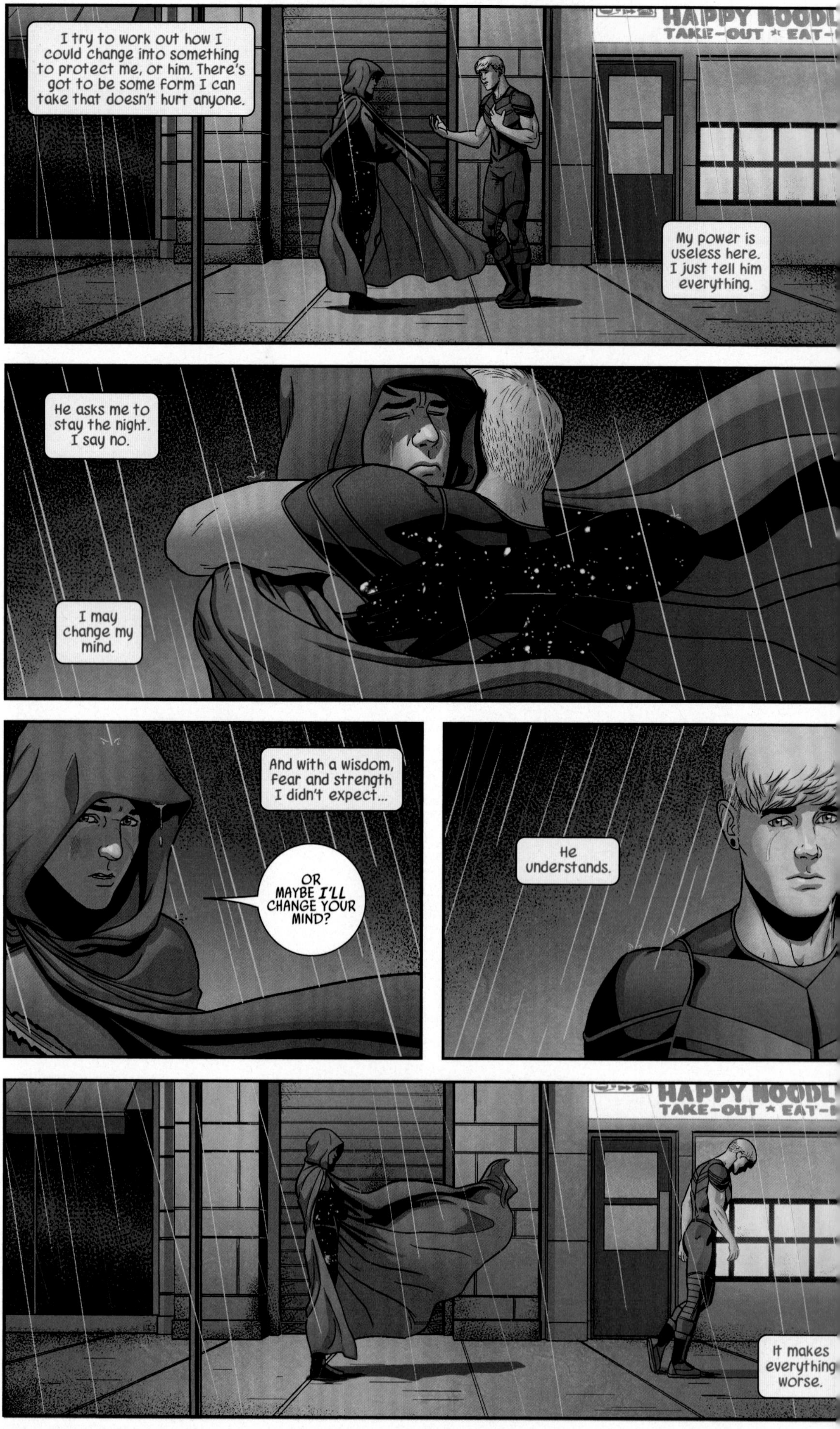
HAPPY NOODL
TAKE-OUT ★ EAT-I
I try to work out how I could change into something to protect me, or him. There's got to be some form I can take that doesn't hurt anyone.
My power is useless here. I just tell him everything.
He asks me to stay the night. I say no.
I may change my mind.
And with a wisdom, fear and strength I didn't expect...
OR MAYBE *I'LL* CHANGE YOUR MIND?
He understands.
HAPPY NOODL
TAKE-OUT ★ EAT-I
It makes everything worse.

THE THERAPIST

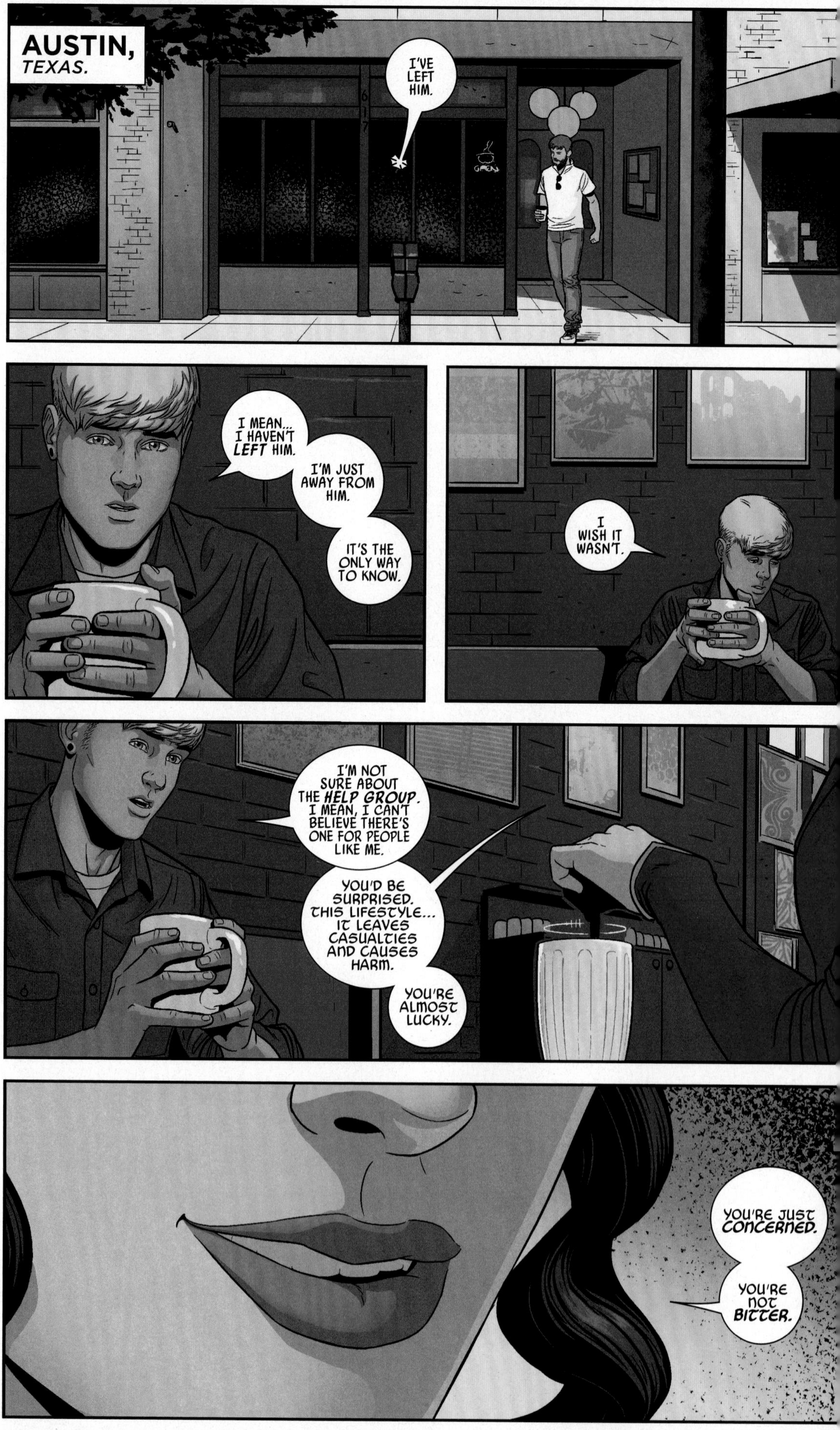
AUSTIN, TEXAS.
I'VE LEFT HIM.
I MEAN... I HAVEN'T LEFT HIM.
I'M JUST AWAY FROM HIM.
IT'S THE ONLY WAY TO KNOW.
I WISH IT WASN'T.
I'M NOT SURE ABOUT THE HELP GROUP. I MEAN, I CAN'T BELIEVE THERE'S ONE FOR PEOPLE LIKE ME.
YOU'D BE SURPRISED. THIS LIFESTYLE... IT LEAVES CASUALTIES AND CAUSES HARM.
YOU'RE ALMOST LUCKY.
YOU'RE JUST CONCERNED.
YOU'RE NOT BITTER.

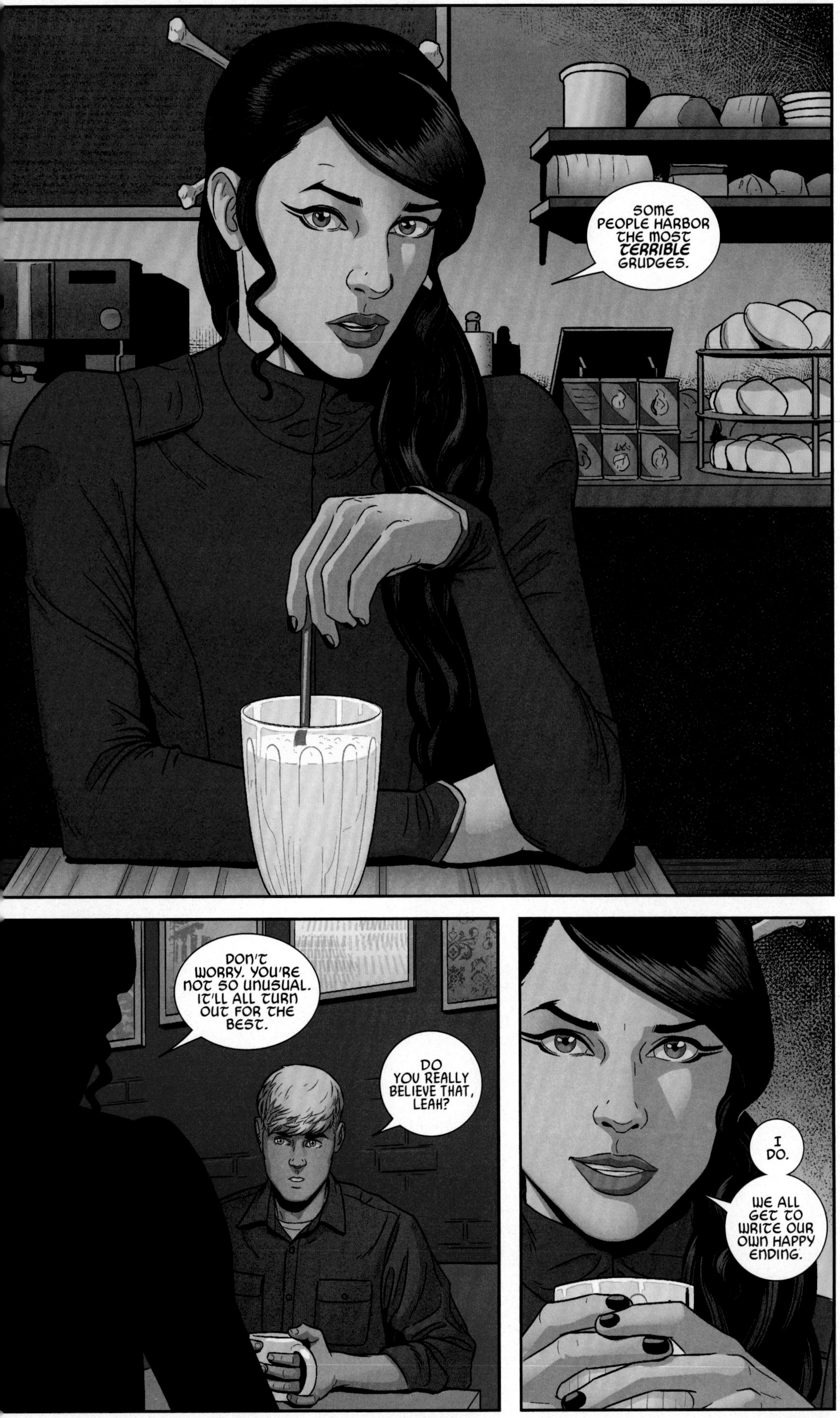
SOME PEOPLE HARBOR THE MOST TERRIBLE GRUDGES.
DON'T WORRY. YOU'RE NOT SO UNUSUAL. IT'LL ALL TURN OUT FOR THE BEST.
DO YOU REALLY BELIEVE THAT, LEAH?
I DO.
WE ALL GET TO WRITE OUR OWN HAPPY ENDING.

10

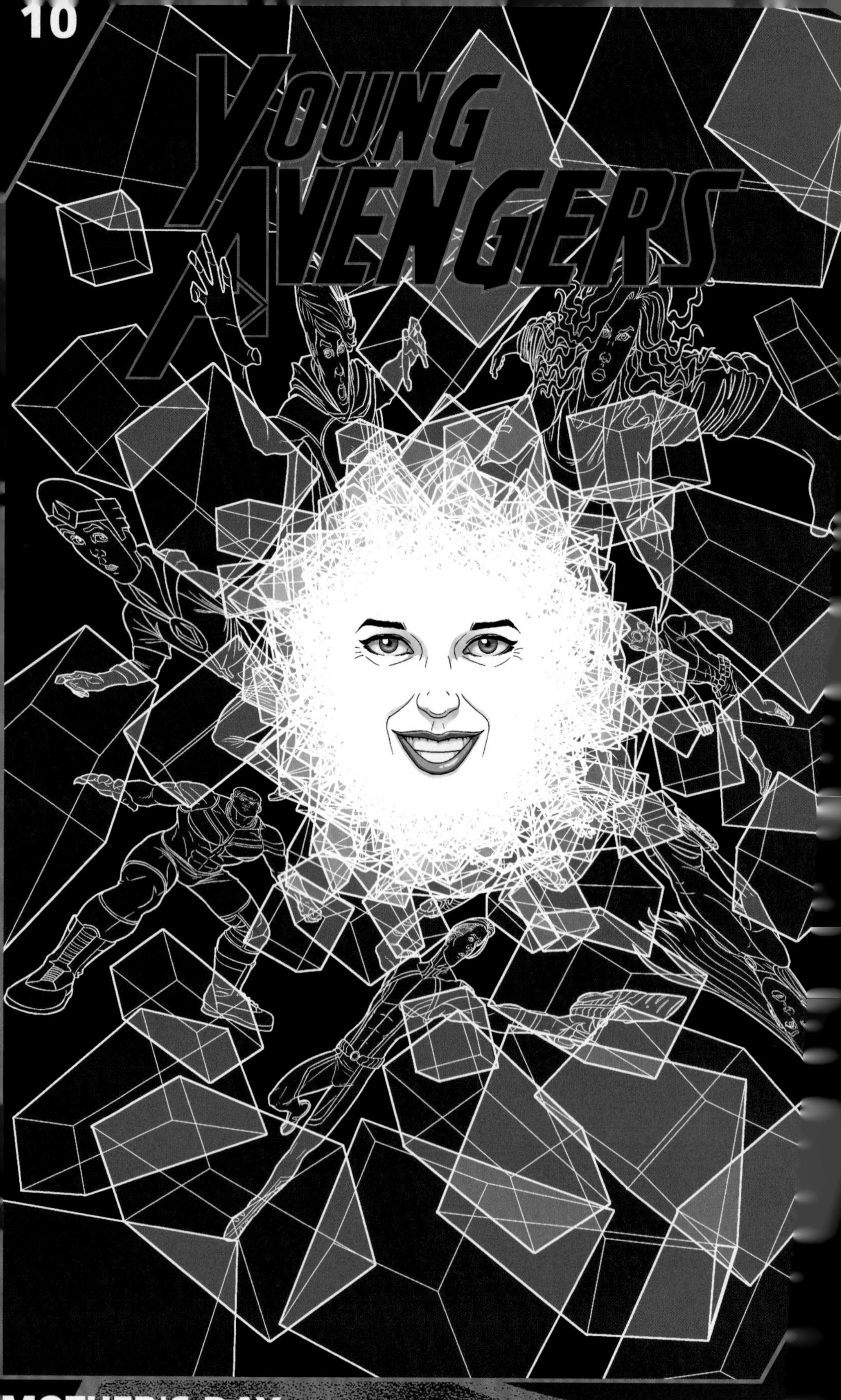
YOUNG AVENGERS

MOTHER'S DAY

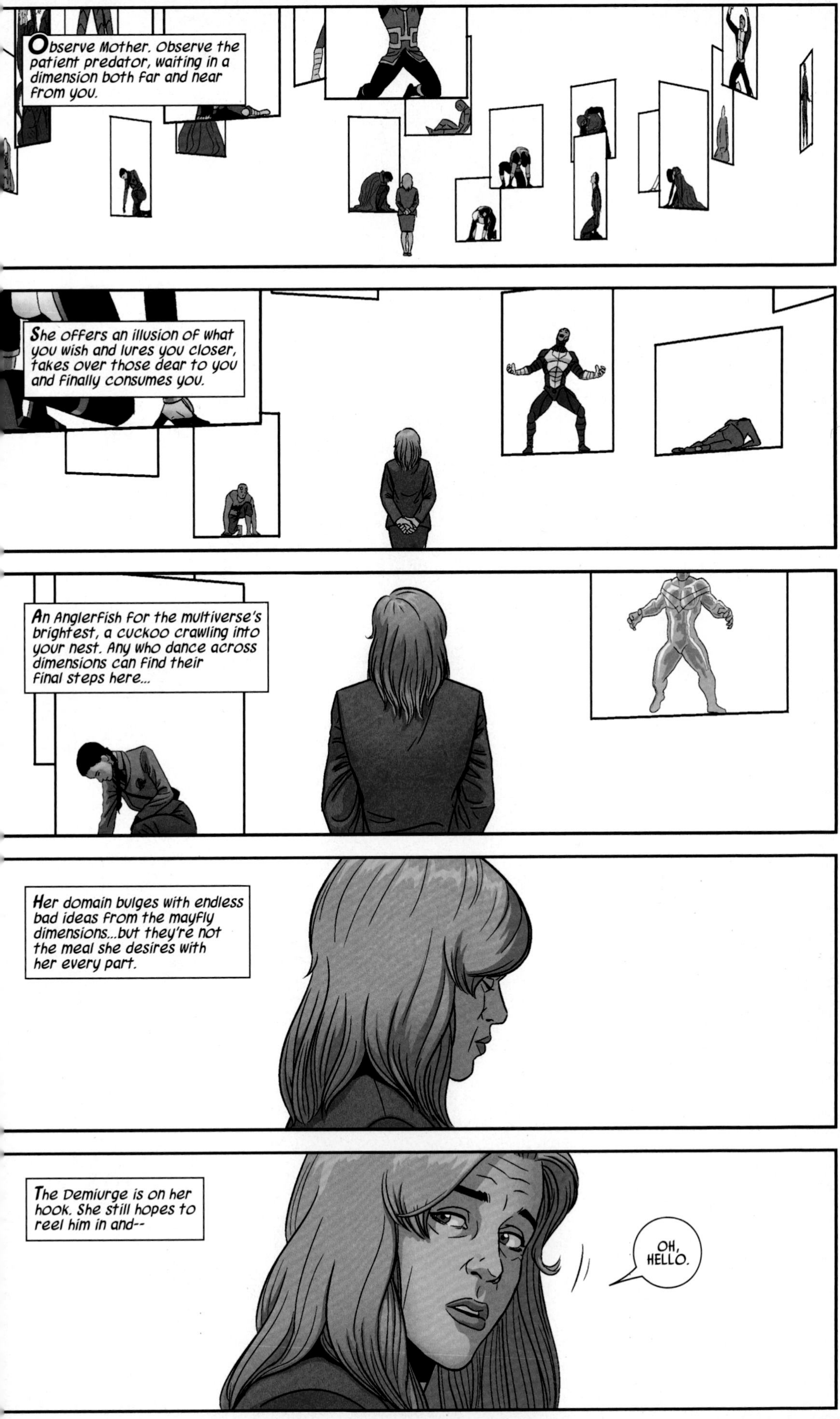
Observe Mother. Observe the patient predator, waiting in a dimension both far and near from you.
She offers an illusion of what you wish and lures you closer, takes over those dear to you and finally consumes you.
An Anglerfish for the multiverse's brightest, a cuckoo crawling into your nest. Any who dance across dimensions can find their final steps here...
Her domain bulges with endless bad ideas from the mayfly dimensions...but they're not the meal she desires with her every part.
The Demiurge is on her hook. She still hopes to reel him in and--
OH, HELLO.

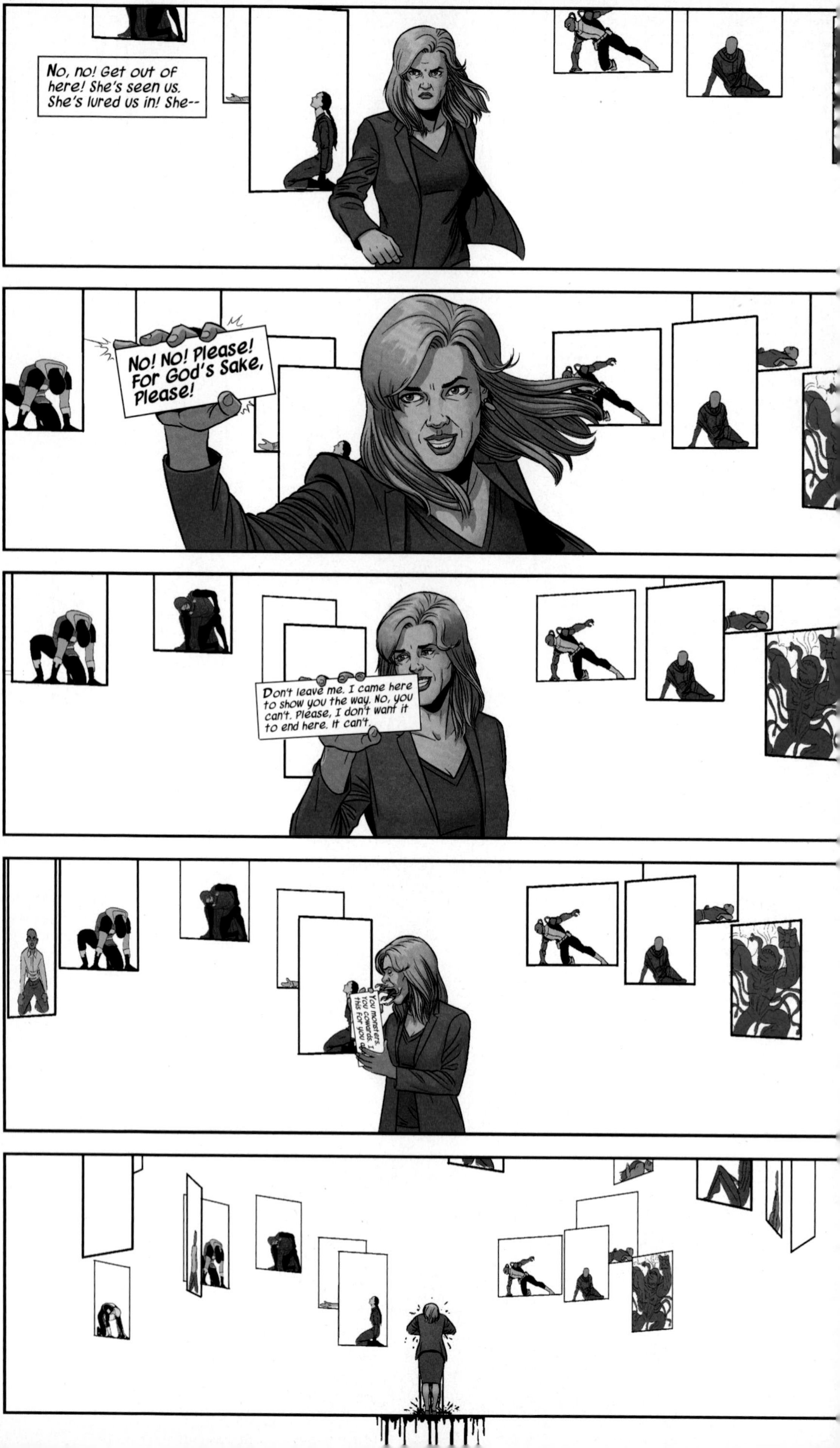
No, no! Get out of here! She's seen us. She's lured us in! She--
No! No! Please! For God's Sake, Please!
Don't leave me. I came here to show you the way. No, you can't. Please, I don't want it to end here. It can't.
You monsters.
You cowards. I
this for you

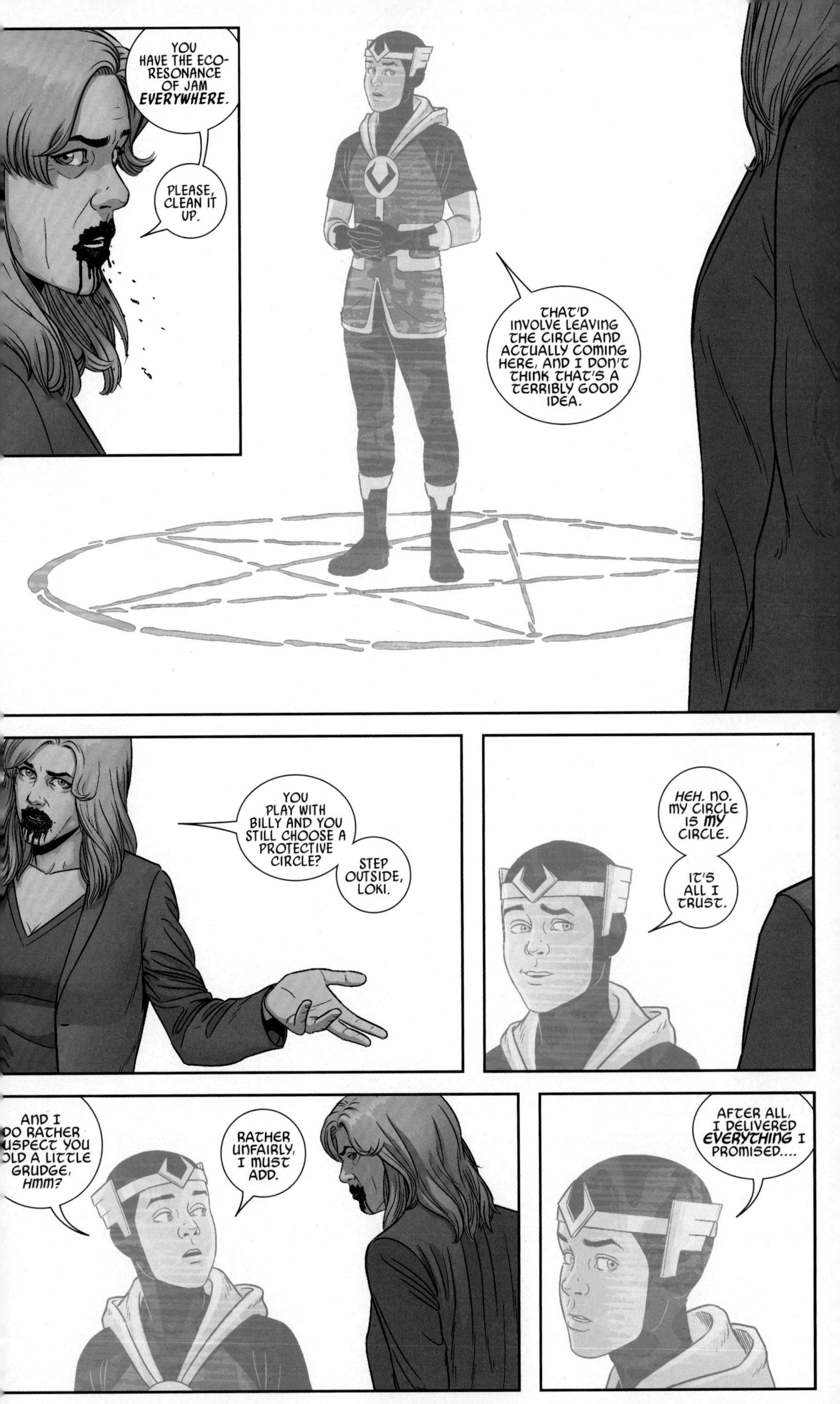
YOU HAVE THE ECO-RESONANCE OF JAM EVERYWHERE.
PLEASE, CLEAN IT UP.
THAT'D INVOLVE LEAVING THE CIRCLE AND ACTUALLY COMING HERE, AND I DON'T THINK THAT'S A TERRIBLY GOOD IDEA.
YOU PLAY WITH BILLY AND YOU STILL CHOOSE A PROTECTIVE CIRCLE?
STEP OUTSIDE, LOKI.
HEH. NO. MY CIRCLE IS MY CIRCLE.
IT'S ALL I TRUST.
AND I DO RATHER SUSPECT YOU HOLD A LITTLE GRUDGE, HMM?
RATHER UNFAIRLY, I MUST ADD.
AFTER ALL, I DELIVERED EVERYTHING I PROMISED....

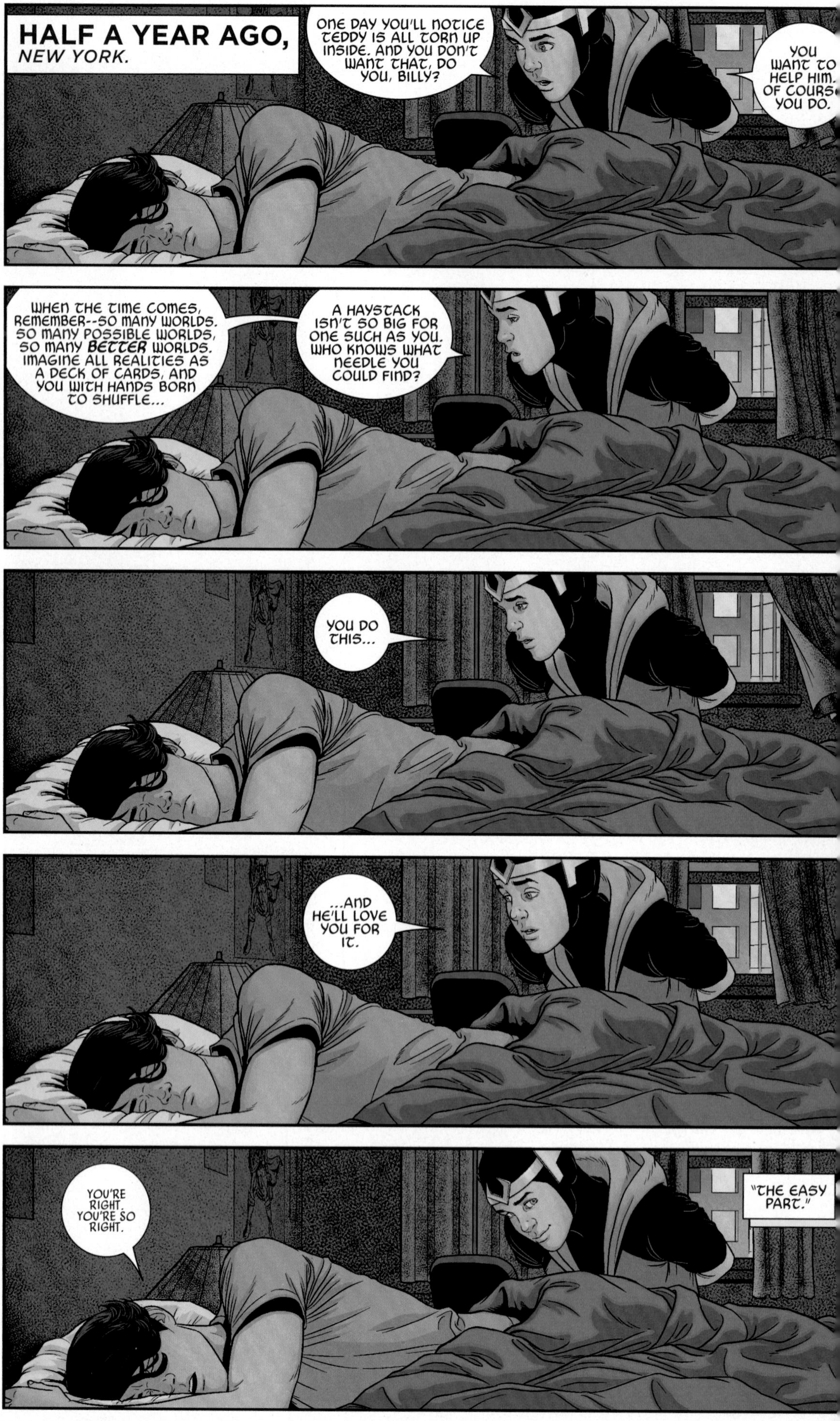
HALF A YEAR AGO, NEW YORK.
ONE DAY YOU'LL NOTICE TEDDY IS ALL TORN UP INSIDE. AND YOU DON'T WANT THAT, DO YOU, BILLY?
YOU WANT TO HELP HIM. OF COURS YOU DO.
WHEN THE TIME COMES, REMEMBER--SO MANY WORLDS. SO MANY POSSIBLE WORLDS, SO MANY BETTER WORLDS. IMAGINE ALL REALITIES AS A DECK OF CARDS, AND YOU WITH HANDS BORN TO SHUFFLE...
A HAYSTACK ISN'T SO BIG FOR ONE SUCH AS YOU. WHO KNOWS WHAT NEEDLE YOU COULD FIND?
YOU DO THIS...
...AND HE'LL LOVE YOU FOR IT.
YOU'RE RIGHT. YOU'RE SO RIGHT.
"THE EASY PART."

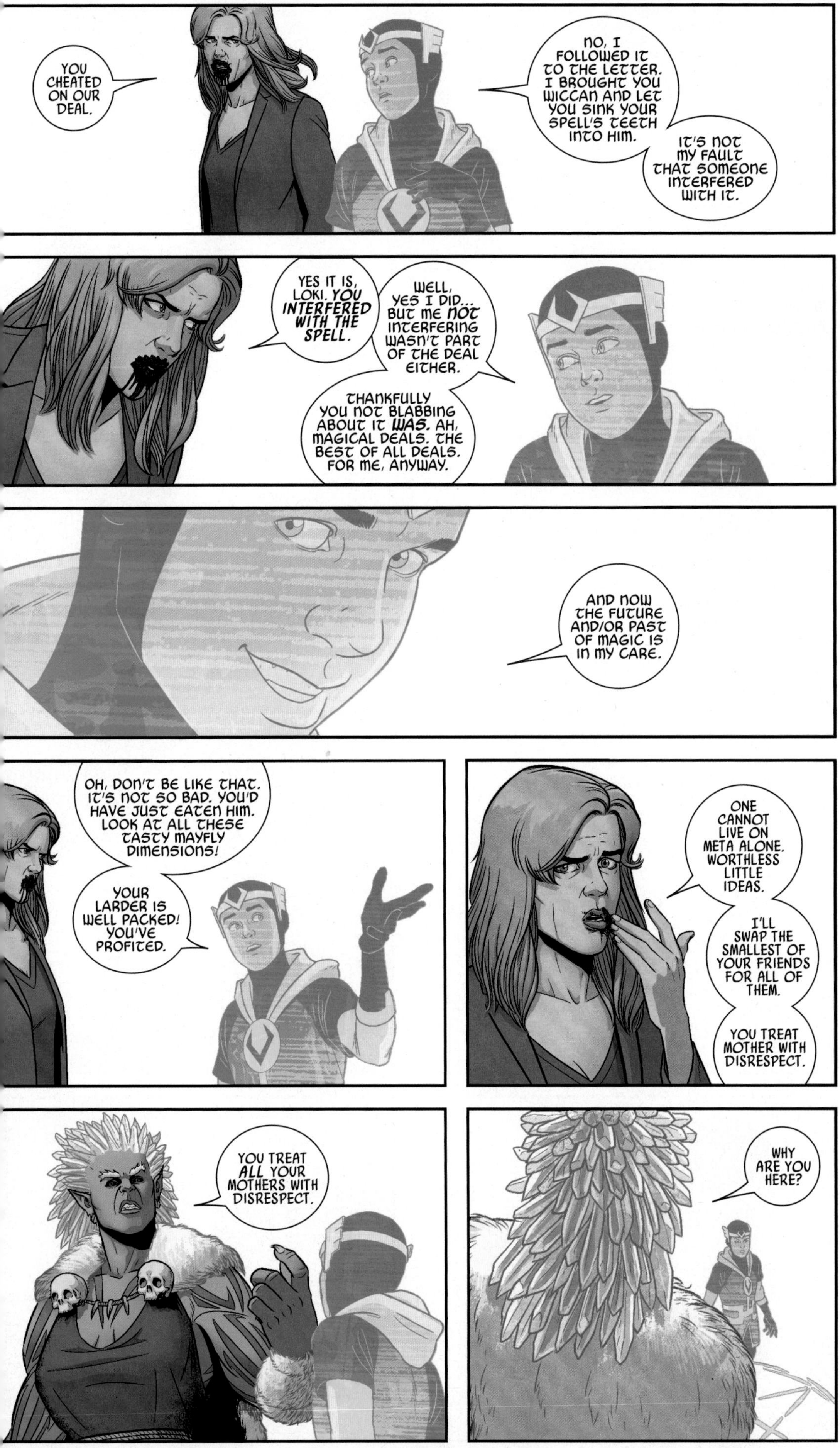
YOU CHEATED ON OUR DEAL.
NO, I FOLLOWED IT TO THE LETTER. I BROUGHT YOU WICCAN AND LET YOU SINK YOUR SPELL'S TEETH INTO HIM.
IT'S NOT MY FAULT THAT SOMEONE INTERFERED WITH IT.
YES IT IS, LOKI. YOU INTERFERED WITH THE SPELL.
WELL, YES I DID... BUT ME NOT INTERFERING WASN'T PART OF THE DEAL EITHER.
THANKFULLY YOU NOT BLABBING ABOUT IT WAS. AH, MAGICAL DEALS. THE BEST OF ALL DEALS. FOR ME, ANYWAY.
AND NOW THE FUTURE AND/OR PAST OF MAGIC IS IN MY CARE.
OH, DON'T BE LIKE THAT. IT'S NOT SO BAD. YOU'D HAVE JUST EATEN HIM. LOOK AT ALL THESE TASTY MAYFLY DIMENSIONS!
YOUR LARDER IS WELL PACKED! YOU'VE PROFITED.
ONE CANNOT LIVE ON META ALONE. WORTHLESS LITTLE IDEAS.
I'LL SWAP THE SMALLEST OF YOUR FRIENDS FOR ALL OF THEM.
YOU TREAT MOTHER WITH DISRESPECT.
YOU TREAT ALL YOUR MOTHERS WITH DISRESPECT.
WHY ARE YOU HERE?

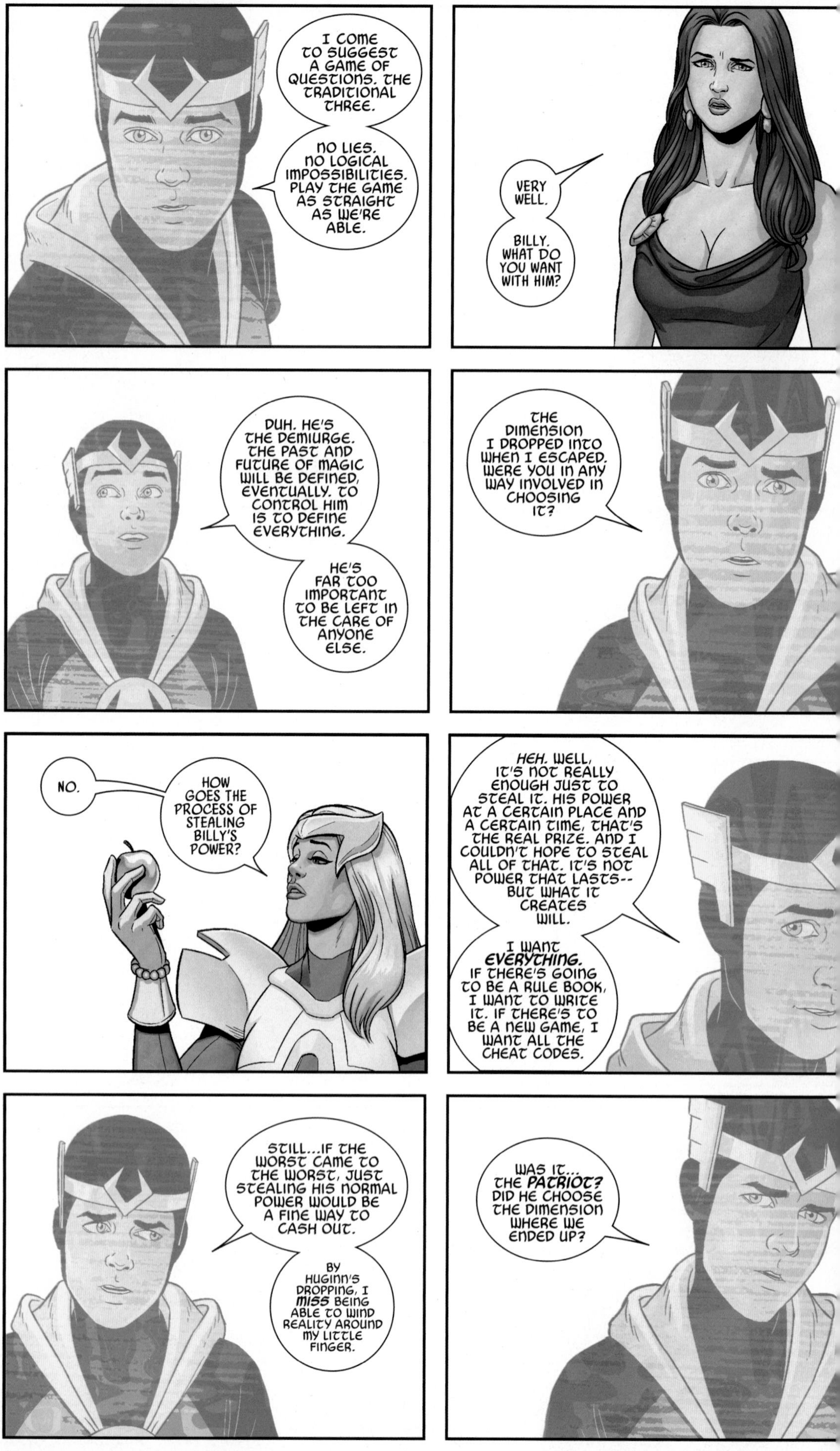
I COME TO SUGGEST A GAME OF QUESTIONS. THE TRADITIONAL THREE.
NO LIES. NO LOGICAL IMPOSSIBILITIES. PLAY THE GAME AS STRAIGHT AS WE'RE ABLE.
VERY WELL.
BILLY. WHAT DO YOU WANT WITH HIM?
DUH. HE'S THE DEMIURGE. THE PAST AND FUTURE OF MAGIC WILL BE DEFINED, EVENTUALLY. TO CONTROL HIM IS TO DEFINE EVERYTHING.
HE'S FAR TOO IMPORTANT TO BE LEFT IN THE CARE OF ANYONE ELSE.
THE DIMENSION I DROPPED INTO WHEN I ESCAPED. WERE YOU IN ANY WAY INVOLVED IN CHOOSING IT?
NO.
HOW GOES THE PROCESS OF STEALING BILLY'S POWER?
HEH. WELL, IT'S NOT REALLY ENOUGH JUST TO STEAL IT. HIS POWER AT A CERTAIN PLACE AND A CERTAIN TIME, THAT'S THE REAL PRIZE. AND I COULDN'T HOPE TO STEAL ALL OF THAT. IT'S NOT POWER THAT LASTS-- BUT WHAT IT CREATES WILL.
I WANT ***EVERYTHING.*** IF THERE'S GOING TO BE A RULE BOOK, I WANT TO WRITE IT. IF THERE'S TO BE A NEW GAME, I WANT ALL THE CHEAT CODES.
STILL...IF THE WORST CAME TO THE WORST, JUST STEALING HIS NORMAL POWER WOULD BE A FINE WAY TO CASH OUT.
BY HUGINN'S DROPPING, I ***MISS*** BEING ABLE TO WIND REALITY AROUND MY LITTLE FINGER.
WAS IT... THE ***PATRIOT?*** DID HE CHOOSE THE DIMENSION WHERE WE ENDED UP?

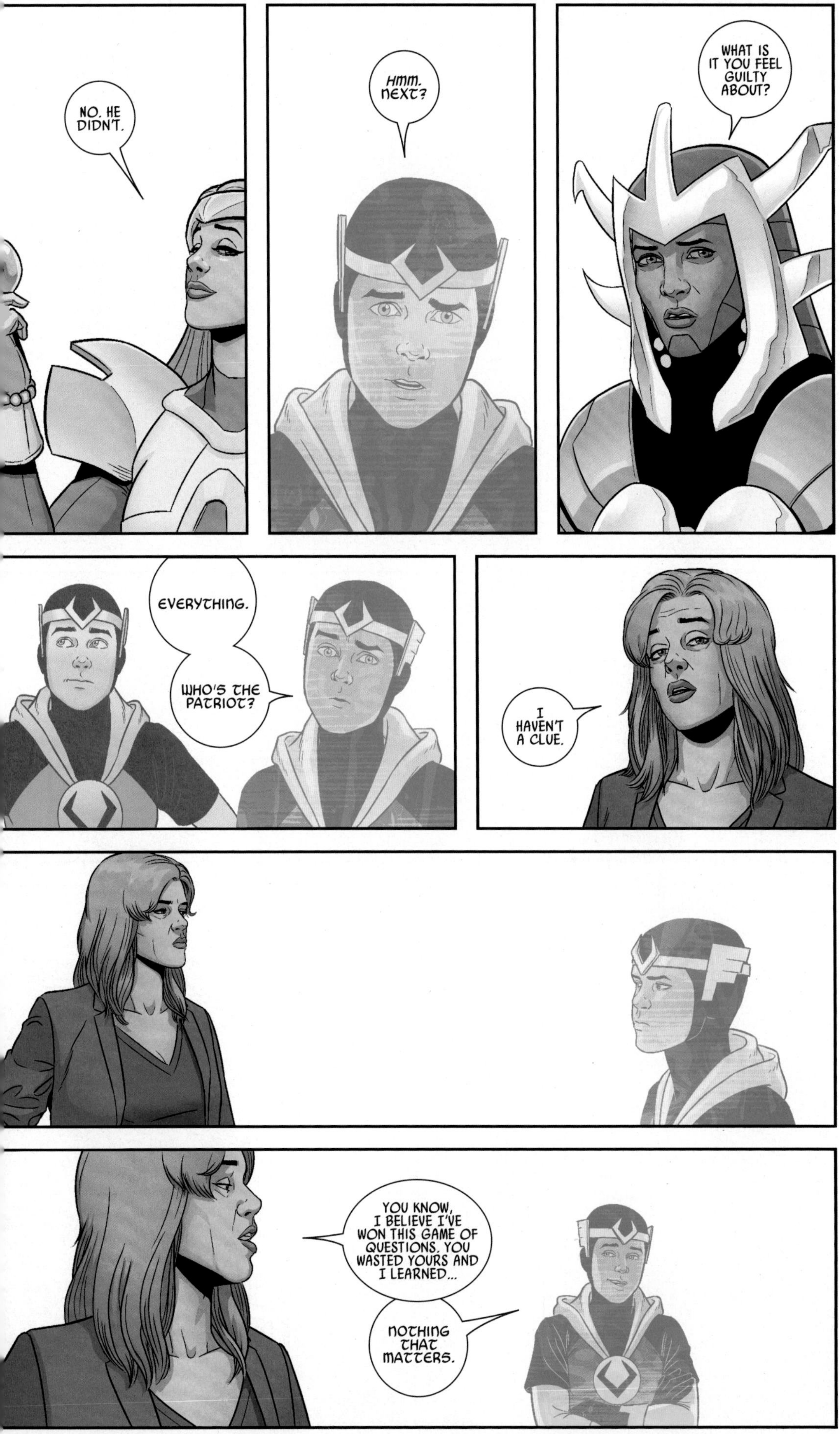
NO. HE DIDN'T.
HMM. NEXT?
WHAT IS IT YOU FEEL GUILTY ABOUT?
EVERYTHING.
WHO'S THE PATRIOT?
I HAVEN'T A CLUE.
YOU KNOW, I BELIEVE I'VE WON THIS GAME OF QUESTIONS. YOU WASTED YOURS AND I LEARNED...
NOTHING THAT MATTERS.

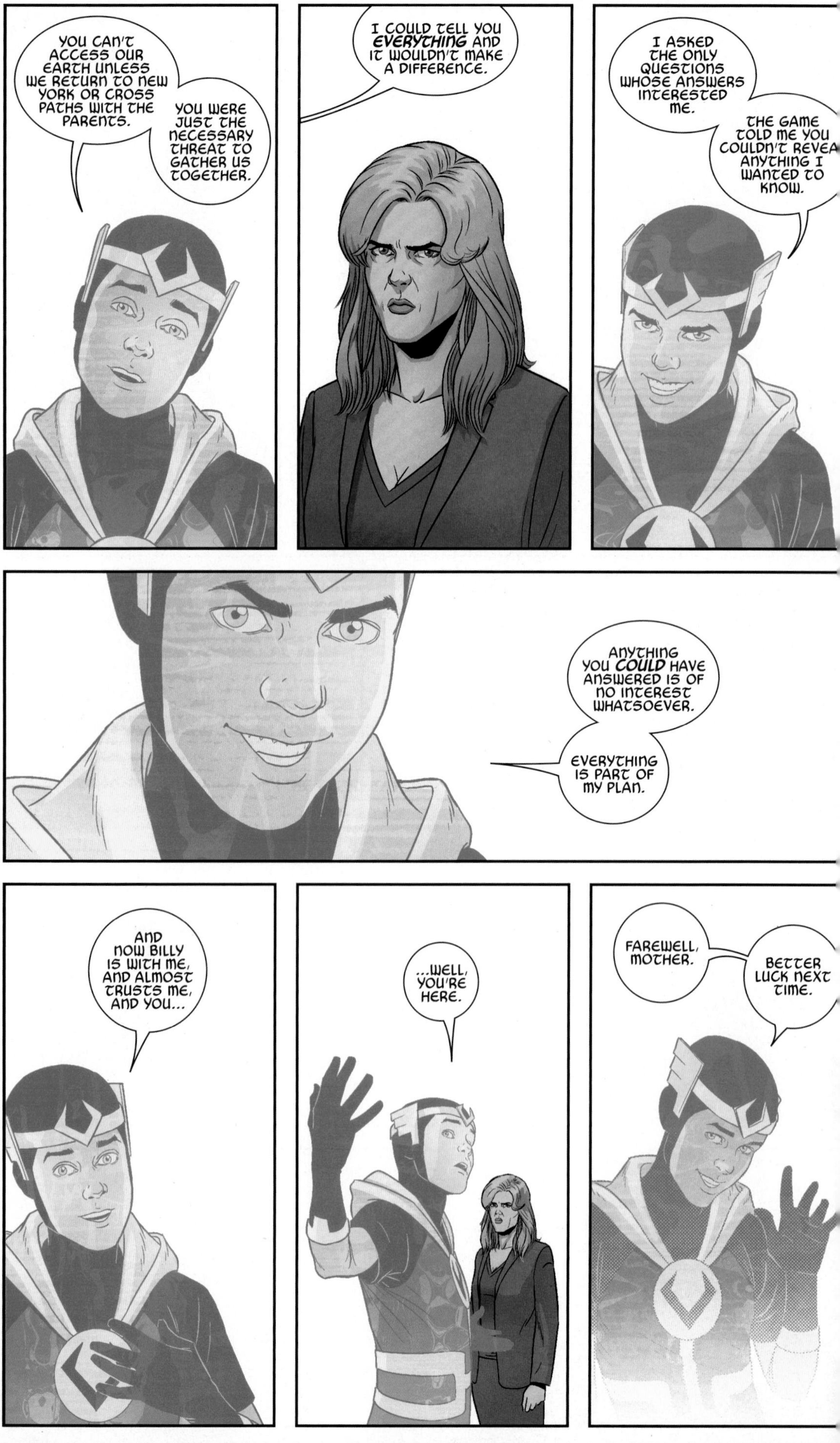
YOU CAN'T ACCESS OUR EARTH UNLESS WE RETURN TO NEW YORK OR CROSS PATHS WITH THE PARENTS.
YOU WERE JUST THE NECESSARY THREAT TO GATHER US TOGETHER.
I COULD TELL YOU EVERYTHING AND IT WOULDN'T MAKE A DIFFERENCE.
I ASKED THE ONLY QUESTIONS WHOSE ANSWERS INTERESTED ME.
THE GAME TOLD ME YOU COULDN'T REVEA ANYTHING I WANTED TO KNOW.
ANYTHING YOU COULD HAVE ANSWERED IS OF NO INTEREST WHATSOEVER.
EVERYTHING IS PART OF MY PLAN.
AND NOW BILLY IS WITH ME, AND ALMOST TRUSTS ME, AND YOU...
...WELL, YOU'RE HERE.
FAREWELL, MOTHER.
BETTER LUCK NEXT TIME.

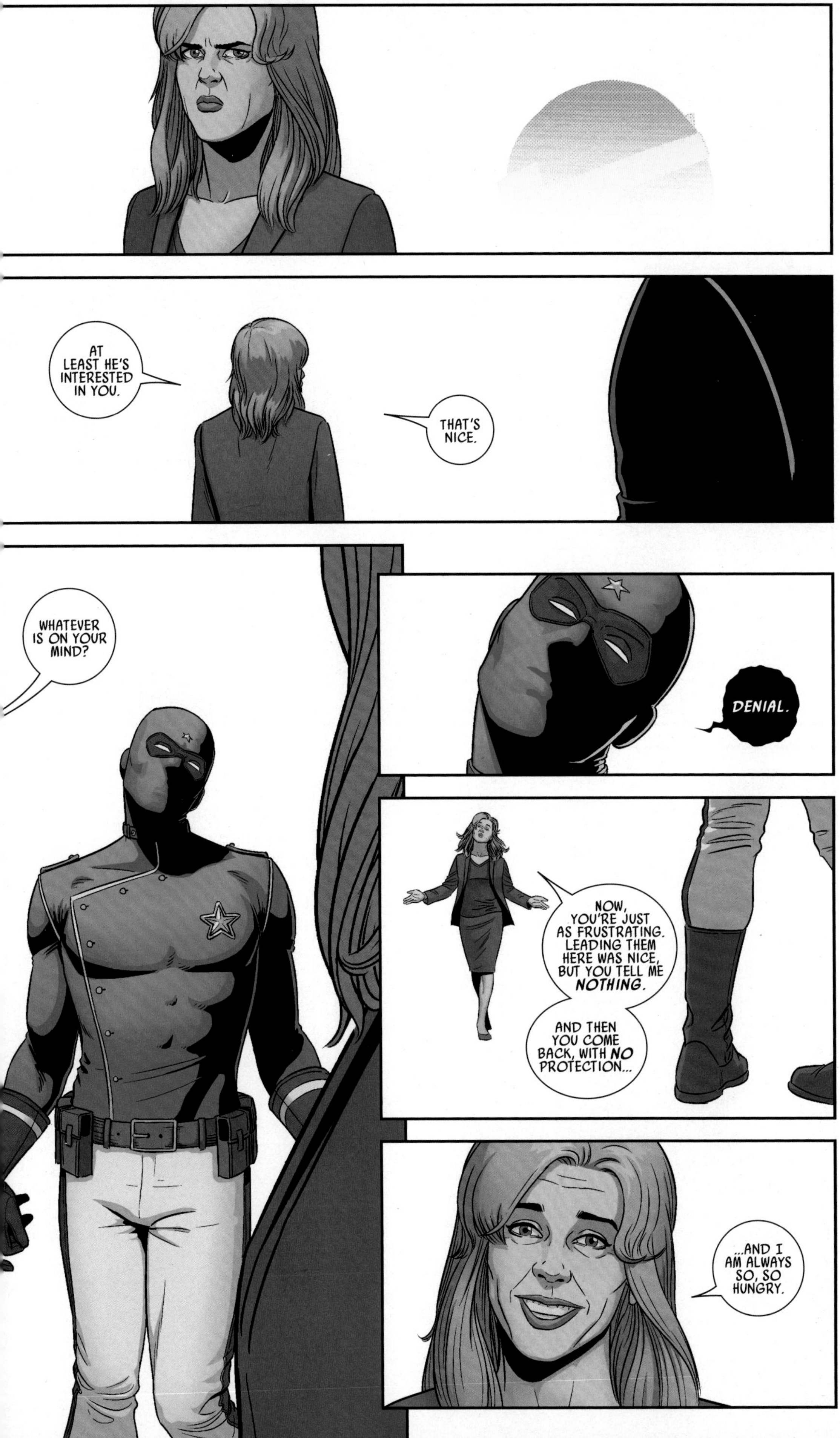
AT LEAST HE'S INTERESTED IN YOU.
THAT'S NICE.
WHATEVER IS ON YOUR MIND?
DENIAL.
NOW, YOU'RE JUST AS FRUSTRATING. LEADING THEM HERE WAS NICE, BUT YOU TELL ME NOTHING.
AND THEN YOU COME BACK, WITH NO PROTECTION...
...AND I AM ALWAYS SO, SO HUNGRY.

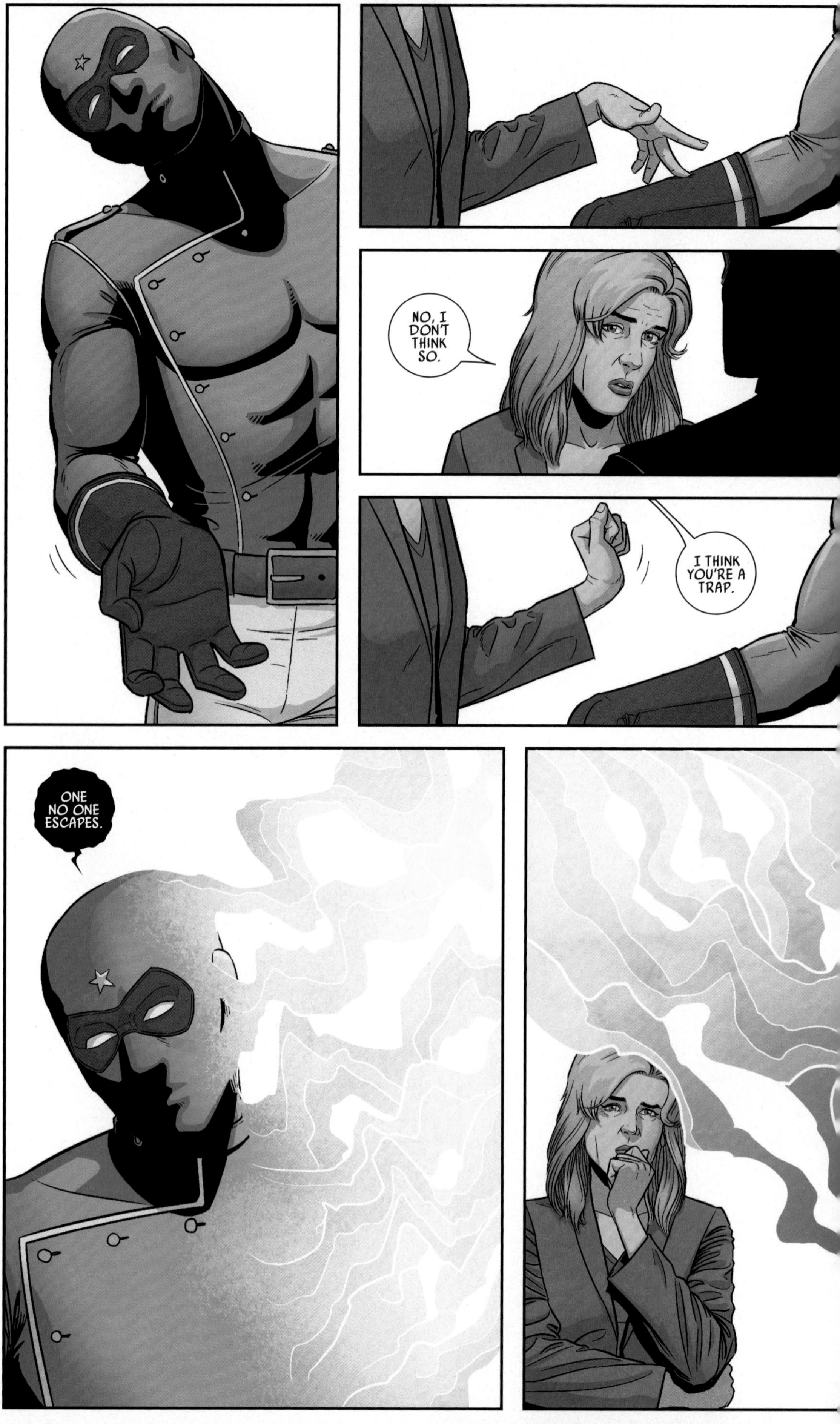
NO, I DON'T THINK SO.
I THINK YOU'RE A TRAP.
ONE NO ONE ESCAPES.

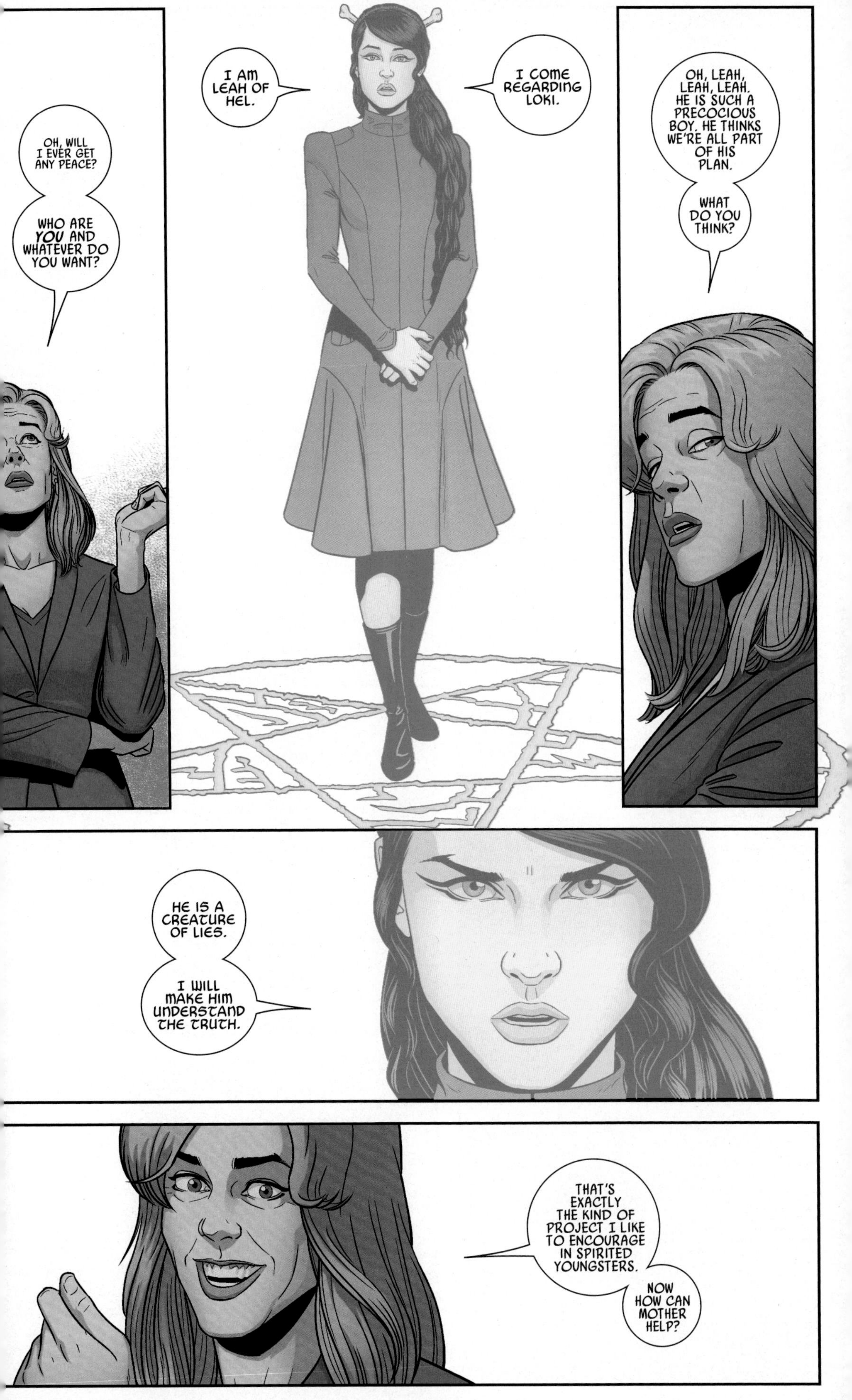
OH, WILL I EVER GET ANY PEACE?
WHO ARE *YOU* AND WHATEVER DO YOU WANT?
I AM LEAH OF HEL.
I COME REGARDING LOKI.
OH, LEAH, LEAH, LEAH. HE IS SUCH A PRECOCIOUS BOY. HE THINKS WE'RE ALL PART OF HIS PLAN.
WHAT DO YOU THINK?
HE IS A CREATURE OF LIES.
I WILL MAKE HIM UNDERSTAND THE TRUTH.
THAT'S EXACTLY THE KIND OF PROJECT I LIKE TO ENCOURAGE IN SPIRITED YOUNGSTERS.
NOW HOW CAN MOTHER HELP?

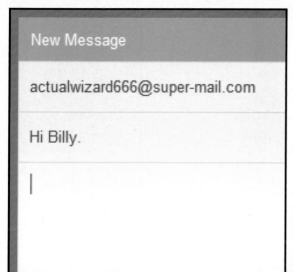

New Message

actualwizard666@super-mail.com

Hi Billy.

|

LATER...

TEDDY, ARE YOU FINISHED?

LEAH, I HAVEN'T EVEN STARTED, BUT I THINK I'M DONE.

I WANT TO SEND HIM A NOVEL.

I CAN'T EVEN FIND A SENTENCE.

WE'RE JUST WRITING TO EACH OTHER. I WANT TO CALL, BUT...MAYBE HIS VOICE IS TOO DANGEROUS, MAYBE? HELL, MAYBE EVEN WRITING IS TOO MUCH CONTACT?

I DUNNO. MAYBE EXISTING IS ENOUGH.

IT'S FOR THE BEST, TEDDY.

YOU NEED THIS.

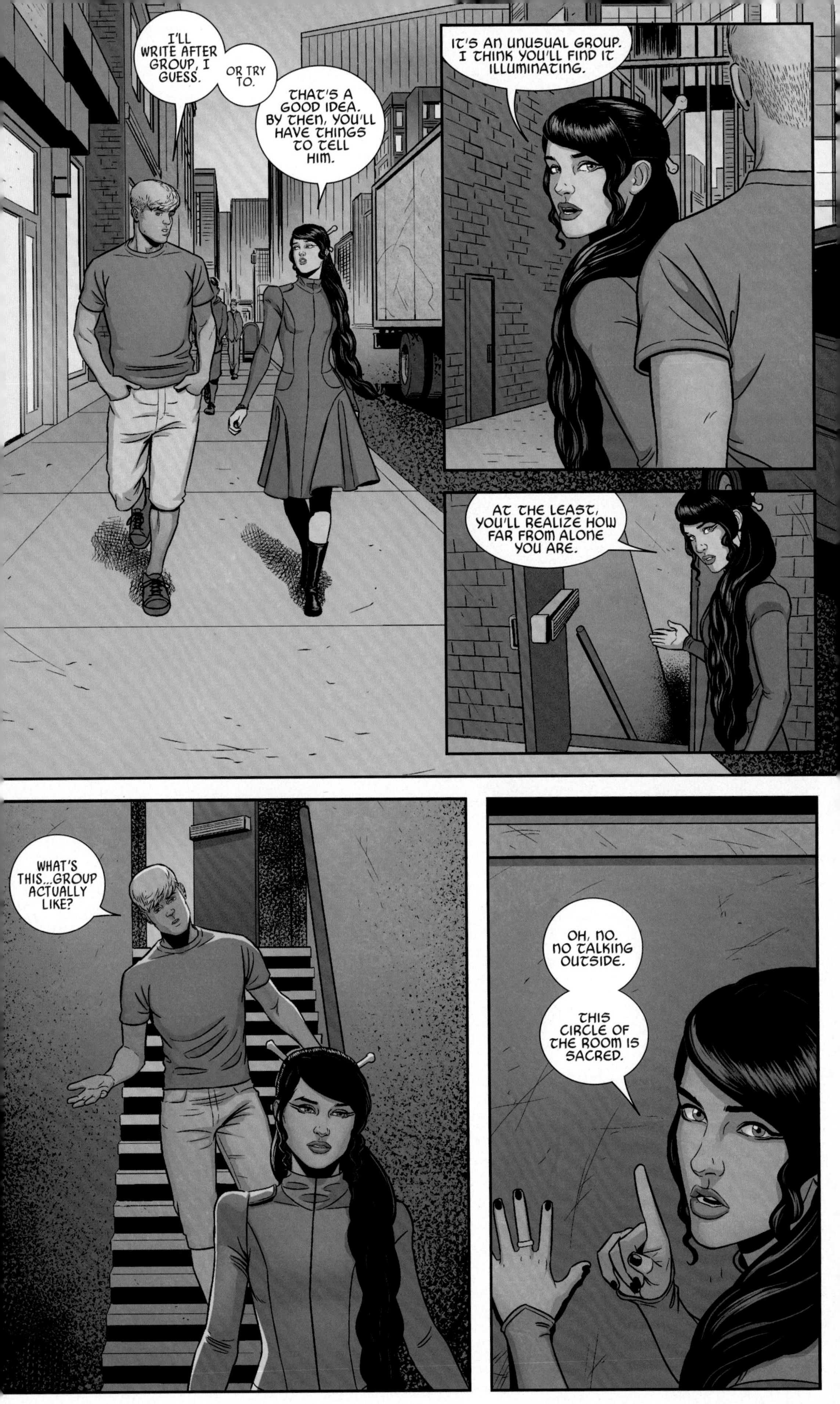

I'LL WRITE AFTER GROUP, I GUESS.
OR TRY TO.
THAT'S A GOOD IDEA. BY THEN, YOU'LL HAVE THINGS TO TELL HIM.
IT'S AN UNUSUAL GROUP. I THINK YOU'LL FIND IT ILLUMINATING.
AT THE LEAST, YOU'LL REALIZE HOW FAR FROM ALONE YOU ARE.
WHAT'S THIS...GROUP ACTUALLY LIKE?
OH, NO. NO TALKING OUTSIDE.
THIS CIRCLE OF THE ROOM IS SACRED.

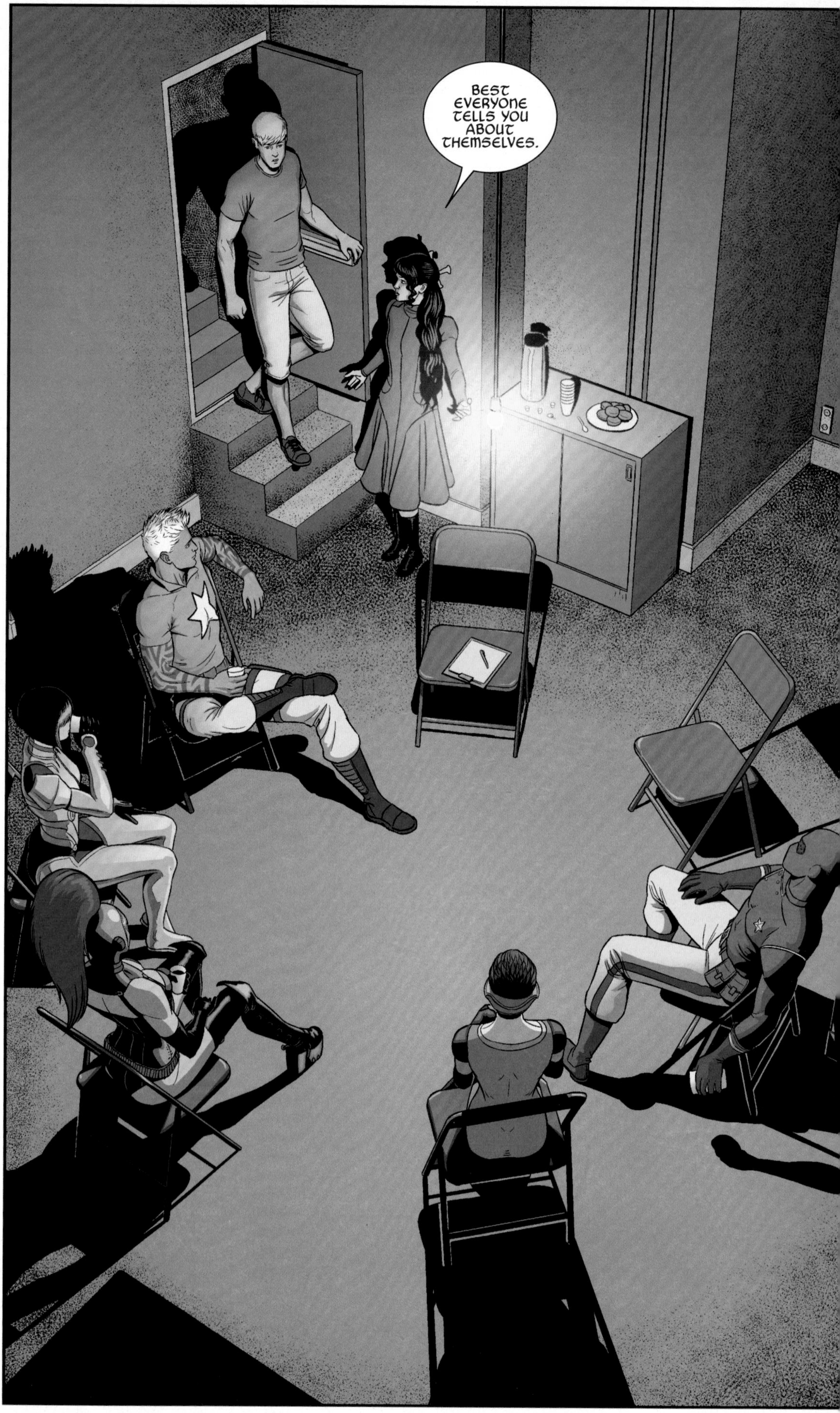
BEST EVERYONE TELLS YOU ABOUT THEMSELVES.

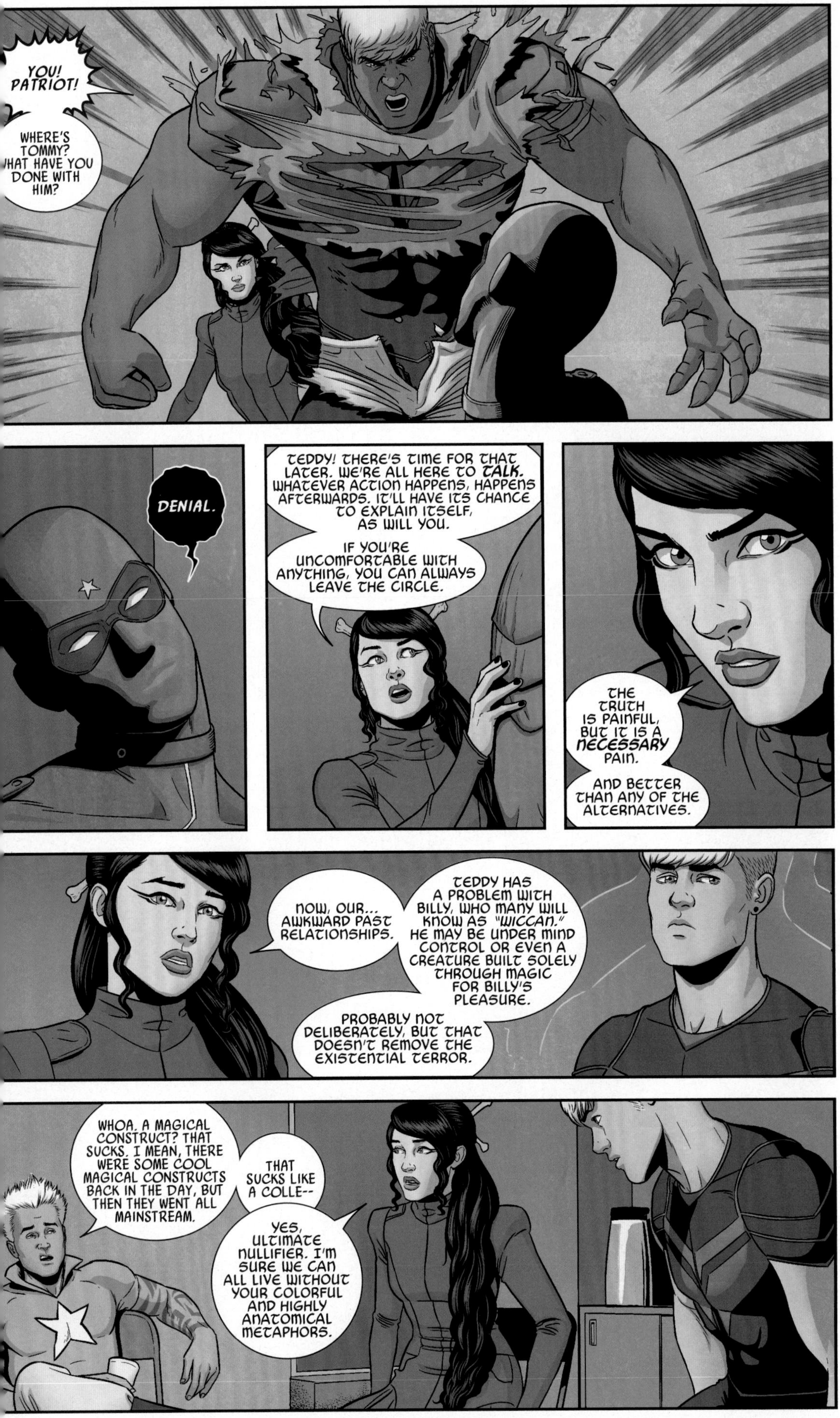
YOU! PATRIOT!
WHERE'S TOMMY? WHAT HAVE YOU DONE WITH HIM?
DENIAL.
TEDDY! THERE'S TIME FOR THAT LATER. WE'RE ALL HERE TO TALK. WHATEVER ACTION HAPPENS, HAPPENS AFTERWARDS. IT'LL HAVE ITS CHANCE TO EXPLAIN ITSELF, AS WILL YOU.
IF YOU'RE UNCOMFORTABLE WITH ANYTHING, YOU CAN ALWAYS LEAVE THE CIRCLE.
THE TRUTH IS PAINFUL, BUT IT IS A NECESSARY PAIN.
AND BETTER THAN ANY OF THE ALTERNATIVES.
NOW, OUR... AWKWARD PAST RELATIONSHIPS.
TEDDY HAS A PROBLEM WITH BILLY, WHO MANY WILL KNOW AS "WICCAN." HE MAY BE UNDER MIND CONTROL OR EVEN A CREATURE BUILT SOLELY THROUGH MAGIC FOR BILLY'S PLEASURE.
PROBABLY NOT DELIBERATELY, BUT THAT DOESN'T REMOVE THE EXISTENTIAL TERROR.
WHOA. A MAGICAL CONSTRUCT? THAT SUCKS. I MEAN, THERE WERE SOME COOL MAGICAL CONSTRUCTS BACK IN THE DAY, BUT THEN THEY WENT ALL MAINSTREAM.
THAT SUCKS LIKE A COLLE--
YES, ULTIMATE NULLIFIER. I'M SURE WE CAN ALL LIVE WITHOUT YOUR COLORFUL AND HIGHLY ANATOMICAL METAPHORS.

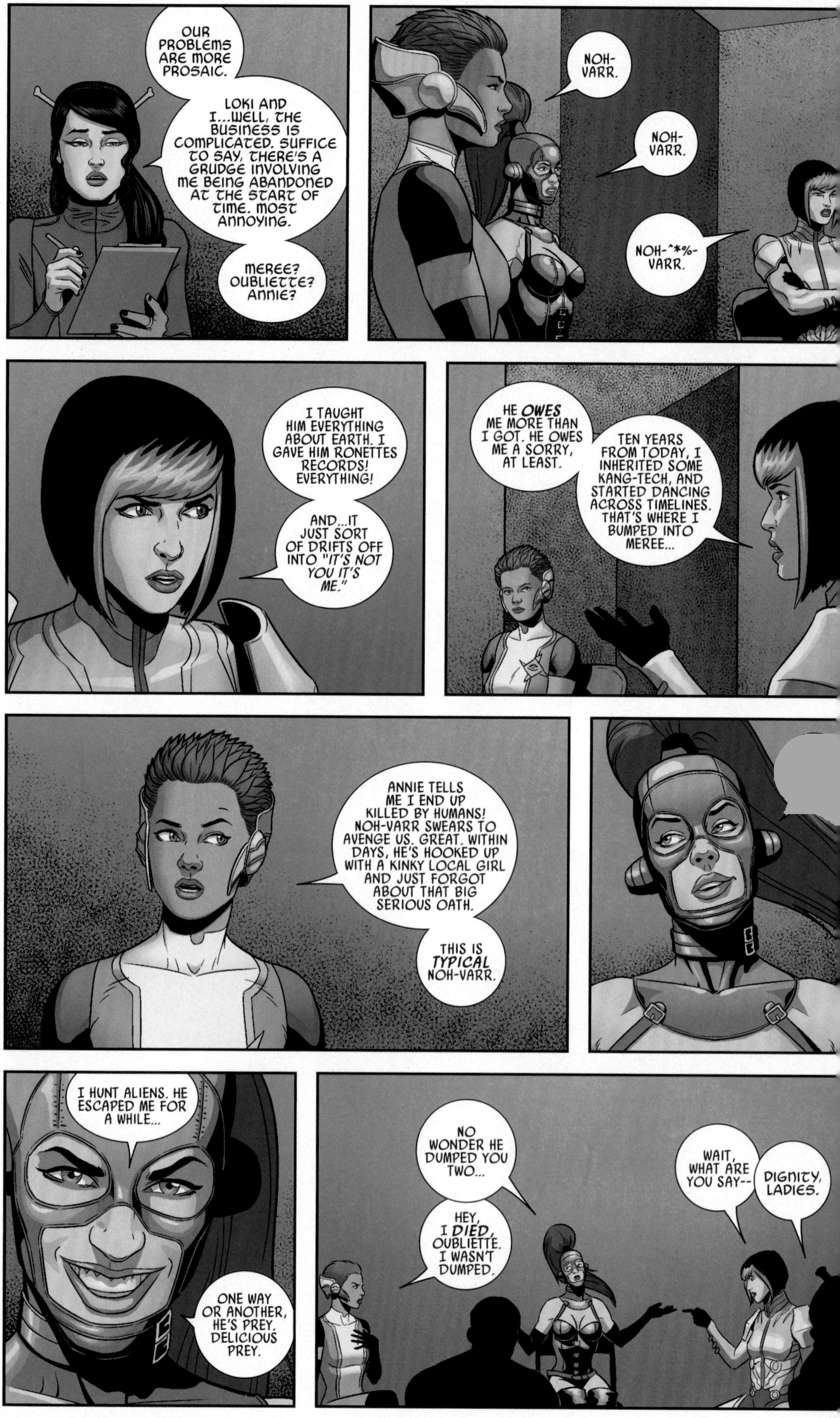

OUR PROBLEMS ARE MORE PROSAIC.
LOKI AND I...WELL, THE BUSINESS IS COMPLICATED. SUFFICE TO SAY, THERE'S A GRUDGE INVOLVING ME BEING ABANDONED AT THE START OF TIME. MOST ANNOYING.
MEREE? OUBLIETTE? ANNIE?
NOH-VARR.
NOH-VARR.
NOH-^*%-VARR.
I TAUGHT HIM EVERYTHING ABOUT EARTH. I GAVE HIM RONETTES RECORDS! EVERYTHING!
AND...IT JUST SORT OF DRIFTS OFF INTO "IT'S NOT YOU IT'S ME."
HE OWES ME MORE THAN I GOT. HE OWES ME A SORRY, AT LEAST.
TEN YEARS FROM TODAY, I INHERITED SOME KANG-TECH, AND STARTED DANCING ACROSS TIMELINES. THAT'S WHERE I BUMPED INTO MEREE...
ANNIE TELLS ME I END UP KILLED BY HUMANS! NOH-VARR SWEARS TO AVENGE US. GREAT. WITHIN DAYS, HE'S HOOKED UP WITH A KINKY LOCAL GIRL AND JUST FORGOT ABOUT THAT BIG SERIOUS OATH.
THIS IS TYPICAL NOH-VARR.
I HUNT ALIENS. HE ESCAPED ME FOR A WHILE...
ONE WAY OR ANOTHER, HE'S PREY. DELICIOUS PREY.
NO WONDER HE DUMPED YOU TWO...
HEY, I DIED, OUBLIETTE. I WASN'T DUMPED.
WAIT, WHAT ARE YOU SAY--
DIGNITY, LADIES.

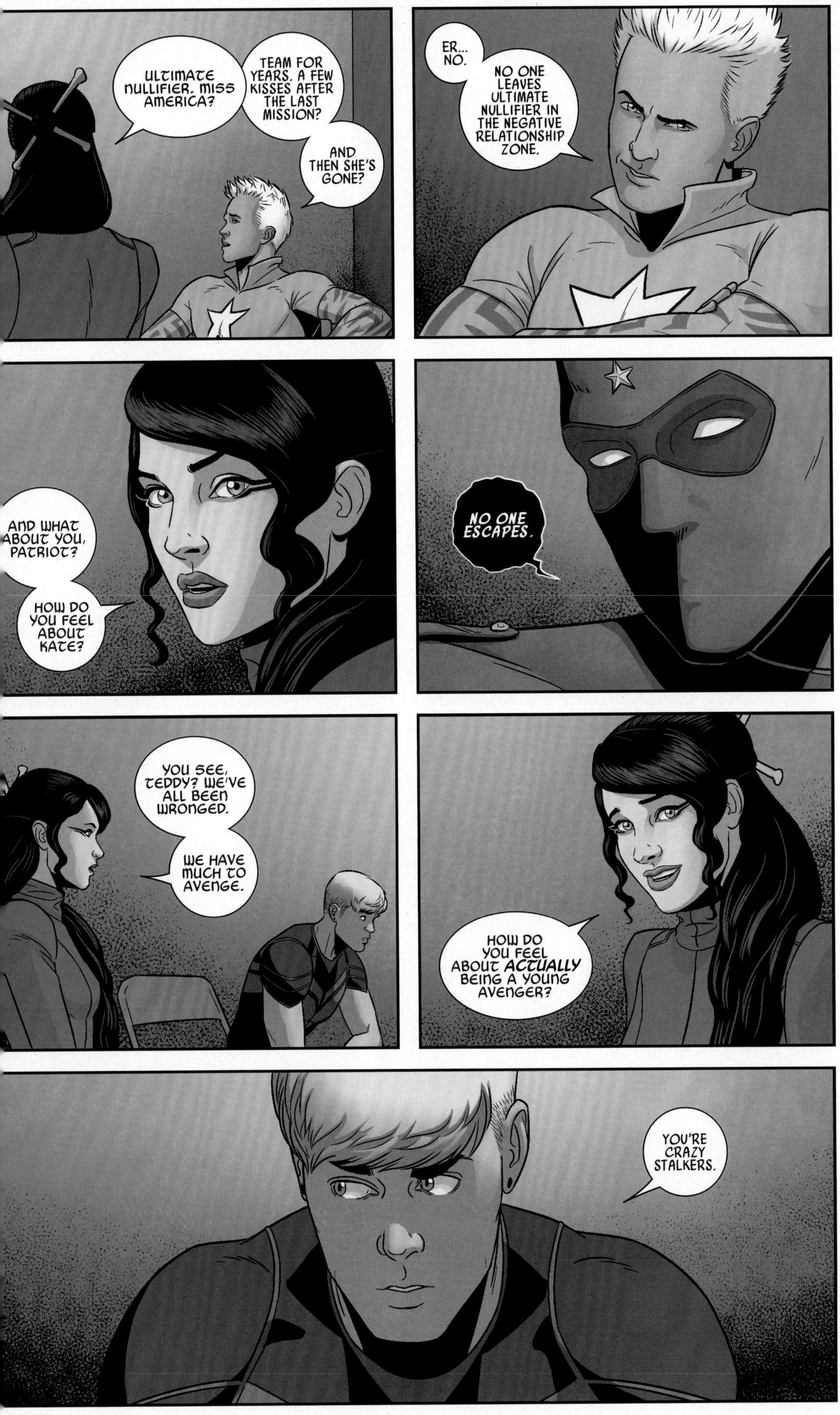
ULTIMATE NULLIFIER. MISS AMERICA?
TEAM FOR YEARS. A FEW KISSES AFTER THE LAST MISSION?
AND THEN SHE'S GONE?
ER... NO.
NO ONE LEAVES ULTIMATE NULLIFIER IN THE NEGATIVE RELATIONSHIP ZONE.
AND WHAT ABOUT YOU, PATRIOT?
HOW DO YOU FEEL ABOUT KATE?
NO ONE ESCAPES.
YOU SEE, TEDDY? WE'VE ALL BEEN WRONGED.
WE HAVE MUCH TO AVENGE.
HOW DO YOU FEEL ABOUT ACTUALLY BEING A YOUNG AVENGER?
YOU'RE CRAZY STALKERS.

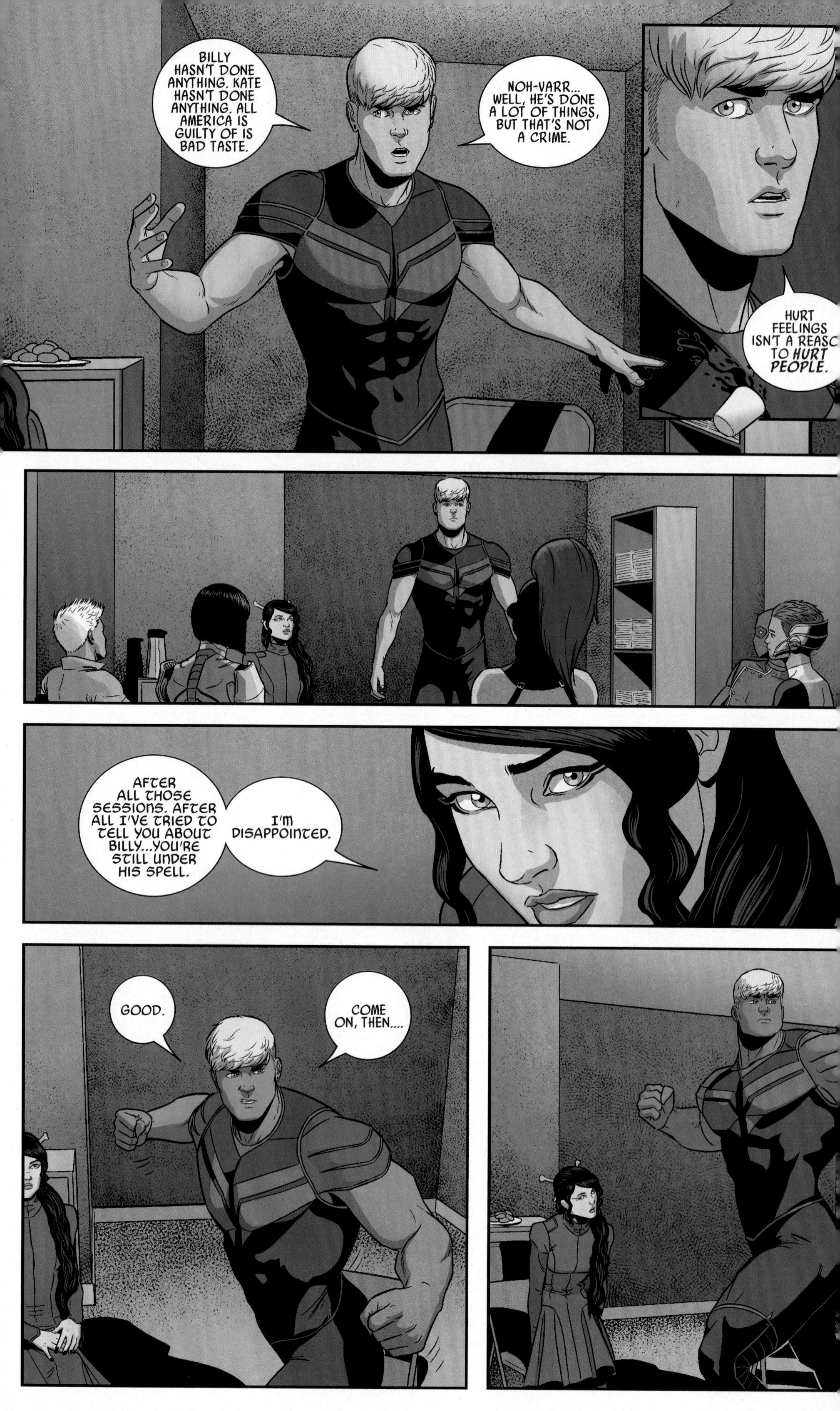
BILLY HASN'T DONE ANYTHING. KATE HASN'T DONE ANYTHING. ALL AMERICA IS GUILTY OF IS BAD TASTE.
NOH-VARR... WELL, HE'S DONE A LOT OF THINGS, BUT THAT'S NOT A CRIME.
HURT FEELINGS ISN'T A REASO TO HURT PEOPLE.
AFTER ALL THOSE SESSIONS. AFTER ALL I'VE TRIED TO TELL YOU ABOUT BILLY...YOU'RE STILL UNDER HIS SPELL.
I'M DISAPPOINTED.
GOOD.
COME ON, THEN....

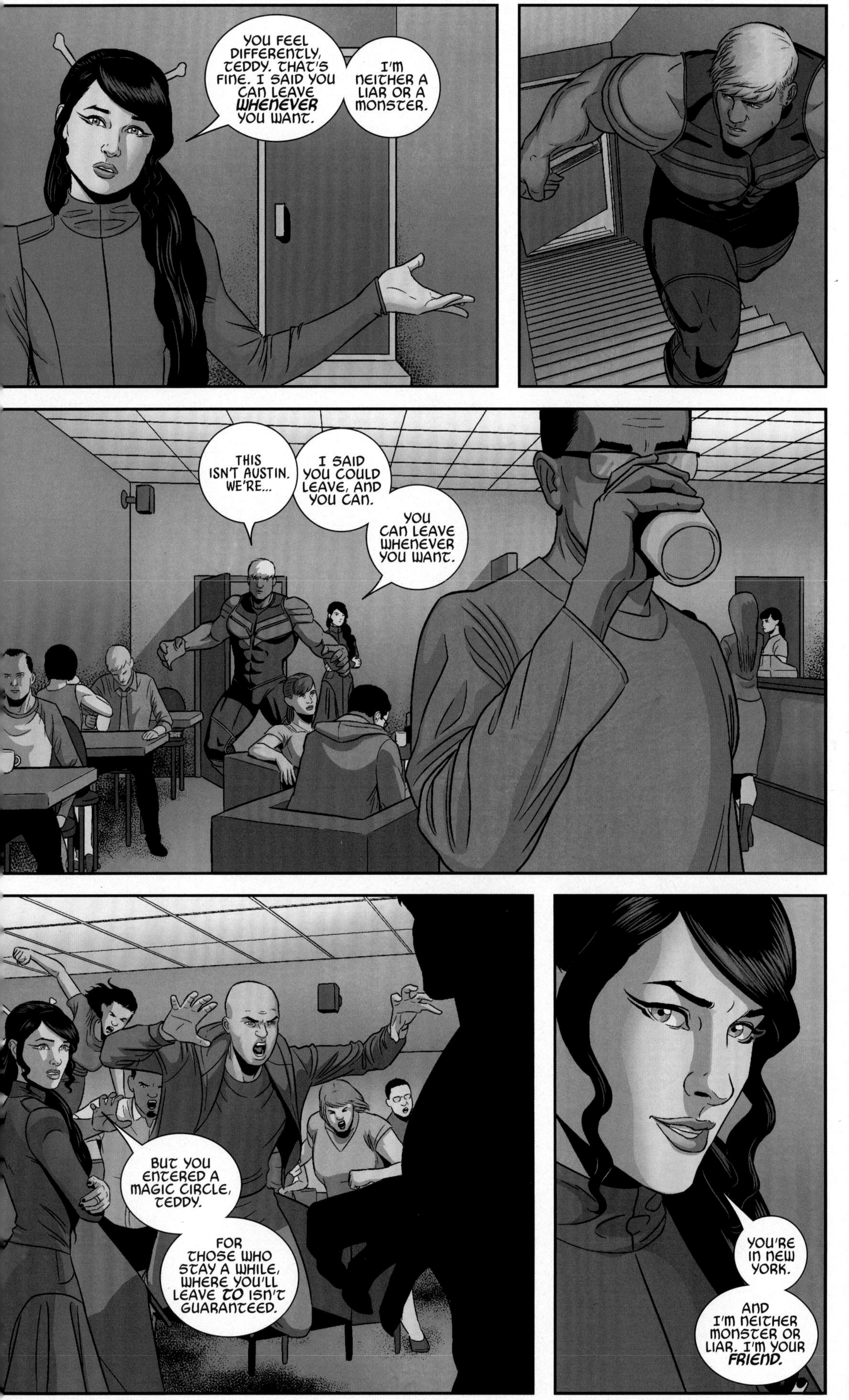
YOU FEEL DIFFERENTLY, TEDDY. THAT'S FINE. I SAID YOU CAN LEAVE WHENEVER YOU WANT.
I'M NEITHER A LIAR OR A MONSTER.
THIS ISN'T AUSTIN. WE'RE...
I SAID YOU COULD LEAVE, AND YOU CAN.
YOU CAN LEAVE WHENEVER YOU WANT.
BUT YOU ENTERED A MAGIC CIRCLE, TEDDY.
FOR THOSE WHO STAY A WHILE, WHERE YOU'LL LEAVE TO ISN'T GUARANTEED.
YOU'RE IN NEW YORK.
AND I'M NEITHER MONSTER OR LIAR. I'M YOUR FRIEND.

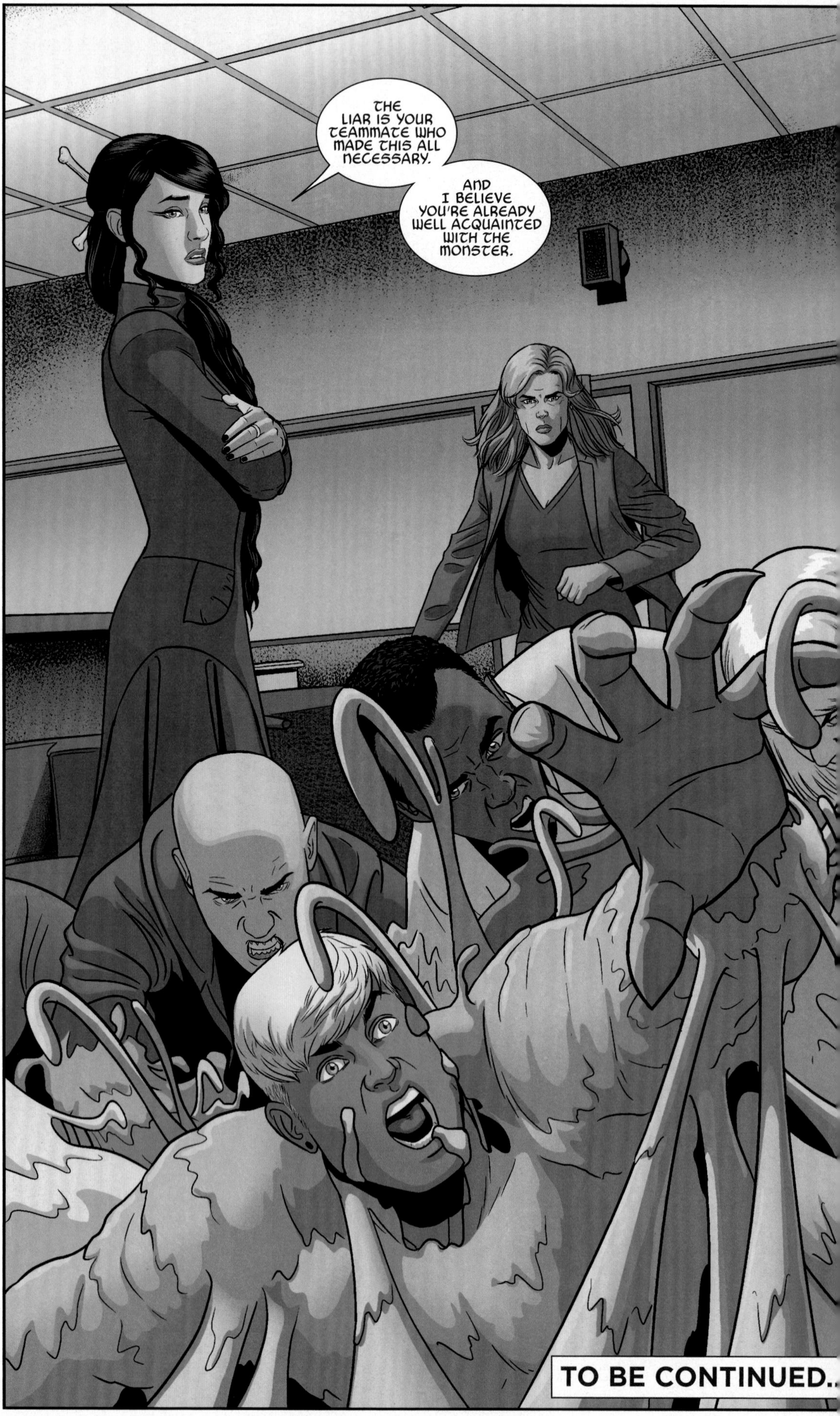
THE LIAR IS YOUR TEAMMATE WHO MADE THIS ALL NECESSARY.
AND I BELIEVE YOU'RE ALREADY WELL ACQUAINTED WITH THE MONSTER.
TO BE CONTINUED...

#6 WOLVERINE THROUGH THE AGES VARIANT
BY MIKE DEL MUNDO

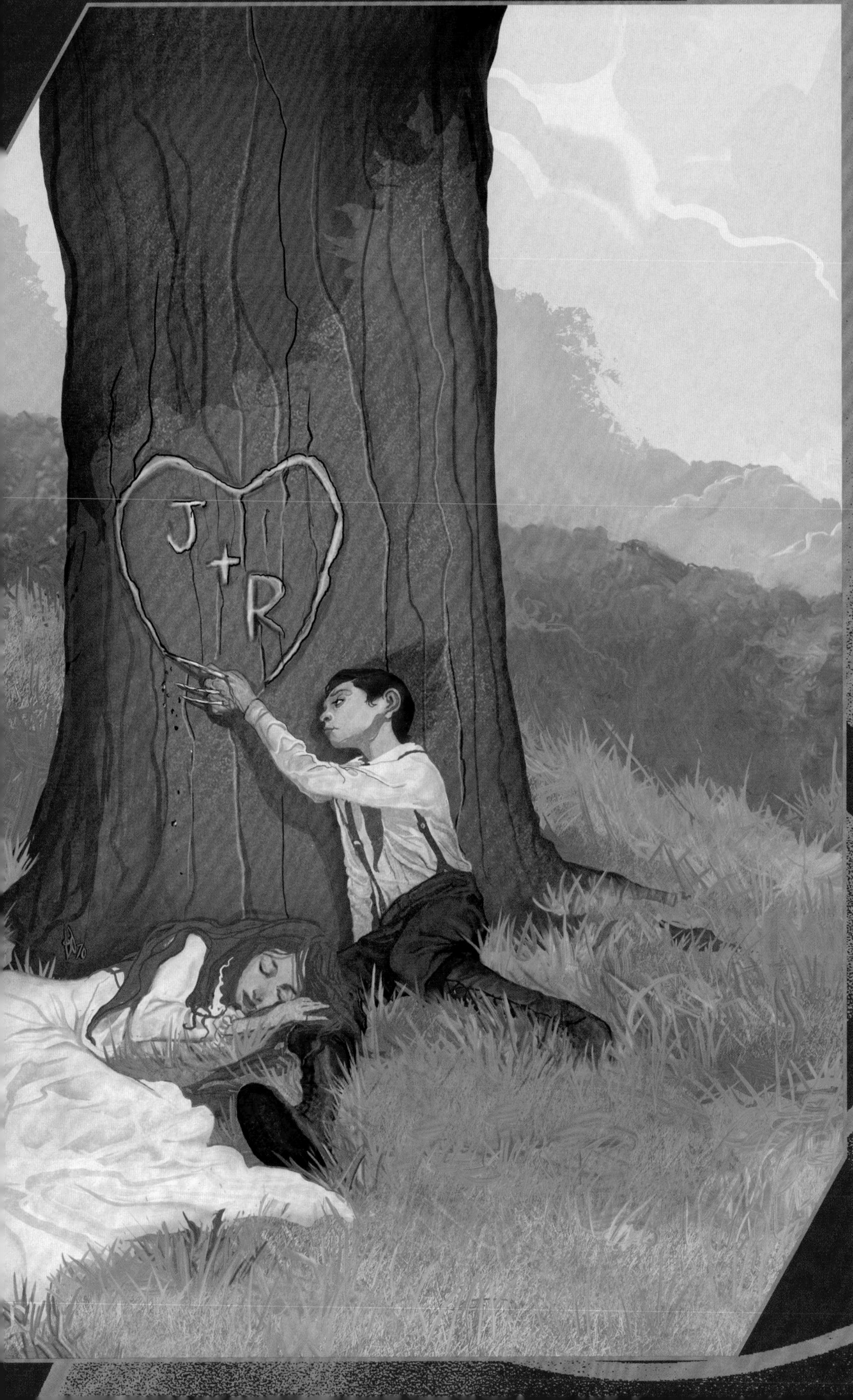
J
+
R

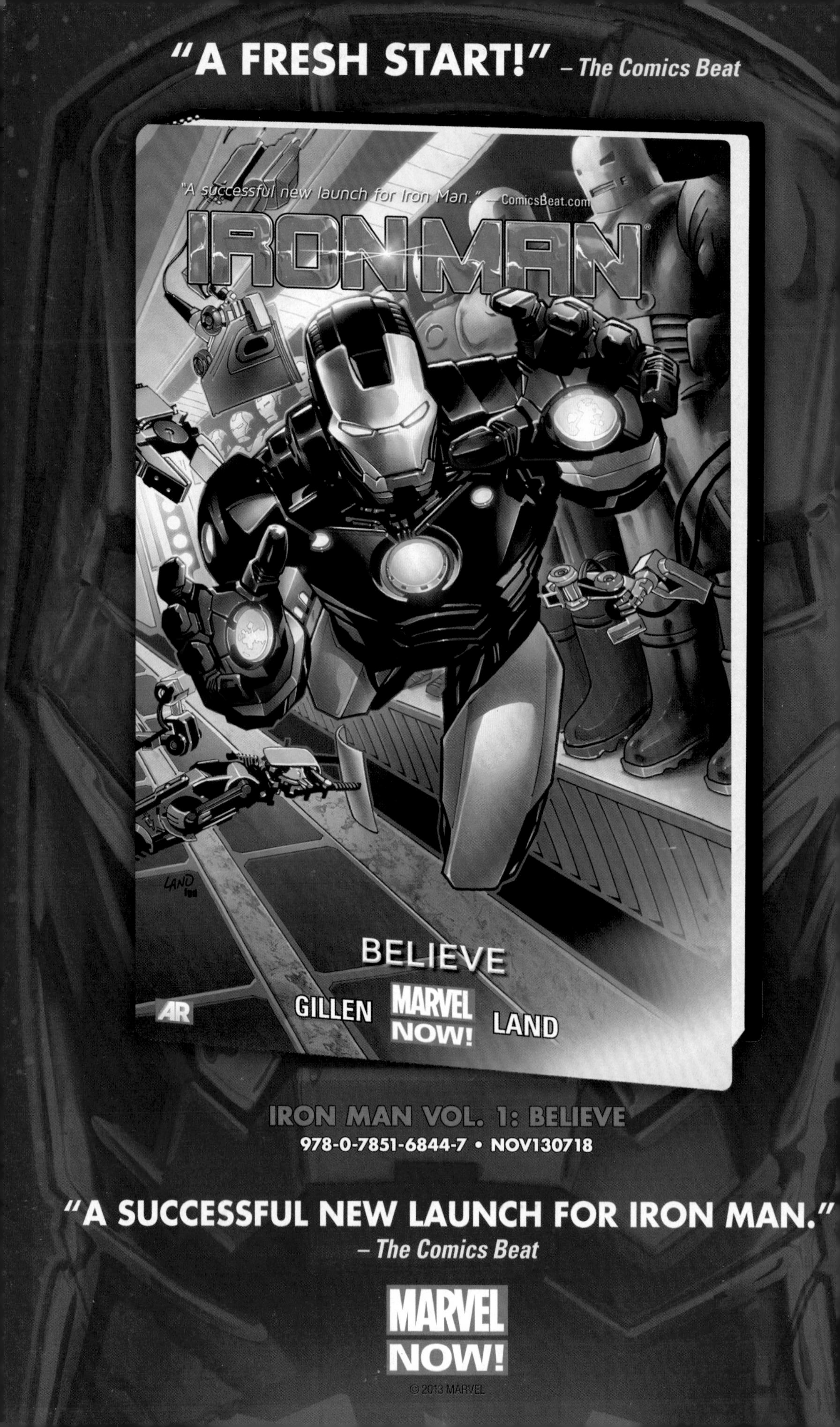
"A FRESH START!" – The Comics Beat
"A successful new launch for Iron Man." —ComicsBeat.com
IRON MAN
BELIEVE
GILLEN
MARVEL NOW!
LAND
IRON MAN VOL. 1: BELIEVE
978-0-7851-6844-7 • NOV130718
"A SUCCESSFUL NEW LAUNCH FOR IRON MAN."
– The Comics Beat
MARVEL NOW!
© 2013 MARVEL